Faulkner On and Off the Page

Faulkner On and Off the Page

Essays in Biographical Criticism

Carl Rollyson

University Press of Mississippi / Jackson

The University Press of Mississippi is the scholarly publishing agency of the Mississippi Institutions of Higher Learning: Alcorn State University, Delta State University, Jackson State University, Mississippi State University, Mississippi University for Women, Mississippi Valley State University, University of Mississippi, and University of Southern Mississippi.

www.upress.state.ms.us

The University Press of Mississippi is a member of the Association of University Presses.

Any discriminatory or derogatory language or hate speech regarding race, ethnicity, religion, sex, gender, class, national origin, age, or disability that has been retained or appears in elided form is in no way an endorsement of the use of such language outside a scholarly context.

Copyright © 2025 by University Press of Mississippi
All rights reserved
Manufactured in the United States of America
∞

Publisher: University Press of Mississippi, Jackson, USA
Authorised GPSR Safety Representative: Easy Access System Europe - Mustamäe tee 50, 10621 Tallinn, Estonia, gpsr.requests@easproject.com

Library of Congress Cataloging-in-Publication Data

Names: Rollyson, Carl E. (Carl Edmund), author.
Title: Faulkner on and off the page : essays in biographical criticism / Carl Rollyson.
Description: Jackson : University Press of Mississippi, 2025. |
    Includes bibliographical references and index.
Identifiers: LCCN 2024061923 (print) | LCCN 2024061924 (ebook) |
    ISBN 9781496856043 (hardback) | ISBN 9781496856050 (trade paperback) |
    ISBN 9781496856395 (epub) | ISBN 9781496858122 (epub) |
    ISBN 9781496856401 (pdf) | ISBN 9781496856418 (pdf)
Subjects: LCSH: Faulkner, William, 1897–1962. |
    Novelists, American—20th century—Biography. | LCGFT: Biographies. |
    Essays. | Literary criticism.
Classification: LCC PS3511.A86 Z96186 2025 (print) | LCC PS3511.A86 (ebook) |
    DDC 813/.52 [B]—dc23/eng/20241230
LC record available at https://lccn.loc.gov/2024061923
LC ebook record available at https://lccn.loc.gov/2024061924

British Library Cataloging-in-Publication Data available

Contents

Introduction: Life as a Text and the Text as Life 3

Part One: Faulkner and Biography
Building a Better Biography. 7
The Historians of Yoknapatawpha 17
Biographical Fiction: A Faulknerian Novel 31
Interview with Taylor Brown 33
The Foreigner in Faulkner. 37
Counterpull: Estelle and William Faulkner 42
"Sole Owner and Proprietor": William Faulkner and Jean Stein 53
Reminiscing about William Faulkner at the University of Virginia:
A Biographer's Outtakes. 68

Part Two: Faulkner, Politics, and History
Faulkner's Conservatism 73
Faulkner the Antifascist. 81
Faulkner as Futurist 86
War No More: The Revolt of the Masses in *A Fable* 91

Part Three: Faulkner and Hollywood
Recreating *Absalom, Absalom!*: *Revolt in the Earth*. 113
Faulkner's Shadow: Hollywood, Hemingway, and *Pylon*. 131
The Stories of Temple Drake 146
"Tomorrow" and *Tomorrow*: Faulkner into Film 150
The Reivers: On and Off the Screen 162

Part Four: Faulkner and Race
The White Man's "Negro" in Faulkner Country. 175
The Twilight of Man in "Delta Autumn". 181
"Shooting Negroes" 189

CONTENTS

Caste from a Faulknerian Perspective: *Intruder in the Dust* 201
What Faulkner Could Not Imagine: The Life of James Meredith 209

Acknowledgments 211
Notes 213
Bibliography 225
Index 231

Faulkner On and Off the Page

Introduction
Life as a Text and the Text as Life

In the modern era, literary biography has been dismissed as unreliable and irrelevant. What to believe in a biography when there are competing versions of events and different biographers come to different conclusions? And besides, what is important is the work, right? But how do you define work? Does it all occur on the page? What about all the work product? What about the pattern of life that remains stable in biographies of the same subject, whatever differences of interpretation remain? And how is biography more unstable, actually, from literary texts that provoke all sorts of alternative readings and disputes about what is happening on the page? It might seem tidier to certain literary critics to remain fixed on the page, but you don't have to be a deconstructionist to understand the page is not as steady as some critics suppose when they are ditching an interest in biography.

So in this book I read Faulkner's life as a constantly shifting text always open to revision, which is how I think he viewed himself—like the characters in fiction, there was always more to know and no written text was sacred, which is why he was not particularly bothered by the discrepancies editors found in the Snopes trilogy. Not only did he change his view of his own characters—set *The Sound and the Fury* beside the *Compson Appendix*, for example—but he invented them again in the medium of film. *Absalom, Absalom!* becomes something quite different in its screenplay version, *Revolt in the Earth*.

The Faulkner we know keeps reinventing himself in the work of others—in Horton's Foote's screen adaptation of "Tomorrow" and in Taylor Brown's novel, *Wingwalkers* in which Faulkner appears as a character in a story that has characters that seem to have grown out of the world of *Pylon*. A similar process of Faulkner reinvention occurs in biographies of him, as biographers bring with them the context of the period in which they are writing, a period which has also been shaped by generations of Faulkner scholars.

But the life as a text means something else as well. Why do writers like Faulkner object to biography? Surely one reason is because they have worked out the text of their own lives and object to biographers who see that life text differently. If the biographers were writing fiction, Faulkner might not have objected. He did not seem to mind and may even have been flattered when Sherwood Anderson modeled the character of David in "A Meeting South" on Faulkner. What troubled Faulkner—aside from his objections about invasion of privacy—is that what appears in a biography is taken as fact, data in a text. Such textifying makes book on the writer's life, and such factifying disturbed a man who told Malcolm Cowley that you could not stand a fact up, that as soon as you began to give it a good hard look it began to wobble.

This book is aware of that wobble but also of the through-line that biography can establish with patience and perspicuity, tracking how literature emerges out of life, and how that literature then has to be factored back into the life text Faulkner created for himself. Part of what I mean by "off the page" is what I have learned from interviews about my subjects. Interviews have taught me about the spill-over effect that destabilizes what seems so fixed on the pages of a book, and I have tried to show that spill-over effect in the interviews I have included in this book.

When I decided to write a Faulkner biography, I had in mind the inclusion of certain events and activities and characters who had not been given their due in previous biographies. Rather than thinking of him as only the great high modernist novelist and short story writer who strayed to Hollywood when he needed the money and stayed home when he didn't, I saw a much more unsettled writer incessantly on the move, incorporating what only looked like alien elements into his work, while maintaining a public persona that disparaged anything that did not fit the narrative of the novelist he created in interviews, essays, and speeches. What this book attempts to do, is to carry on that work of biography, of finding the man on the page even as he is shaping a life off of it.

Part One
Faulkner and Biography

Building a Better Biography

William Faulkner (1897–1962), winner of the 1949 Nobel Prize for literature, has not lacked for biographers, beginning with Joseph Blotner's two-volume, two-thousand page monument in 1974, followed by comprehensive lives in 1979, 1980, 1984 (Blotner's one-volume revision), 1987, 1989, 1993, 2004, 2009, 2017,[1] as well as compact biographies in 2006, 2007, 2008, 2016, 2018,[2] and biographical chapters in literary studies.[3] In spite of all this work, I felt compelled to write yet another two-volume biography, which, by my standards, is the first to come to terms with all the significant aspects of Faulkner's life and work. A concise account of the full-length biographies that preceded mine will highlight my own biographical method and practice.

Blotner's work is the bedrock of Faulkner biography. A professor at the University of Virginia during Faulkner's residence there (1957–1962), Blotner became a kind of Boswell but also the authorized biographer with exclusive access to Faulkner's wife Estelle and other family members and friends. Blotner provided a thorough accounting of the origins and development of Faulkner's writings and collected documents and other data that scholars are still digesting. Except for recounting his own friendship with Faulkner, Blotner adopted an objective voice, withholding comment on vital scenes in his subject's life. For example, he recounted Estelle Oldham's apparent suicide attempt during her honeymoon with Faulkner without noting its impact on her husband or reporting her own comment on this episode. It is not clear from his papers or from his subsequent articles about his biography that Blotner even asked her about several important aspects of her marriage. While reviewers were grateful for Blotner's massive treasure of biographical data, several deplored his apparent unwillingness to shape all this material into a coherent interpretation. His one-volume revision provided a more focused narrative, but the lack of candor and even curiosity about certain aspects of Faulkner's life remained a problem.

As if supplying an antidote to Blotner's agnostic account, Judith Wittenberg delivered a highly speculative psychological biography, making much of Faulkner's unconscious attitudes that influenced his creation of characters and his way of presenting his own biography. Whatever one makes of her interpretations, she opened up Faulkner biography to the kind of searching analysis Blotner eschewed. But she also disarmed herself as a writer of biographical narrative by allowing her critical judgments of Faulkner's work to prevail over a full understanding of his whole life. She repeated an opinion, already well established by certain critics of Faulkner's work, that his greatest period as a writer ranged from 1929 to 1942. That left twenty years of a downward trajectory that are a dismaying prospect to behold in her book. In short, she let her training as a literary critic block her from an immersion in what those twenty years meant to Faulkner and how he lived them.

David Minter, next up, avoided psychobiography, preferring to focus on the culture in which Faulkner fashioned a sense of himself as an artist. An insightful literary critic, Minter, like Wittenberg, did not do much original biographical research, relying instead on the Blotner bedrock—as did historian Stephen Oates, who saw an opening for a "pure biography," using "novelistic techniques." Oates is a throwback to nineteenth-century romantic biography:

As the train roared through the Mississippi countryside, the boy and his two brothers sat transfixed at the open window of the passenger coach, watching the shadowy forests, the hazy fields of corn and cotton, the occasional farm houses and barns, all slide backward toward Holly Springs. It was an arduous trip for their mother, a small prim woman with auburn hair and stern eyes. The coach was oppressively hot, and cinder flakes from the locomotive swirled through the open window, sullying the boys' faces and clothes. But Billy, the oldest, had seldom been so excited. Already he had a love for the steam locomotive that rivaled his father's. The sharp burst of its whistle, the hum of its wheels, the throb of the exhaust exploding from its stacks—all thrilled the boy to incandescence.

Biographers usually write this way for children.

After Oates, an astringent needed to be applied, which is what Frederick Karl supplied in a thousand-plus-page biography portraying the man, the myth, his family history, his work and sense of his own life, as demonstrated in this wonderful concatenating first paragraph:

When Faulkner (Family name, Falkner) was born in New Albany, Mississippi, on September 25, 1897, there was still a mythical America; and it was still possible for an individual to wrap himself in that myth. Part of the myth had attached itself to the Falkner family well before the writer was born—its violence, its frontier qualities, its efforts to relocate itself as part of the Southern planter aristocracy—but Faulkner also created his own. Those famous silences which characterized his public pose were an essential part of the mythmaking; they seemed to locate him on some mystical or magical ground where no one else could tread. Faulkner desperately wanted to be a great writer, but he wanted just as desperately to be an epic hero. But nature and nurture reinforce that willed sense of self.

Then historian Joel Williamson provided an in-depth exploration of Faulkner's southern heritage, including a fresh and revealing investigation of the Faulkner family history. Richard Gray rectified Williamson's failure to deal adequately with Faulkner's fiction by showing how a sense of history suffused Faulkner's work. What could Jay Parini add at this point? A dutiful biographer, he acknowledged the most recent trends in Faulkner criticism, mentioning, for example, that "feminist and poststructuralist critics have tended to look at the story ["The Fire and the Hearth"] as a 'subtle defense of the southern status quo in which African-American challenges to oppression either are defused through humor or are displaced to the margins of the text (and thereby trivialized)." Such awkward asides may win elections, but they doom biography.

The "one matchless time" referred to in Parini's title is the period between 1929–42, when Faulkner "found not simply his own voice but a teeming chorus of voices, each of them distinct, whole, and authentic." So we return to Wittenberg and the supposition that after 1942 we are left with the indistinct, fragmentary, and inauthentic. The same bias prevails in André Bleikasten's biography (first published in French in 2009), which seems like another work up of Blotner. Estelle Faulkner appears in Bleikasten as a lamentable marriage partner, fey and on the periphery of what matters to the critic eager to get on with explications of texts. That Estelle Faulkner wrote fiction, that Faulkner even submitted fiction under both their names and rewrote at least one of her stories, does not interest Bleikasten, even though such facts suggest why at certain times Faulkner found Estelle to be an indispensable partner, no matter how much he complained about her as a burden and an irrelevance. Biography is not supposed to take subjects at their word—at least not without the scrutiny that Faulkner's own characters aim at one another—but that is essentially what Bleikasten does.

Perhaps believing that yet another chronological biography of Faulkner would not yield significantly new results, Philip Weinstein decided on a more radical approach in *Becoming Faulkner*, dividing Faulkner by topics and shifts back and forth in time. While Weinstein makes astute comments on his subject's life and work, he also fragments and dislodges Faulkner from his time and place. Only a chronological, historically based narrative of Faulkner's evolving and contradictory statements and treatments of race, for example, can hope to align the man and his art.

Nagging at my own need to write a Faulkner biography was the work of Carvel Collins, whose immense collection at the University of Texas, is a treasure of primary sources, including interviews with many people who had passed away by the time Blotner began his work. Judging by the notes in previous biographies, I am the first biographer to look at every one of the 105 boxes in the Collins collection. Several Collins interviews also corroborate Blotner and add a good deal of texture to my biography. Collins was unusual in many respects. Unlike most academic biographers of his era, which began in the late 1940s, he collected everything, not just what pertained to the writer's work. By the summer of 1967, he had made more than thirty visits (over a twenty-year period) to Oxford, Mississippi, and he would continue to work on his biography until his death in 1990, never even beginning to write a narrative, so far as I have been able to ascertain. He spoke with the notable figures in Faulkner's life, including Faulkner himself, but also with anyone who had contact with his subject. In that respect, Collins is superior to Blotner, especially for a biographer who values the minute particulars that help to reveal the man as well as the writer.

Nearly as important was *Faulkner and Love*, Judith Sensibar's biographical study of the women in Faulkner's life. She finally restored Estelle Faulkner to an important place in Faulkner biography, showing the impact of Estelle's fiction on her husband, although still not placing Estelle firmly and chronologically in the frame of Faulkner's life. Sensibar dealt with Faulkner's mother and his African American caretaker, Caroline Barr, but the biographer did not go beyond those relationships to explore the importance of other women in Faulkner's life, especially Meta Carpenter, Joan Williams, Else Jonsson, and Jean Stein, who become central characters in my biography.

Faulkner spoke parsimoniously about his private life and disparaged his screen work, some of which he took home from Hollywood. His fiction and film, together with the women he loved, including the wife he could not live without—had not been integrated into a unified narrative of an intertextual biography—a back and forth between different kinds of writings and lives in Oxford, Mississippi, in Hollywood, in New York City, New Orleans, and in various locations abroad. Overlooked also was the testimony of his wife's and stepson's letters, and other records of what family and home life meant to him. And there were people still alive who had observed him as a father and neighbor, and these people had never been interviewed until I arrived on the scene.

A recent biographer, Kirk Curnutt, has termed Faulkner's work in Hollywood "lackadaisical," even though as early as the 1970s, Bruce Kawin began comparing Faulkner's fiction and screen work, and Kawin's scholarship has been carried on by Robert Hamblin, Peter Lurie, Ben Robbins, Sarah Gleeson-White, Stefan Solomon, and others.[4] But no biographer had taken up Robbins's insight: "Faulkner both reshaped and was shaped by the alien territories of commercial film." No biographer had taken seriously Meta Carpenter's memory of Faulkner's enthusiastic work on scripts about World War II, or seemed to know that Faulkner and director Howard Hawks at one time considered forming a production company.[5] No biographer saw how Faulkner's work on *Drums Along the Mohawk* (1939) had seeped into the writing of *The Wild Palms* (1939), or that one of his last screenplays, *The Left Hand of God* (1955), spoke directly to his own plight as a Nobel Laureate in an atomic Cold War world.

It is difficult to wrench from my two-volume life an extended example of how I have tried to overturn the typical narrative of Faulkner biography because each moment in my book calls on the whole of Faulkner's experience that went into the creation of, for example, his screenplays. Perhaps the closest I can come to a demonstration of my method is an account of his screen adaptation of *The Left Hand of God*. In her memoir, *A Loving Gentleman*, Meta Carpenter Wilde said Faulkner did not think much of the novel as the basis of a film. But he voiced his skepticism before he wrote the screenplay, and the results show that he changed his mind. What I aim to show in the following discussion of *The Left Hand of God* is how Faulkner came to terms with his own stature as a writer, confirmed by the Nobel Prize, in a film script that has been neglected by Faulkner critics and biographers.

Todd McCarthy boils down the director Howard Hawks's pitch to Faulkner: A picture based on William E. Barrett's "timely and inspirational novel, *The Left Hand of God*, about an American flier trying to escape the embattled China of 1947 disguised as a priest. The trappings of the story— the resourceful pilot hero, a gorgeous young nurse, the endangered outpost of humanity [a Catholic mission] trying to stave off violent and unpredictable forces—had obvious appeal to Hawks, who certainly would have played up the adventure and romance angles." But what was the appeal to Faulkner? The money was good: $2,000 a week and a bonus if Faulkner finished the work in a month. But did he need the money after the $30,000 Nobel award? In fact, he did, because he had set up a $25,000 trust fund. Much of the Nobel wealth would go to doing good works so that Faulkner would become the benefactor of his community, just like the hero he would fashion for *The Left Hand of God*.

But would money alone be enough to entice a Nobel Prize winner's return to the site of the Hollywood horror show and memories of the Ward, where he bent over his typewriter turning out products for the two-headed Warner Bros. monster he had drawn in a cartoon for his daughter Jill? In a hand-written discarded draft of the Nobel speech, he had recorded his humiliation and outrage: "A few years ago I was taken on as a script writer at a Hollywood studio. At once I began to hear the man in charge talking of 'angles,' story 'angles,' and then I realized that they were not even interested in truth, the old universal truths of the human heart without which any story is ephemeral—the universal truths of love and honor and pride and pity and compassion and sacrifice."[6] Why collaborate with the enemy? What could Hawks have said that would have moved Faulkner to return? Well, it was Howard Hawks, and Faulkner believed he owed a man whose work Faulkner respected and perhaps even learned from. How could he deny Hawks, who had been responsible for Faulkner's most important screenwriting credits: *To Have and Have Not* and *The Big Sleep*?

And what if *The Left Hand of God* abetted Faulkner's own work? What if Faulkner's adaptation of this "inspirational novel" fulfilled his script for *Battle Cry* (an ambitious feature film covering every front in World War II), and *Requiem for a Nun*, both of which dealt with the theme of redemption and of individuals asserting a newfound integrity in the midst of history? Hawks biographer Todd McCarthy calls Faulkner's first draft screenplay "craftsmanlike" but "rather dull and sincere, with an abundance of narration." But his work is superior to the film eventually released starring Humphrey Bogart and Gene Tierney.

Like so much of William Faulkner's life, what was deeply personal and what motivated his writing remain mysterious, one of those "trade secrets" he begrudgingly confided just once in a letter to his mother in 1925.[7] What Faulkner gave to his work he wanted to stay there, as if to share too much of himself even with his intimates would have robbed him of his powers—forces that had to be kept inside. At all costs, he had to avoid spillage, the leaking out of energies that more properly belonged in the books. Consequently, the biographer, like one of Faulkner's own characters, has to, at some points, speculate in order to complete the story of that character, William Faulkner. With Faulkner, one detects, surmises, infers, imagines, and ratiocinates.

From Hollywood, while working on *The Left Hand of God*, Faulkner wrote to his former lover Joan Williams: "Fantastic place, fantastic work." He went at the screenplay in what looks like a Hollywood be damned mood even as this old Hollywood hand of nearly twenty years standing, perfected certain Hollywood/Hawksian conventions, such as the John Wayne-Walter Brennan dialogues in *Red River* and *Rio Bravo*.[8]

Faulkner conceived of the film, although set in China, as a Hollywood western: "Evening after sunset. A small gorge or mountain pass, barren solitary. A rough trail along which pass a column of mounted men and heavy though crudely laden pack animals with their drivers." The studios wanted audiences to identify with foreign characters and situations as though the world abroad was American. So in the released version of the film, Lee J. Cobb plays a Chinese warlord. Faulkner did not suggest actors for the roles, but in creating Hank, he seemed to have Walter Brennan in mind, one of the stars of two Faulkner scripts, *Banjo on my Knee* and *To Have and Have Not*. Hank is not in Barrett's novel. He is a singular Faulkner creation but also a Hollywood creature. He is the wisecracking sidekick so often employed in the Brennan-Gary Cooper films and, even more notably, for Faulkner's purposes, in Hawks westerns the director was always trying to remake, Faulkner said, even in films like *Land of the Pharaohs* (1955), which Faulkner worked on as well.[9] After the first appearance of Jim Carmody, comes the "second white man," Hank, subordinate to Carmody but also his critic, functioning as Brennan does in *Red River* as Wayne's conscience. In one version of the film, Brennan also narrated the story, providing a perspective on the hero—by turns serious and comic, just as Hank does—who supports Carmody but also questions his decisions. As for the Chinese, well, they are make-do American Indians and even sometimes sound like refugees from Faulkner's script for *Drums Along the Mohawk*.

Without Hank, the released film lacks humor and tension, so that even an actor as great as Humphrey Bogart can seem if not exactly boring, then without enough to do, since he has no one, really, to answer to.[10] Listen to Hank narrate the story and you can hear Walter Brennan talking about China: "for my nickel you could have had the country and the job both two years ago, and by now even Jim too was going around to that idea." Soon the Communists would take over the country, but their encroaching power is only an off-camera phenomenon alluded to in the dialogue.

Hank's voiceovers are uncommonly long for the screen, but they could have been compressed while retaining his mordant humor. His narrative interludes function like the introductory sections of *Requiem for a Nun*, a draft of which Faulkner was writing on the reverse side of the *Left Hand of God* script.[11] Without Hank's narrative, the released version of the film lacks the background necessary to savor Carmody's developing moral consciousness, which he works out under Hank's intense scrutiny.

Jim and Hank are downed pilots now working for a Chinese warlord, Yang, their rescuer who will not let them go. They are also in the midst of a civil war trying to avoid "soviet gangs" who are moving across Yang's territory. When one of Yang's men kills a traveling priest, Carmody whips the murderer across the face—assuming an authority that Yang accords to himself. When Yang orders Carmody to do the same to Hank, the two white men escape, knowing full well that Yang, not daring to lose face, will come after them.

Carmody, wearing the dead priest's clothes, and Hank, dressed as a servant, find refuge in a Catholic mission, which has been expecting the arrival of a priest. Carmody, who has said, "Religion is for children," is called upon to perform mass, hear confession, administer communion, attend to the dying, and, in general, take care of the mission which becomes his mission—at first only as an effort to save himself but, in the end, to serve humanity. Carmody, for all his reluctance, performs well as a priest inspiring reverence among his congregation—rather like the recalcitrant Nobel laureate who found, to his surprise, that he could fulfill his public responsibilities with considerable success. It had not been easy. "Billy has gotten so touchy we don't dare mention his fame, and believe me, we edge off. He is so very proud and happy over winning the prize, but is his own shy self about publicity," his mother explained.[12]

In Faulkner's speeches at his daughter's graduations from high school and college, and in his Nobel address, Faulkner had insisted the world could change only if individuals, one by one, changed themselves and protested injustice. Carmody mentions he was an altar boy but is now a lapsed Catholic, and the dying priest replies, "There is no such thing." He might as well say, as Gavin Stevens does in *Requiem for a Nun*, "The past is never dead. It's not even past." Although Carmody jokes when he calls himself "an American white devil" when rejecting the attentions of a courtesan, he regards himself as unredeemed.

What matters, however, is Carmody's courage, loyalty, and self-sacrifice. Hank has injured himself in an avalanche—an episode not in the novel—and cannot walk. When they arrive at the village mission, Hank explains why he serves Carmody. Earlier, after their plane crashed: "It must have taken him days to keep me alive and still get me down that mountain to where he could find help. I don't know how he did it." But Carmody has not yet figured out how to save himself. That the mission welcomes Carmody as a priest becomes less significant, ultimately, than his understanding that their faith in God and humanity is what will redeem him. When the village comes to Carmody he is so moved that he kneels to them—a spontaneous gesture that Hank is sure came as a surprise: "I don't guess he knew why, either. But it was the right thing to do. It was exactly right. It was as if the Lord himself was taking care of him—of us—." The "us" is everyone, white and Chinese alike, and Carmody's spontaneous submission to his fate, to saving the village, seems like a gift of grace, not an action of his own volition. Was Faulkner thinking of the grace he had shown in the Nobel ceremony, the deft pirouetting that his lover Else Jonsson noticed—not aware that this was the same man who had doused himself with liquor in the days approaching the Nobel event? When Faulkner said the award was not just to him, he meant it. Accepting the prize signified that he could no longer go it alone, as he had done so often in Hollywood, in New York, at home, acting as his own soldier of fortune.

By all accounts, Faulkner's presence at Stockholm inspired awe. In *The Left Hand of God*, Anne, a devout Catholic and the wife of a lost American pilot (presumed dead) watches Carmody perform as Father O'Shea, and exults: "Never in my life did a Mass move me as that one did. He was so deliberate—so reverent—so sincere. It was as though it could go on forever . . . ." She is speaking of a moment but also of eternity and universality, the very terms of Faulkner's Nobel sermon. The Communists in the film are described as godless—not only in the disbelieving sense but in their obliteration of individuality, which Faulkner deplored in his anti-Communist speeches.

Carmody is Faulkner in character: "The whole Chinese family is watching him with the same air of complete trust. He sees the family and speaks to them in the hill dialect, indicating that he is learning even something of that." Hill dialect? That is precisely the dialect used in Faulkner's patriotic short stories such as "Shall Not Perish," written during World War II. That Faulkner had an impact similar to Carmody's is undeniable. Perrin H. Lowrey, Jr., writing to a Faulkner friend while Faulkner was in Hollywood working on *The Left Hand of God*, testified that "as a young writer, I wanted to tell someone close to him how much his speech of acceptance in Stockholm meant to those of us who are trying to turn out something good. The dignity and selflessness and awareness of that speech must have been particularly meaningful and encouraging to all the young writers of my generation. . . . So I wanted him to know . . . I simply wanted to thank him for doing so generous and so fine a thing."[13] Faulkner had to know through other aspiring writers such as Joan Williams and Shelby Foote, and many others that his words inspired generations of writers.

Hank who has kidded Carmody all along, calling him "Father," admits "something has happened to you." Carmody concurs: "something happened to me. I don't even know myself what it was. Yes, I do know—an old Buddhist priest—a man dying of leprosy—a woman dying in childbirth who held my hand and believed in me while she died—the patience, the suffering, the hope, but above all the trust—You see, I can't tell you," he says to Dr. Marvin, the priest who comes to relieve Carmody after he has saved the mission. Like the marshal (Gary Cooper) in *High Noon*, one of Faulkner's favorite pictures,[14] Carmody is full of doubt but acts so as to save himself and the community.

Carmody deals with the head villain, Yang, one-to-one. Carmody proposes a throw of the dice. If Carmody wins, the mission is saved. If Carmody loses, Yang will withdraw from the village but at the price of enslaving Carmody. Before they roll, though, Carmody says he has already won, telling Yang why the warlord will lose: "If I stood the torture well, people would say that I was stronger than Mieh Yang, since he could not break me. And if I stood it badly, they would marvel that such a weak man commanded your troops. They would wonder if maybe you too were not weak." Yang concedes to Carmody and withdraws his threat against the mission.

William Faulkner's *Left Hand of God* never got made because of production code violations and the Catholic Church's opposition. Even with his redemption, Carmody, in Faulkner's script, was too unsavory for the production code, which forbids, for example, scenes with a character pretending to be a priest and actually performing holy services. After two decades in Hollywood Faulkner knew that his mixture of the profane and the sacred could never be approved. His best screenplays, as I show elsewhere in my biography, were ambitious in scope, but since he could not control their production, he also could not take full ownership of his Hollywood achievements.

For a writer customarily viewed as fiercely independent and even recalcitrant, Faulkner's collaborative work in Hollywood, especially with Howard Hawks and his actors, is a revelation. It casts significant light on his later fiction, in which his characters collaborate in creating the communal narrative history of Yoknapatawpha, a history he also brought to Hollywood in scripts like "War Birds" and "Country Lawyer," which extended the range of his mythical county beyond what is essayed in his novels and stories.

In an essay on Faulkner biography, published in 2004, Kevin Railey called for a new biography of Faulkner that would emphasize not the monument to a great writer established by Joseph Blotner and his successors,[15] but rather a biography that would "renounce its affiliation with the myth of the coherent personality and explore the ways in which subjects are many-sided and multifarious entities."[16] That Faulkner—agile and adaptable—is the figure I track in my biography.

The Historians of Yoknapatawpha

Jay Parini

Overstatement is one reason why biographies miss their mark as literature. Thus Jay Parini, describing the perilous plight of World War I pilots, has to add that Faulkner's mother, bidding her son goodbye as he departed for flight training in Toronto, "must have thought she might never see her firstborn again." Describing the scene, evoking the atmosphere of a time when aviation had both a romantic and harrowing allure, is not enough. The biographer steps in to wreck the moment, compelled to comment on what he cannot possibly know.

It is odd that Parini, a novelist, doesn't seem to know better. Too many paragraphs in this bloated biography are ruined with this sort of tagline: "A faint adolescent mustache darkened the area above his lips, a hint of manhood in potentia." The sentence refers to Faulkner, the young flight cadet, who "walked on a cloud now, delighting in the uniform, which proclaimed his elevated status to the world." This built-in redundancy in the imagery is fatiguing—as are the clichés: "Faulkner (having permanently deep-sixed Falkner)."

That all of these examples are drawn from a single page gives you some idea of Parini's relentlessly bad prose. It is beyond me to explain how someone can teach Faulkner for thirty years—Parini reports in his preface he did—and begin his biography with banalities: "This book represents a particular journey, a series of discoveries, an attempt to reach through Faulkner to find him in his work, the work in him, without reading crassly backward from the work into the life."

Parini is a dutiful biographer—too dutiful. He acknowledges the most recent trends in Faulkner criticism, no matter how misguided. He is nothing if not politically correct, mentioning that "feminist and poststructuralist critics have tended to look at the story ["The Fire and the Hearth"] as a 'subtle defense of the southern status quo in which African-American challenges to oppression either are defused through humor or are displaced to the margins of the text (and thereby trivialized)." Such asides may win elections, but they doom (to use a favorite Faulknerian word) biography.

The "one matchless time" of Parini's title refers to the period between 1929 and 1942, when Faulkner "found not simply his own voice but a teeming chorus of voices, each of them distinct, whole, and authentic." This is generally regarded as Faulkner's greatest period of creativity, which Parini handles competently but with little fresh insight.

Parini correctly sensed that a new biography of Faulkner was needed—there are new letters and other documents to be integrated into a fresh account of the novelist's life and art, and because there has never been a wholly satisfying biography of reasonable length for the general reader.

Postscript: My review of Parini's biography was first published in the *New York Sun* (November 10, 2004). It is harsh and reflects my disappointment in a biography I had expected to like. Parini's book had a favorable reception from others, and it may well be that for all the faults I find, his work remains the single, most accessible full-length but not unduly long biography of Faulkner yet written. That Parini's work has a value that my initial review does not acknowledge, is also evident in the use I put Parini to in other parts of this book.

M. Thomas Inge

What does it mean to be a Faulknerian biographer? In his new book *William Faulkner* M. Thomas Inge supplies the answer right off: "Faulkner wrote as if there were no literature written in English before him, no century and more of convention and literary tradition established before he put pen to paper. He recreated fiction anew and set the novel free to better serve the twentieth century through a powerful, discordant, and irresistible torrent of language that crashed through time, space, and experience to tell the story of modern mankind in ways both tragic and comic. Faulkner would have written the way he did whether or not James Joyce, Virginia Woolf, Joseph Conrad, and the others had ever existed." To be a Faulknerian biographer, one has to be bold, to realize that source studies (what Faulkner absorbed from other writers), social and cultural context, psychological analysis—indeed all the staples

THE HISTORIANS OF YOKNAPATAWPHA   19

of modern literary criticism and biography—do not avail when it comes to portraying the greatest writer in the English language save Shakespeare.

Inge, a southerner steeped in southern literature and history, and eyewitness to a Faulkner lecture at the University of Virginia (the biographer includes a charming sketch he made of his subject), understands that it is best just to stand back, so to speak, and simply describe the career of a writer who admitted that his genius was a gift he could not explain.

The lesser Faulkner—the one who wanted to be a poet—failed precisely because he was derivative and wanted to show that he could write like A. E. Housman, T. S. Eliot, Keats, and the other greats he worshipped. Only when Faulkner decided to put away his books did he rise to the magnificence of *The Sound and the Fury, As I Lay Dying, Light in August, Absalom, Absalom!, The Wild Palms, The Hamlet,* and *Go Down, Moses*—works that defy categorization, products of savage humor and searing tragedy, embodying an epistemology that has enticed generations of scholars and general readers.

Faulkner has often been described as a "difficult" author. His answer to that charge was to suggest reading his work again. There is no better advice to be had. What certain reviewers decried as chaotic was in fact writing of exquisite order and perception. Faulkner is fathomable, but you need to take the time to take him at his word. I was heartened to find on amazon.com a lively volume of chatter about *Absalom, Absalom!*—not among academics but among readers who had found their way to greatness and wanted to share their knowledge of it with others.

Faulkner appeals to us on a gut level. We want to know who his characters are, why they are telling their stories, why others contradict their stories, why, in the case of *Absalom, Absalom!*, all of them are fixated on Thomas Sutpen, who came to Jefferson, Mississippi, where he built himself a mansion and started a dynasty and then somehow destroyed it all. Albert Camus was right when he said Faulkner had brought Greek tragedy into detective fiction.

Although I was introduced to Faulkner back in my undergraduate days by Inge and went on to publish my own first book on Faulkner, I still had much to learn from this deft, cogent book, which is certainly the definitive introduction to Faulkner. Inge dispels a few myths and misperceptions.

Myth No.1: Faulkner was a neglected writer whose reputation needed rehabilitating by the critic Malcolm Cowley, whose publication of *The Portable Faulkner* in 1946 set off a reevaluation of the novelist that led to a Nobel Prize in 1950. Not so. Until reading this biography, I did not fully appreciate the cumulative impact Faulkner made on readers in the 1930s and 1940s, even as Hemingway and Fitzgerald outshone him in the public eye. Faulkner's original and "difficult" novels received discerning reviews. Certainly Cowley's "Portable" was propitious, but it was not decisive.

Myth No.2: Faulkner was an acquired taste among the literati, and sales of his work did not pick up until after the Nobel Prize. In fact, *Sanctuary, Pylon*, and *The Wild Palms* sold well. It is true that Faulkner went through a dry period in the mid-1940s when most of his books were out of print, but by 1948 his novel *Intruder in the Dust* was a bestseller.

That Faulkner had his detractors is hardly worth mentioning, although Inge scrupulously gives them their due. An unconventional man, Faulkner was bound to irritate some reviewers because of his relentless quest to shatter the norms of storytelling. Who would dare to begin a novel from the point of view of an idiot? And yet having Benjy Compson do so in *The Sound and the Fury* produced some of the greatest imagist prose of this century. Who would create a novel by alternating chapters with a passionate love story, rather like *A Farewell to Arms* with those devoted to the tall tale of a convict caught in a Mississippi flood? And yet the emotional entanglements evoked in these juxtaposed narratives suddenly collide in the convict's terse concluding word, "Women!"—which makes *The Wild Palms* such a powerful tragicomedy.

Inge's book is a wonderful addition to the Overlook Press series of illustrated biographies. His selection of photographs is astute: He puts together sequences of images that suggest the rhythms of Faulkner's life

This biography is a miracle of compression, made possible only because its author has distilled a lifetime of devotion to his subject into this small gem of a book.

André Bleikasten

In his Foreword to *William Faulkner: A Life through Novels*, Philip Weinstein calls André Bleikasten the "most distinguished interpreter of America's greatest twentieth-century novelist." Weinstein's own impressive work on Faulkner entitles him to make such a sweeping claim. But when he advances a similar claim to superiority for this biography, I have to dissent. Bleikasten's book, published in French in 2009, is barely a biography at all. Weinstein scarcely mentions other Faulkner biographies, preferring to contrast Joseph Blotner's standard account of "day-by-day and year-by-year doings" that avoids what Faulkner "means: why we should read him, what we will find there" with Bleikasten's "capacity to say, again and again, exactly how Faulkner's work works." I doubt any critic can do exactly what Weinstein asserts, but, more importantly, Bleikasten fails to show what biography can offer to Faulkner readers or why biography matters.

As Weinstein reports, Bleikasten rejected the idea of writing a Faulkner biography more than once, suggesting "there were already too many biographies of Faulkner out there." It is a commonplace of critics to complain about the plethora of biographies on the same subject, as if biography has only one story to tell, whereas Faulkner's work demonstrates, again and again, that biography, as in *Absalom, Absalom!*, depends crucially on who is telling the tale and when that tale is told. Style, structure, point of view, and, of course, evidence and proximity matter and differ from one biography to another of the same subject. What to select, how to say it, when it is said, yield a William Faulkner markedly different in Blotner, Frederick Karl, Joel Williamson, Jay Parini, Judith Sensibar, or Philip Weinstein—to name just some of the Faulkner biographers. Take any page from these biographies covering the same time in Faulkner's life, and you will see a different man—recognizable, of course, from one account to another, and yet subtly and importantly at odds with the figure presented in one biography after another.

So why did Bleikasten relent and write yet another biography of Faulkner? He decided he could "synthesize what he had come to know about Faulkner over the years," and this much Bleikasten does brilliantly while acknowledging and relying on the work of his predecessors. But what synthesis means, on the Bleikasten page, is summary. So, for example, we get a judicious assessment of all that Faulkner said about race, with notations of his inconsistencies, his paternalism, and racism, juxtaposed against the much more profound explorations of color and the color line in his novels. Fair enough. But where are Faulkner's interactions with blacks and whites? The evidence is there, collected, for example, by Robert Cantwell in the 1930s and available not only in his publications but in his papers at the University of Oregon. The visceral, palpable sense of who Faulkner was, the man we want to read about in a biography, is absent from this fastidious account of those "doings" that Blotner detailed.

Bleikasten wrote his biography before the full force of Judith Sensibar's work on the women in Faulkner's life became available to biographers. As in all the other biographies, Faulkner's wife, Estelle, appears in Bleikasten as a lamentable marriage partner, fey and on the periphery of what matters to the critic eager to get on with the explication of the text, at which the French are best. That Estelle Faulkner wrote fiction, that Faulkner even submitted fiction under both their names and rewrote at least one of her stories, does not interest Bleikasten, even though such facts suggest why at certain points of his life Faulkner found Estelle to be an indispensable partner, no matter how much he complained about her as a burden and an irrelevance. Biography is not supposed to take subjects at their word—at least not without the scrutiny that Faulkner's own characters aim at one another—but that is essentially what Bleikasten does. And of course he is not the first astute critic to have no feel, which is to say, no understanding of what biography can contribute to an understanding of the mentality that shaped the subject's work.

Too often biographers get mired in source hunting, trying to show how a character like Faulkner's Gavin Stevens is modeled after his friend Phil Stone. Critics rightly groan at such one-to-one comparisons, since in so many ways a character like Stevens is not Phil Stone, even if Stone provided a few tics and behaviors and background usable in a novel. Bleikasten spares us that kind of simple-minded alignment of life and work. But what he does not search for and cannot supply are the deep biographical threads that unify the subject's life and the biography written about him.

One example will have to suffice. Bleikasten provides a standard dismissal of *A Fable*, a work that Faulkner hoped would be his crowning masterpiece. It is a work set during World War I, the war of the novelist's youth, the war that was over before he finished flight training in Toronto, the war that he pretended to have served in as he hobbled about on a cane, acting the part of the walking wounded for Sherwood Anderson. Bleikasten suggests the novel does not succeed because Faulkner did not participate in the war and was too removed from the setting in France to provide a convincing narrative.

A critic, then, may applaud this summary judgment: "Weighted down with long and confusing commentaries and similarly interminable descriptions (there is page upon page about uniforms), his prose becomes bloated and winded, the rhetoric so rehashed and jaded that it no longer touches us." A biographer, reading such a passage, will wonder: why all the uniforms? A Faulkner biographer, ought, at this point, to intervene, noting that Faulkner's favorite doll was an Irish policeman in uniform with a cap. Faulkner not only bought a carefully tailored RAF uniform with decorations he did not earn, he kept that uniform and wore it proudly when he returned home from Toronto and on special occasions. His stepson Malcolm Franklin first saw Faulkner at a piano recital wearing that uniform and cap and thought Faulkner was a policeman. Faulkner in his fifties was proud that he could still fit into that uniform. That uniform, in pristine condition, was on display in a Faulkner exhibition at the University of Virginia. Uniforms triggered Faulkner's imagination—so much so that his stories about World War I were taken as accounts of his own firsthand experience by veterans who had seen action on the western front. Knowing all this does not make *A Fable* a better novel, but it does explain why a consummate craftsman like William Faulkner could not see that what had so impressed and engaged him would not thrive on the page.

Biography, in short, does not just show how the subject's work works or even why it does not. Biography shows how a subject like William Faulkner made literature out of his life, a literature of and from himself. This is what Bleikasten's subtitle, *A Life Through Novels*, ought to mean but does not. This is a biography that speaks powerfully to critics but that will disappoint those looking to understand why the man wrote as he did.

Michael Gorra

The Saddest Words: William Faulkner's Civil War

Michael Gorra, Mary Augusta Jordan Professor of English Language and Literature at Smith College, and editor of the Norton Critical Edition of *As I Lay Dying*, is well prepared to take on the subject of William Faulkner and the Civil War. He has read the relevant literature on Faulkner and race—so much of which inevitably deals with the legacy of the Civil War—but he also realizes that no scholar has looked squarely at what Faulkner knew about the war and its aftermath in the American psyche. This lacuna in Faulkner scholarship is due, in part, to Faulkner's refusal to write a historical novel about the war. He comes closest to the subject in *The Unvanquished*, as Gorra observes, but much of the action in that novel is on the periphery of the war. Faulkner never described a major Civil War battle or included any of its major figures in his fiction as significant characters. What we have instead are fitful scenes set in the war, as in *Absalom, Absalom!* and memories of the war that suffuse novels such as *Flags in the Dust*, originally published as *Sartoris* and *Light in August*.

While Gorra draws on the work of notable Faulkner scholars, his book is aimed at the general reader. For that reason, he often retells the plots of Faulkner's novels and actually reconstructs Faulkner's Yoknapatawpha County, drawing together his data from several different works of fiction. As a result, he provides something like the compendium Malcolm Cowley assembled, with Faulkner's approval, in *The Portable Faulkner* (1946). A reader new to Faulkner will find the back matter of Gorra's book helpful since it includes maps of Faulkner's Yoknapatawpha County, a William Faulkner chronology, a list of his major works, and "Yoknapatawpha County: A Brief History of an Imaginary Place."

Gorra takes his title from *The Sound and the Fury* (1929), in which Jason Compson, the son of a Confederate general, tells his son Quentin that "was" is the saddest word. We cannot change the past, since it is over. But Quentin cannot take "was" that way because the past is inescapable: it happens over and over again in memory. Or as Gorra puts it: "What *was* is never over." Not only Quentin but Gail Hightower in *Light in August,* young Bayard Sartoris in *Flags in the Dust,* and other characters cannot to seem to live fully in the present because the past of their defeated land is a constant reminder of human failure, of what the South came to call the "lost cause."

All this is quite familiar to Faulkner readers and has been the subject of scholarly inquiry now for more than seventy years. But much of that inquiry has been within the parameters of Faulkner's own fiction. Not enough atten-tion, Gorra argues, has been focused on what Faulkner left out—not merely the Civil War battles but the very idea of the war—what it was about and how the South and the rest of the nation dealt with its defeat. In *Flags in the Dust,* old man Falls, a Civil War veteran, says he never did figure out the war's purpose. Gorra suggests that at one time Falls probably did know, but like southerners and northerners alike he preferred to forget in a spirit of reconciliation. A whole school of historiography—in the South and North—elided the issue of slavery in favor of explanations dealing with sectional conflict and the incompetence of regional leaders. Faulkner, schooled at the turn of the twentieth century, never quite surmounted the deep South view that Reconstruction was a terrible mistake, foisted by the North not only on whites but on the ill-prepared African Americans who could not govern let alone vote with any true knowledge of how to reconstitute a society.

Contemporary scholars have rejected that revanchist historiography of the Reconstruction period, but much earlier, in the 1930s, W. E. B. Du Bois went against the tide of the sentimental version of slavery propagated by Margaret Mitchell in *Gone with the Wind,* Ulrich Bonnell Phillips in his histories of slav-ery, and sometimes, alas, perpetuated by Faulkner in some of his short stories. Du Bois wanted to debate Faulkner after the novelist had become a public figure in the 1950s and began making statements about integration, which he supported but also consigned to a nebulous future when southerners would somehow in a new generation throw off the racism of their ancestors. Du Bois would have confronted Faulkner with an array of data about Reconstruction, showing how both Northern and Southern leaders set it up to fail. Du Bois would have refuted Faulkner's patronizing suggestion that Black people might not yet be ready for equality with whites—hence the need, as the novelist said, to "go slow" where integration was concerned. In short, Gorra deploys Du Bois as a major counterpoint to Faulkner's purblind narratives of war.

Gorra's book, however, is not meant to be a debunking of Faulkner. Gorra realizes that no American novelist has treated race in quite so profound

THE HISTORIANS OF YOKNAPATAWPHA

a manner that puts it at the core of what we think about the Civil War. Faulkner's fiction, as Gorra demonstrates, often gives the lie to what Faulkner the public figure said. This passage from *The Saddest Words* embodies a nuanced view of the man and his work and why both still matter:

> Faulkner could not see the racial ideology of his world—could not even really think—except when writing fiction. He could stand outside that ideology only by first assigning it to a character. He inhabited those beliefs by inhabiting another person. Then he saw them clearly, and in that act he became better than he was. Another way to say this is that Faulkner could not have written so clearly of mob psychology in "Dry September" without knowing it from within, without feeling or recognizing the force of its communal roar. One of his few adequate pieces of nonfiction is a loose autobiographical sketch called "Mississippi" (1954), an essay written in the third person, as though it were about somebody other than himself. There he describes the "middleaged novelist" as a man who loves his "native land . . . even while hating some of it." Loving the river and the hills, the fields and the voices, but hating "the intolerance and injustice": hating, among other things, the fact that black people "could worship the white man's God but not in the white's man church"; hating above all the irrevocable evil of lynching itself. There the novelist recognizes that its victims are chosen simply "because their skins were black" and feels the sting of shame. I spoke in my preface of a civil war within Faulkner himself. In reading these words I wonder if it was only Mississippi that he hated.

The passage suggests that Faulkner directed that love and hate at himself, which might certainly account for some of his self-destructive drinking, although Gorra does not do much speculating about his subject's biography.

Gorra does not consider other reasons Faulkner avoided a frontal treatment of the Civil War. In general, Faulkner had a bias against historical fiction and did not believe an entire novel could be sustained set entirely in the past—or at least such a novel could not attain the high art that he aspired to create. He also showed remarkably little interest in the historian's desire to know what actually happened in the past. He favored good stories and the lore he absorbed as a child listening to Civil War veterans and to his family and teachers. By the time he was called upon to deliver opinions on civil rights and other matters pertaining to the Civil War, his orientation toward fiction made it impossible for him to analyze the actual history of his region. To have

FAULKNER AND BIOGRAPHY

accounted for the Civil War as Robert Penn Warren did in *The Legacy of the Civil War*—another book Gorra makes excellent use of—Faulkner would have had to address his northern audience with a specificity he had been careful to avoid. In 1918, on his first trip North, he began to understand how peculiar his way of thinking and speaking could seem outside his native land, and he became watchful about how he expressed himself. It may seem simplistic to say he shaped his fiction to please his paymasters in the North, the New York publishers who were entranced by his southern manners and his gentlemanly mystique on his frequent trips to the city, but his letters show a canny ability over more than two decades to extract lucre from those publishers by pleading poverty (often he was close to bankruptcy) even as his novels failed to return a profit. Until the Nobel Prize (1949) made him a moneymaker, the nobility of Random House's devotion to him might even be called "a lost cause," a theme he knew how to orchestrate with exquisite precision.

Interview with Michael Gorra

An Edited Excerpt, February 6, 2021

MG: I wanted to unkink Yoknapatawpha, straighten it out, tell what Faulkner himself would not do, was probably incapable of doing because that's not the way his mind worked. I wanted to provide a sort of history of Yoknapatawpha from the days of white settlement on up to about 1930.

CR: You can talk about what he does to the Civil War, but there's lots of things he doesn't do. Why is that he doesn't do certain things?

MG: What he doesn't do is big battle scenes, and there were certainly plenty of big battles in Lafayette County, where he grew up and lived. Oxford was occupied twice by Union forces. He lets the war be an off-stage echo. It will come into Jefferson briefly and recede.... He's interested in the lingering effects of the war. You'll remember that passage in *Absalom, Absalom* where Quentin thinks "Maybe happen is never once." Like ripples in water, and then the event that is that stone ripples out. And you can see those ripples long after the stone has sunk. Well Faulkner is interested in those ripples.... With his characters he often doesn't dramatize the big events in their lives.... We don't get the moment itself. We don't actually get Henry Sutpen's killing of Charles Bon. We get the report of it. What people say about it, remember about it. What Faulkner does with characters he does with history—the ripple of the event not the momentary flash of the event itself.

CR: You can see why this happens, since he grew up in the aftermath of the Civil War. He heard about it, but he was not a participant. He writes from the point of view of someone whose Civil War is his heritage but it didn't actually happen to him. Even so, his contemporaries are writing historical novels. Stark Young is writing about the Civil War. The only time Faulkner does that in a book is *The Unvanquished.*

MG: He wrote it for money, although Faulkner never did anything purely for money, or he would write things for money and then revise them until suddenly they were much more complicated. He did that with *The Unvanquished.* He's writing *Absalom, Absalom!* and is immersed in the past, and then he finds he needs a bank balance to go on. So he takes that knowledge of the Civil War to get himself a bank balance, draws on family experiences in the Civil War, sells the stories to *The Saturday Evening Post*, invents a twelve-year-old boy who sees events that he does not fully understand, and maybe that he does not understand is a kind of ripple effect. . . . Faulkner's stories build up one another until we get to that extraordinary story, "An Odor of Verbena," in which the young man who's grown up in the Confederate South and its heritage and says, "No, I'm not going to take on everything that heritage tells me to do. . . . I'm not going to kill for it."

 . . . In the third story of that book, when they go in search of the silver that the Union army has taken from their family, they come upon columns of newly freed people marching across the landscape—they were called contrabands—Black people who have left slavery behind but didn't know where to go yet, so they were marching in the path of the Union army. Bayard Sartoris doesn't really understand, but I think Faulkner understood it, and we read that story now, in the light of more recent historiographical work on what the exit from slavery was like, it gains an extraordinary power.

CR: It's part of a great migration, and its happening in the 1930s.

MG: That's true. I hadn't really thought of it that way, but to think of that story, "Raid," as an early iteration of the great migration—that makes a great deal of sense. I like that.

CR: To go back to "An Odor of Verbena," I wonder about the extent to which Faulkner is like that main character, Bayard Sartoris, in that, when you look at his work—not just the Civil War but his whole southern heritage—he honors it in so many ways and yet he's clearly not what other members of his family are—segregationists for example. . . . At the University of Virginia he said about his grandson: "He can have a Confederate battle flag if he wants one, but he shouldn't take it too seriously."

MG: That analogy between Bayard and Faulkner makes a lot of sense to me. . . . He knows his father did things that are unconscionable. Faulkner

28   FAULKNER AND BIOGRAPHY

is like that with his knowledge of the southern past, his sense of the difference between himself and the other white people around him. . . . I spent yesterday afternoon with your own book and what struck me was the racism of Faulkner's mother. You have a moment when she likes listening to Nat King Cole but when she finds out he's Black, she breaks all his records. It's a terrible moment. And Faulkner is seeing her everyday. But he is listening to "That Evening Sun." Faulkner likes the blues.

CR: What we don't know. What no one is ever going to know is *did* he ever have a conversation with his mother about race and slavery. I suspect not.

MG: I suspect you are right.

CR: I want to tie this to something you say in your book: You say he is "drawn to the outer edge of the unsayable." We can talk about that in terms of his fiction. We can talk about that in terms of his family. For example: Black Faulkners.

MG: There are Black Faulkners all through that part of Mississippi. It's not like Thomas Jefferson where people have done a genome. . . . Although it doesn't much matter. They inhabit the same world. They would have grown up on different sides of a racial dynamic that nevertheless bound them to each other. . . . I'm not certain Faulkner would have had many conversations about race with anybody close to him. He would have talked to University of Mississippi historian James Silver about race, but with blood relatives I think probably not. There are such enormous reticences on his part. Did he talk about it with publishers, other writers outside the South? He and Stark Young had conversations in New York City when they were young. That would be interesting to know. You say that Young's family had a consciousness of slavery as a burden they were uneasy with. I think Faulkner himself was uneasy with it, but not to the point that he could talk about it with other people—with his own family, in particular.

CR: I did a lot of work in the Floyd Watkins archive and read transcripts of conversations between him and Faulkner's hunting buddy, John Cullen, and one of the things Cullen says is that he was just amazed when Faulkner started making public statements about civil rights and race, because he had just assumed that Faulkner thought just the way Cullen did. Cullen, by today's standards, would certainly be called a racist. His view was "They're doing pretty good for people who came out of Africa as savages." That was a very common opinion that whites had, and you see vestiges of this occasionally when Faulkner makes comments about Reconstruction, where you can see he was taught this kind of thing. In the fiction—and you do a really good job of this—he is a very different man. He can free himself from these familial attachments. The fiction, the life of the imagination takes over. When Shreve says at the end of *Absalom,*

Absalom!—I'm paraphrasing: "I who look at you now will have descended from the loins of African kings"—that's an absolutely astounding statement.

MG: It absolutely is. Two things come to mind: One is thinking of John Cullen, *Old Times in the Faulkner Country*, as a young man part of the group that hunted down Nelse Patton and participated in the lynching. The other line, "doing pretty well for people who might have been in Africa"—a few months after my book came out I got a five-page single-spaced letter from a retired physician, no less, who essentially voiced the same idea: Being a slave in antebellum America, this man said, didn't I think that was better than being hungry and naked in Africa? It went on and on asking questions like this.

CR: Cullen describes much more graphically than in *Old Times in the Faulkner Country* the castration of Nelse Patton at the same time as he is talking about African Americans with a history of savagery—with no irony, no sense that this is terrorism that whites are practicing.

MG: It's the sort of attitude you see in "Pantaloon in Black," where the white sheriff is talking about the lynching of Ryder and just shaking his head and saying, "Well, they don't feel things like we do." The story shows the moral poverty of that sheriff and of the social order he is upholding

CR: At the same time, I've always had the sense that that White Man is rattled. He's seen things that he can't quite comprehend and he's got these bromides and cliches and the ideology. . . .

MG: That makes sense. At a certain point, when faced with experience, with an actual fact, they just run away into ideology. They don't have a language to define what they see and feel about what they see. So they fall into what they feel they ought to feel.

CR: Before we finish I want to say that one of the things about your kind of book, if it's done badly, is to simply abstract from Faulkner a message: "This is what Faulkner thought about the Civil War." What makes your book work for me is your attention, when it is necessary, to deal with individual works with nuances that are different from *The Unvanquished* to *Absalom, Absalom!*

MG: Thank you, yes: The war in *Go Down Moses* is not the same as the war in *Flags in the Dust*, or the trace of the war in *The Sound and the Fury*, let alone *Light in August*. The characters are different. Faulkner is always attuned to the particular way in which a character's experience and memory has shaped the world around them. There are more memorable characters in Faulkner for me than in any other American writer. The variety of their responses to what is yet a tightly contained social and physical landscape.

CR: Is there anything else I should have asked you?

MG: No, but I want to say some things about your own book. One of the things that has really struck me is just how good you are with women in Faulkner's life—on his mother, on Estelle. You talk more openly about Estelle's alcoholism than anybody does, and also the glamour of Estelle— dancing with the Prince of Wales and what she brought back with her to Mississippi. And then the way you talk about Faulkner's own alcoholism. You say quite rightly that he was not interested in investigating it. It was just a fact of life to him. "I drank, and now I'm drying out, and that's just the way it is."

CR: Thank you, thank you. It's what happens when time goes on, things change, we see different values. I've learned a lot from Faulkner scholars— Judith Sensibar, for example. If I hadn't read her, I don't think I could have done the kind of biography I've written. Biography is that kind of cumulative, incremental experience.

MG: I think it's hard to make the secondary characters in a biography vivid, and your book really does that.

CR: Thanks again.

MG: It's really been fun, Carl. I've enjoyed the talk

CR: So have I.

Biographical Fiction
A Faulknerian Novel

William Faulkner wanted to fly as much as he wanted to write. In his post–World War I novel, *Soldier's Pay*, he has a young cadet, who just missed serving in the war, claim he would rather have been mortally wounded than not to have flown and fought. So it was for Faulkner, stuck in a Canadian RAF camp, when the war ended—so distressed that he returned home with wings he had not earned and a factitious limp. In short, he created himself as a work of fiction.

In *Wingwalkers*, Taylor Brown, steeped in Faulkner biography, uses that Faulkner persona to create a novel that is an original portrayal of a world gone wild over flying, watching barnstormers and wingwalkers and paying for the privilege of taking flight from the mundane and miserable circumstances of their lives.

Brown invents Captain Zeno Marigold, World War I ace, and Della the Daring Devilette, crisscrossing the country, living on the coinage of their aerial exploits, until they come upon disaster in an air show when Zeno disobeys Della's command that he should refuse to fly an experimental plane that . . . well, I shouldn't spoil the story for you.

Does it all sound familiar? The rootless aviators, their mad intense love, and the writer who meets them and quietly, almost submissively, inserts himself into their company? Zeno and Della are Faulknerian characters, right out of *Sartoris* (1929), *Pylon* (1935), and *The Wild Palms* (1939). Wingwalkers is a brilliant mashup of Faulkner, the man and the writer. The facts are taken from Joseph Blotner's magisterial *Faulkner: A Biography* (1974), but the way Brown matches Faulkner with Zeno and Della is ingenious.

Brown's Faulkner watches Zeno and Della and announces he is going to write about the air show in New Orleans, as he did in *Pylon*, but their passion and commitment to one another, which depends, in Zeno's case, on the couple's life in the air comes to ground fatally, since of course, flight can only be a temporary solution to the agony of existence.

I'm trying to write about this exquisite novel without giving it all away—much as Faulkner suspends conventional narrative in novels that make us want not only to read but reread his characters' actions. Their lives and motivations have to be pieced together and depend on our own persistent desire to understand what is going on with them.

When Faulkner meets Zeno and Della, Brown resists the temptation to tell us what Faulkner thinks of them. Faulkner remains, as in biographies of him, a man of mystery, who gives away very little of himself. It all goes into the writing, you see. To go off the page and confess, so to speak, never appealed to him.

But a telling scene in *Wingwalkers* reveals more about Faulkner than he is willing to say. In a rowdy New Orleans bar, he scribbles something on a napkin when he is told the couple is on the way to California. You will have to read the novel to learn what the napkin note says. Suffice it to say that Faulkner understands Brown's characters.

Wingwalkers is, to an unusual extent, an extrapolation of Faulkner's fiction. The form of Brown's novel is reminiscent of *The Wild Palms*, which tells two separate, yet intertwined stories: the doomed love affair of Harry Wilbourne and Charlotte Rittenmeyer, on the one hand, and, on the other, the epic efforts of a Mississippi convict to save himself and a pregnant women during the Great Mississippi Flood of 1927.

At their best, biographical novels extend the work of biography. Brown has taken familiar stories from Blotner, like Billy, an avid reader of *The American Boy* magazine, building a plane with his brothers that crashes but only stimulates their desire to take flight.

Faulkner liked to believe his characters kept changing and evolving and he was just trying to keep up with them, just as we try to keep up with Faulkner, and as he tries to keep up with Brown's characters, who have emerged out of his imagination via Brown.

The symbiosis of fact and fiction in *Wingwalkers* is vertiginous. Reading this book will give you a thrill.

Interview with Taylor Brown

Edited Excerpt, May 21, 2022

TB: I was in Oxford, Mississippi, in Square Books, one of the most storied bookstores in the country, definitely in the South. The walls are just covered in all this literary memorabilia. When I was on the staircase landing, I looked over and I saw this shadow box on the wall, and it had a photo of Faulkner inside of it. But it wasn't the Faulkner we are used to seeing with a pipe and looking very distinguished with silver hair and who had won the Nobel Prize. He looked like he was barely out of his teens, and he was in his flying uniform, and he cut a pretty rakish figure. He has his flying cap cocked on, a rattan cane, a hand-rolled cigarette stuck in his mouth. Come to find out later that his mother took those photographs. It really sparked my imagination. I remembered how much aviation was in his early work. I was always interested in aviation myself. My Dad was a pilot, and I was what he called a "waffle belly," a kid who always wants to go to the airport and watched the airplanes take off and land. If you do it enough and you lean against the chain link fence, you become a "waffle belly." I started picking up the Blotner biography and memoirs by Faulkner's brothers and as you know were all pilots. Faulkner had been a "waffle belly too." It felt like digging up buried treasure: the hot air balloonist who came to Oxford whom they called the "balloonatic" who landed on the Faulkner henhouse one year, and building this boy-sized airplane out of bean poles and wrapping paper and trying to fly it off a bluff behind the house. But I didn't have enough for a novel until I came across this tidbit in Blotner about the opening of the Shushan airport in New Orleans in 1934, which they open during Mardi Gras with all this fanfare. The Blotner biography says he showed up, hung over, that morning at the family he was staying with and told them a wild tale of the night he'd spent with aviators from the meet: a man on a motorcycle he rode with spending the night drinking and carousing with them. I could find out nothing else about who they were or what kind of night they had. That to me was a story waiting to be told. Who were these pilots/motorcyclists, and how did their lives intersect with Faulkner's? What might the consequences have been?

CR: That's fascinating, as you say, because we don't know any more about the story than Faulkner was willing to tell. Faulkner used the material about the flyers and the air show, and that's all in *Pylon*. He's telling a different story there. There's no motorcycle there, but the novel is so close to the grain of Faulkner's experience that anyone who knows his biography will be fascinated to see what you make of this. I don't know if you like the term biographical novel. Such novels stretch the facts—they have to—because there are things biographers can never know. But you're doing something much more specific. You are really getting to the grain of his experience, the way he looked at flying, as opposed to telling a more external story. It's like a novel Faulkner could have written, a kind of parallel universe to *Pylon*.

TB: It's interesting that you say that because there are ways that I thought of it as that as I was writing. As we know *Pylon* is not Faulkner's best work, right? He wrote it in something like six weeks, taking a break from *Absalom, Absalom!* Part of me wanted him to put more into *Pylon*. Zeno and Della—I wanted them to be Faulkner's characters. There seems to be some awareness of that on Della's part that she is part of a story that someone is weaving that she is not in control of. Maybe we all are, but who is in control of it?

CR: I felt when I was reading *Pylon* that the reporter who is observing the flyers and is never given a name is kind of like Faulkner, a "waffle belly." His experience is vicarious. He is fascinated with people who have no roots and are not tied to the ground. What you do in the novel, it seems to me, is that you take that reporter and you make him Faulkner—the way Faulkner meets them and observes them. He even writes a note to the characters on their way to Hollywood, a kind of tip. Was it a hard novel to write?

TB: At times, yes, but there are novels that have a tailwind. I felt as if I was sure I was on the right track, just going with it. I felt I had found something that I was uniquely qualified to tell by having the affinity with Faulkner and his interest in aviation that I didn't choose but was just the way I grew up. For me it was healing. In January 2016, my first novel had come out. I had been working pretty much my whole life to have a novel published by a big New York press. That was my dream. Who knows how many rejections? Novels I had written and thrown away. I had a spreadsheet of something like five hundred submissions with thirty of them accepted. So in January of that year I had achieved what I set out to do. I did end up feeling very alone soon after that. I felt "now what?" You've worked so hard for this dream, and I'd lived a somewhat monastic existence for several years, gone through an early divorce, and didn't really have anyone to share it with. In studying and getting deeper into Faulkner's biography, and seeing all of the critical, romantic, emotional—all the hardships that he went through, in some ways I took a lot of strength from that. "I'm not alone. This is the story of being an artist." We look back at legendary figures like Faulkner, and we think of them as just geniuses and it was easy for them. Going through that process and getting deeper into it, was good for me somehow.

CR: Your writing experience parallels Faulkner's. He wrote an early novel, *Elmer*, which he never published, the first two published novels were certainly respectable, but the Faulkner we know does not appear until his third and really his fourth novel, *The Sound and the Fury*, a work of genius. So he's got a good ten years there of struggle before he, in any sense, makes it, and he's still worried about money for a good part of his career, but he had that sense of early failure and why am I doing this, and how am I going to support myself. What you said about having a tailwind, I don't think there is any correlation between how long it takes to write a novel and the quality of it. Faulkner struggled for years over certain novels, but he said he wrote *As I Lay Dying* in six weeks—maybe a little longer than that. There were some revisions. But it came very, very quickly. As you say, it fell into place.

TB: I agree, and I've learned to remember that myself when things come really fast and wonder "is this too fast and not good," or it takes a really long time, and think "is it not good because it's taking me so long?" Both ways can work out.

CR: Sometimes biographers look at Faulkner's later letters—as Faulkner got older he worried that he was losing his inspiration and wondered "am I as good as I was before"—and latch onto that as the truth, because he has these *feelings*, maybe whatever book he is writing is not as good as some of the earlier stuff—that he knows something. But he doesn't know something. He's checking himself, so to speak.

TB: Absolutely. He's just being an artist. If he didn't have that doubt, it wouldn't be natural. Or he wouldn't be writing as well, since he would just be thinking everything he is doing is amazing.

CR: Your book, I say in my *New York Sun* review is Faulknerian, but it is not just an extension of Faulkner's work but of the form—the way you create these intersecting stories: on the one hand, the flyers, Zeno and Della, and on the other of Faulkner, reminds me of *The Wild Palms*. You need one story to counterpoint or lift the other story.

TB: It's not something I thought about from a bird's eye view: "This is how I want to structure this." It happened organically, and just felt right. Somehow the interplay of the story lines is going to bring more out of each of them. Readers are not always so patient, and the story lines don't intersect until pretty late in the book. They have to feel like they are related without actually touching each other: dancing around each other all the time.

CR: That's the same in *The Wild Palms*. Faulkner went back and forth between two stories and objected to separating them in a paperback edition. Your fictional characters are so obsessive, and there is an obsessiveness, a devotion to the life they have until almost the end when it becomes too much for one of the characters. That's Faulkner, that kind of obsession and involvement with the characters. But we never lose sight that this is the story of a writer.

TB: Absolutely. Along the way I discovered that writing is like wing-walking. You have Della up there without a parachute. If she falls, everyone one sees it. There is something with celebrity going on, and it seems to me that the story of writing and Faulkner is putting yourself up there on the wing. You face all of this potential criticism, the praise and the opposite of that, and you are putting it all up there.

CR: And people are watching to see if you will crash!

TB: Exactly. Sometimes there's the sense that they want you to, because that would be even more drama. The daring of it.

CR: You preserve some of Faulkner's mystery. You don't try to tell us what he is thinking as he's looking at these flyers.

TB: There is something that remains enigmatic about him. He fostered that, to a large degree, playing with truth and fiction in his own life. It's almost as if in telling his tales he was practicing them so that they could find their way into his work. What's true, what's not true. He's playing with the audience.

CR: So are you done with Faulkner?

TB: For now, until I find another entry point. My relationship with Faulkner is stronger than it ever was. His story is a guiding light.

The Foreigner in Faulkner

In April 1918, William Faulkner wrote to his mother from New Haven, Connecticut: "I am here safely and am about to freeze."[1] It was his first trip North in the company of his mentor, Phil Stone, enrolled in Yale's law school. Twenty-year-old Billy Faulkner felt out of place. He had no idea just how different Connecticut temperatures were from Mississippi. The heat was not on: "Phil and I went straight to bed." Thus began his experience of the cold, iron New England dark described in *Absalom, Absalom!* In New York City, later in the spring of 1918, he reported home: "These people are always saying things to me to hear me talk." His soft southern drawl was hard to make out and a curiosity.

In New Haven, Faulkner gravitated toward foreigners—English and Scottish soldiers and an ex-German soldier, who drank and sang together. "It's funny to walk the streets and look at these people—Poles, Russians, Italian communists, all with American flags in their lapels," Faulkner told his mother. In July 1918, he enlisted in the Royal Air Force in "an English place," Toronto. His "certification of service" (issued December 31, 1918) stated he had been "born in the parish of Finchley in Middlesex, England," a member of the Church of England. So he became a foreigner twice over: an American playing an Englishman in Canada.[2]

In early November 1921, Faulkner spent a month in New York City, a stay that began by his losing all his ready cash—exactly how he did not say, although his pocket may have been picked. He washed dishes in a Greek restaurant and was "looked down on" because the Greek and Irish dishwashers thought he was a "wop," a valuable experience for the novelist who would have Quentin Compson spend part of the day with a little Italian girl who is herself looked down on as a "furriner." But the world to come, what Quentin calls the "land of the kike home of the wop," is more than Quentin in *The Sound and the Fury* can bear. His brother Jason is even more vehement about aliens: "But I'll be damned if it hasn't come to a pretty pass when any dam foreigner that cant make a living in the country where God put him, can come to this one and take money right out of an American's pockets."

At home and abroad Faulkner displaced himself, identifying with and sometimes playing the part of a foreigner. In August 1925, on a six-month European tour, accompanied by artist William Spratling, Faulkner claimed to have gotten into trouble with Mussolini's fascist police. Appropriating Spratling's misadventure, a Genoa nightclub brawl, during which the artist had stomped on, or perhaps spit on, Italian bank notes with the king's image, Spratling was arrested and released in the afternoon of the next day, making the newspapers: "Exploits of a Drunken Foreigner" and "Foreign Rabble." Faulkner said it all had happened to him.

The great fear of the Other, embodied in the immigrant influx, in the very idea of foreignness that is so palpable in the responses to the little immigrant girl in *The Sound and the Fury,* becomes the crucible in which Joe Christmas is forged as a man who is an Other to himself and a perplexity to his community. Does he rape Joanna Burden as a Black man or as a white man? He thinks he might be Black, and others say so, and thinking and saying make it so in the tautological universe of *Light in August.* Faulkner later said that in *Light in August* he created a Nazi in the figure of Percy Grimm, who must castrate Joe Christmas and take a Black life in order to feel in full possession of his own whiteness. Grimm, like Christmas, has felt like a foreigner in his own community until he mobilizes a lynch mob.

In Hollywood, Faulkner played the role of foreigner, regarding movie making as a mad Yankee operation. He favored eating at Musso & Frank because of its decent prices and what Meta Carpenter, his lover, called in *A Loving Gentleman* its "honest ambience" and "friendly, unaffected waiters, most of them foreign-born." To be served by the displaced, so to speak, appealed to his own foreign sensibility. In 1925, in New Orleans he had frequented Italian restaurants that also get some attention in *Mosquitoes.*

Estelle thought of Sir Walter's Scott's "The Lay of the Last Minstrel" because of her husband's seemingly endless departures from home "wandering on a foreign strand!" Faulkner wrote a good deal of *Absalom, Absalom!* on the foreign soil of Hollywood while thinking of his fleeting moments with Meta Carpenter, and then writing in the voice of another foreigner, Shreve, a Canadian imagining the passion of another foreigner, the New Orleans bon vivant Charles Bon, spending his first spring in northern Mississippi, walking in fugitive moments with his beloved Judith Sutpen just as Faulkner walked Hollywood Boulevard with Meta Carpenter. Faulkner in Hollywood was a man out of order, like Charles Bon, who is sophisticated, elegant, self-assured, handsome, and too old to be attending a "small new college in the Mississippi hinterland and even wilderness, three hundred miles from that worldly and even foreign city," New Orleans, where Faulkner himself had shed the last vestiges of his provinciality.

Faulkner's fictional county of Yoknapatawpha is often upset by foreigners—Homer Barron courting Miss Emily Grierson in "A Rose for Emily," Sutpen's French architect who lays out the ground plan and structures not only for Sutpen's Hundred but also for Jefferson itself as revealed in *Requiem for a Nun*. Often the foreigner appears "without warning out of nowhere," like Thomas Sutpen, or like the Argentine Captain Gualdres in "Knight's Gambit." Gualdres renounces his Argentine citizenship and army commission and enlists in the American army after Pearl Harbor, transforming himself from a figure of foreignness into a familiar, marrying into one of Yoknapatawpha's old families. That process of assimilating the stranger, called the outlander in *Requiem for a Nun* is accelerated in that novel, reflecting Faulkner's own sense that his society had to reinvent itself even as it hallowed its past.

Who is to say how Faulkner's work in Hollywood and meeting European émigrés may have speeded up his awareness that absorbing the foreign facilitated a dynamic process of change. In his film scripts like *The Big Sleep* and the unproduced "Dreadful Hollow," he adapted the genres of the detective story and horror/vampire tale to his vision of a postwar America undergoing the velocity of progress that propels the pages of the narrative prologues in *Requiem for a Nun*, in which his narrator speaks directly to "outlanders," who encounter the power of the past even as they progress into a new era that seems to leave that past behind. In *The Big Sleep*, Faulkner's detective Philip Marlow via Raymond Chandler meets with the family's patriarch, General Sternwood, in a hot house of the past only to emerge as the hero who seems ready to restore the family's fortunes. Similarly, in "Dreadful Hollow," Faulkner employs the character of Jillian Dare, the heroine of Irina Karlova's novel, to create a modern English woman engaged to serve but also to expose a Central European female vampire whose own unnatural youth is dependent on preserving a past that never changes. Jillian, like Faulkner's Marlowe, stands in a hall that has "an air of wealth and decayed splendor with a faint foreign flavor." That decayed splendor is bound to collapse with Jillian's entrance, because she is the foreign element that proves resistant to the vampire's bloody voracity.[3]

Faulkner, feeling like an outcast, wrote against the resistance his own fiction aroused in his neighbors: "I fear some of my fellow Mississippians will never forgive that 30,000$ that durn foreign country gave me for just sitting on my ass and writing stuff that makes my own state ashamed to own me."[4] Writing itself became a form of dispossession, of expatriation without having to leave home.

But then came the opportunity to turn Faulkner's sense of alienation on its head and become what so many of his characters represented: the foreigner. In Brazil, on a State Department tour he had what amounted to a conversion experience, as he explained to Harold E. Howland, a cultural affairs officer: "I became suddenly interested in what I was trying to do, once I reached the scene and learned exactly what was hoped from this plan of which I was a part." He wanted to do more—not just give an oral report when he was next in New York but to call on Howland to "discuss what further possibilities, situations, capacities, etc. in which I might do what I can to help give people of other countries a truer idea than they sometimes have, of what the U.S. actually is." Faulkner had been impressed with the "high type of men and women" who ran the Foreign Service and singled them out by name to convey his gratitude. He commended their "tact and dignity and good taste"—all in terms befitting the gentleman diplomat.[5] It had come as a revelation—this new opportunity to spread a code of conduct. In Brazil, he had lamented: "We Americans once had the beautiful dream of every man's being free. What happened to that dream? . . . We failed in that we forgot the needs of the rest of mankind, perhaps we are too self contented and too rich." By going abroad, he was calling on Americans to return to first principles because nothing less than the entire world depended on it. He wasn't built for this kind of work that vexed and weakened him, but he would not relinquish this new role, and he would triumph over his setbacks by calling on his sense of duty and obligation. In a sense, by becoming a foreigner in foreign lands, Faulkner had repatriated himself.

Howland replied enthusiastically to Faulkner's offer of service, saying "reports from Peru and Brazil have been most glowing. . . ." Muna Lee, a poet and foreign service officer who had invited Faulkner to Brazil, told his Random House editor, Saxe Commins, that the Faulkner visit had inspired several favorable articles and described how the reticent writer had opened up, impressing everyone with his "high idea of the purpose of writing and his deep faith in humanity."[6]

Later, on a trip to Japan, Faulkner took to Japanese ways, wearing a kimono. Did he mention Estelle's own experiences in the Orient and that the food was not exactly foreign to him? During a European tour of duty, Faulkner issued a characteristic salvo: "the people in our State Department in Europe are intelligent people. They have learned by hard experience that the enemy, the opponent, is not the foreigner, it's in the State Department in Washington, the bureaucrats in Washington."

Faulkner had traveled a long way to get in his say. In fact, he could affirm abroad, and in his fiction, what he could not say to his own mother at home. She had instructed his niece, Dean, that all men were created equal "with the exceptions of nigrahs, foreigners, Catholics, and Jews."[7]

Counterpull
Estelle and William Faulkner

Estelle Faulkner cannot be neatly separated from Faulkner's way of writing about her, or from his claim that she invented her version of him. She remained part of his whole esthetic, and like Meta Carpenter, a part of his creation—nearly inseparable from his fiction-making. In *The Wintering*, Joan Williams transforms her lover into Jeffrey Almoner who says to Amy Howard: "I like to think I made you, as you made me over." The women in Faulkner's life appear to have been strongly talented, and able to give in return as much as he gave them. Estelle Faulkner painted, so did Helen Baird, an excellent craftsman; Joan Williams and Jean Stein became published writers. Each woman seems to have been determined to leave her mark on Faulkner even while succumbing, often enough, to his guidance and commanding presence.

Judith Sensibar has explored the dominance of Maud Falkner in the novelist's life, but I would like to focus on Estelle to delve more deeply into her side of things. Such an investigation may help us better understand why Faulkner found it necessary to leave his wife on so many occasions, only to return to precisely the relationship from which he had tried to escape.

One answer, surely, to the question of Faulkner's estrangement from Estelle was the repetitiveness of her behavior and of their marriage together, in which over and over again he had to contend with her alcoholism and with what seemed to him her outrageous depletion of his income. Her erratic conduct suggests a frustration with herself that is perhaps explainable by the interruption of the twenty-two-year-old Estelle's romance with Billy Faulkner on April 18, 1918, when she married Cornell Franklin (a more respectable suitor than the pretentious Faulkner, the "Count No 'Count" of local legend). A woman in her twenties—Meta Wilde, Joan Williams, Jean Stein—excited Faulkner's deepest erotic and esthetic desires, and it is precisely this decade of potential growth in Estelle that he missed.

COUNTERPULL: ESTELLE AND WILLIAM FAULKNER

Estelle wrote one unpublished novel and several short stories, and these abortive creative efforts may have stemmed from her sense that she was, in a way, the missing person in her husband's life. Judith Wittenberg goes so far as to designate Estelle William's "twin," and the biographer calls attention to the way Faulkner was sometimes drawn to emulate her fastidious manners and elegant appearance. Perhaps she stood for sides of himself he was just beginning to discover as a young man. She played the piano for him, and he drew pictures and wrote stories and poetry for her. As Wittenberg notes, it cannot be established exactly when "the relationship changed from that of fraternal childhood playmates to that of romantic sweethearts," but it is clear from all accounts that he was devastated by her desertion, and a gap opened up between them which they could never quite fill. In some of Faulkner's poetry an Estelle figure is portrayed as frozen in youth and as flighty and substanceless as the Estelle his mother, a "down- to-earth" woman, deplored.[1]

In a letter to his favorite Aunt Bama written probably in the spring of 1928 (about a year before his marriage on June 20, 1929), Faulkner describes a girl that is almost certainly Estelle: "I would like to see you taken with her utter charm, and intrigued by her utter shallowness. Like a lovely vase. It isn't even empty, but is filled with something—well, a yeast cake in water is the nearest simile that occurs to me. She gets the days passed for me, though. Thank God I've got no money, or I'd marry her."[2] Faulkner associated Estelle with his youthful, irresponsible alter ego; she would be a lovely possession but would also be essentially insubstantial. Like yeast in water, she was a leavening or enlivening agent, which is exactly the way this vivacious young woman presented herself at parties and in the company of young men. She was a showpiece and one did not take what she had to say seriously—such was the judgment of Faulkner's mentor, Phil Stone, and Faulkner's own opinion, so that at least on one occasion his daughter Jill had to plead with him to treat Estelle like a responsible adult.[3] Estelle, according to Jill, never did present Faulkner with the image of a whole, self-sufficient woman: "Now one of the qualities about my mother that my father claimed distressed him was her lack of independence," Jill told Judith Sensibar: "In part I think this was because for him she was the idealized figure in his poetry, and he saw everything about her through romantic haze."

The spirited, dancing Estelle, during her first marriage to Cornell Franklin, caught the eye of a British prince,[4] and even earlier of her devoted companion, Billy Falkner, who rarely danced or exhibited the social charm that made her the cynosure of male company. It is difficult not to see both of them in his poem, "The Dancer" from *Vision in Spring*. She personifies and speaks as "Youth." She is "so swift, so white and slim." She haunts him, tempts him, and bids him to fly and to possess her. But he complains that she has "mazed" his life "with swiftness," for she is apparently no more than movement itself or "the phantom that I thought was you." She is intangible like music, and his mind, "like water, wrinkles back where your face mirrored was." The ephemeral image of a face mirrored in water, of a youth quickly vanishing before it can be possessed or before it can be brought to fruition, suggests the frustrations of Faulkner's attraction to Estelle. The wrinkling of water also suggests the passage of time as an aging process, as a return to a "Youth" that can only be viewed in the past tense as "was." Compulsive, repetitive—which is to say, neurotic—behavior is often a part of a person's attempt to return to a point of origin in order to recover an element of the self which has been abandoned or never fully exercised.

Evidently Estelle despaired of recovering that source of vitality that her "Billy" had taken up so fervently in their early life together, as her plaintive letters in the 1950s to Faulkner's editor, Saxe Commins, express. Estelle remained flirtatious and attracted the attentions of Faulkner's sometime screenwriter-collaborator, Buzz Bezzerides, and no less than Justice Felix Frankfurter,[5] but it was never enough for William Faulkner. In his memoir. *Flashbacks to Faulkner*, Ben Wasson reported that Estelle continued to charm, prolonging the promise of youth. But to Faulkner, marrying her on the rebound, she was in breach of promise.

During the decade (1918–1928) that took Estelle away from William Faulkner—all the way to the Far East, with a few brief returns to Oxford that excited and enervated him—he entered his early thirties coming into possession of the genius he had been cultivating, without really knowing it, in his troubled twenties. As he said of *The Sound and the Fury*: "It taught me what I had already discovered, in a series of repercussions like summer thunder, the Flauberts and Conrads and Turgenievs which as much as ten years before I had consumed whole without assimilating at all." In that same decade, his love for Estelle languished for lack of a plan or idea that would unite them. In his twenties he could falter as an artist, as he did in the unfinished *Elmer*, without feeling the kind of fatality that overcame Estelle's creative projects in her thirties. She was coming to their marriage, to herself, too late, so that she could not handle the repercussions of an art or a life for which she had not prepared. She could not, therefore, reciprocate her husband's intense erotic and esthetic feelings. She had been paralyzed on the eve of her marriage to Cornell Franklin, weeping because of her parting from Faulkner and because of her loss of freedom. As Joseph Blotner observed: "The men had flocked about her, and she had loved it. Talking charmingly, dancing enchantingly, she had flitted on her brightly colored careless wings. She had laughed and said what she pleased, and suddenly the net had closed around her." The biographer's words evoke an ethereal and evanescent figure who could easily entrance a romantic like William Faulkner.

But Estelle, the social butterfly, aged very quickly and metamorphosed into a wraithlike presence. Faulkner sometimes portrayed her as a kind of specter haunting his hours with Meta Carpenter. And in his most private reveries, she may have lingered like the shadowy emanation of the absent person he once adored. In her memoir, *A Loving Gentleman*, Meta Carpenter Wilde's provocative description of "a pale, sad, wasted creature" and photographs of Estelle's hollow-eyed and skeletal face and body certainly add to this impression.

This view of an attenuated Estelle drew heavily on Faulkner's reports about his wife's heavy drinking and extravagant spending. Here was a wife who had just about consumed herself and might very well expire. To hear Faulkner tell it, he was the only force capable of holding his household together. In *A Loving Gentleman*, he is both romantic and stoic, family man and staunch individualist. Drawn to men of genius and also desirous of a man who would cherish her, Meta Carpenter found nearly the perfect consort. She did not want to believe that what her lover deplored in his wife was also true of himself, even though on more than one occasion she saw him "inebriated"—a phrase she still used, when I met her, as a kind of euphemism for the drunken mess Faulkner could make of himself.

More characteristic of him in her view was his mental and sexual vigor, both of which brought her to a new pitch of maturity. Loving him was a way of establishing herself. "He was sort of the Rock of Gibralter for me," Carpenter said in a 1982 *Southern Review* interview with Panthea Broughton.[6] This Gibraltar fixity in Faulkner was not always there for Carpenter, but she needed to believe in his unshakable character. Carpenter echoes Joan Williams in telling Broughton: "I could live up to everything Bill expected of me and felt was there; the making of a woman was there." He wanted to see in her, as in Williams, "the potential of something that would develop into a mature woman who could reason and use judgment and live a full life."

These young women were attracted to Faulkner, as Estelle apparently realized, because he could accelerate the achievement of their maturing ambitions: "Certainly I do not blame Joan—In all probability, had I been an aspiring young writer and an elderly celebrity had fallen in love with me—I would have accepted him as avidly as Joan did Bill," Estelle wrote to Saxe Commins. Because Faulkner stood for the goal of maturity he was, for Carpenter, "the all encompassing figure—the friend, the lover, the mentor, the guide, the mature father figure—all melded into one." Later on, she admitted to Broughton, she did not need him to play all of these different roles. In retrospect, at least, she viewed him as hastening but not actually beginning her development into adulthood: "So when I met Bill, it was at a period in my life of delayed growth; certainly he contributed to whatever maturity I was beginning to achieve." She did not lean on him for help but gradually learned to accept his advice. For his part, he seemed (she thought) to acknowledge that she would grow away from him, even though he did not want to lose her. It is a dynamic he would repeat with Joan Williams and Jean Stein.

Faulkner took a tragic view of his relationships with women. Joseph Blotner reported that Faulkner quoted to Meta Carpenter, to Joan Williams, and to Jean Stein, Harry Wilbourne's line in *The Wild Palms*: "Between grief and nothing I will take grief." Because Faulkner is on record so many times with harsh and seemingly unequivocal criticisms of his wife, his favorite line has not been applied to what he may have felt about his marriage. Robert Hamblin raises the possibility that "despite the suffering and cruelty they had imposed upon one another over the years, Faulkner and Estelle did indeed continue to love one another."[7] For all her complaining about her husband in her letters to Saxe Commins, Estelle clearly felt great compassion and love for her difficult mate and believed, at one point, that they had "lived more amicably, and with better understanding the past year than ever before." Her letters suggest she acquired a tragic wisdom of her own, so that—as Hamblin surmises—they may have lived together in recognition that it was important to remember the youthful, ideal love they had lost.

Other members of the Faulkner family evidently realized that Estelle was far more of a significant figure in the novelist's life than he would ever admit. That William did not give Estelle her due is acknowledged in a letter from Gloria Franklin (the wife of Faulkner's stepson, Malcolm) to Dorothy and Saxe Commins. Writing on October 27, 1954, she notes Faulkner's attitude after his wife's departure for a trip abroad: "Pappy is doing fine, so far, he has been in good spirits and I think utterly amazed that Mama really left him. Perhaps a taste of being alone in that house would serve him right and do him good.[8] Estelle's loyalty was unquestionable. No matter how emphatic her husband's rejection of her seemed to be, she never wavered. She was "hurt, but not despairing—Nothing can alter my love and devotion—nor upset my faith in Bill's actual love for me—although right now, he swears he doesnt." Indeed, by March of 1954, if not before, she had come to a seasoned perspective on Faulkner as writer and husband that contradicts his own pejorative evaluation of her narrow-mindedness in his letters to Saxe Commins: "Bill's article, 'Mississippi,' in next month's *Holiday* explains the two Bills—He is so definitely dual I think." Perhaps artists had to be, she reasoned. She would hardly have been surprised at Meta Carpenter's comment to Panthea Broughton about Faulkner's attitude toward the extinction of their love affair: "In the losing of it, he valued it more." In his last letters to Carpenter, he suggested that what had been between them "could remain only as a dream." Putting it another way, she speculates, "he may have needed the insecurity that somehow sparked whatever it was in him that kept him looking for, yearning for, something he couldn't have."[9]

Faulkner would not divorce Estelle, although she told Commins she offered her husband an opportunity to do so late in their marriage. Much earlier, after Meta's first romantic hopes for a life with Faulkner were dashed by what she came to regard as his indecisiveness, she realized he was fatally caught in the "counterpull" of his character—as she put it to Panthea Broughton—never wholly happy with her in Hollywood or with his family in Oxford. In other words, he tended to bifurcate his biography, to give it a counterpoint, in much the same way as he juxtaposed "The Wild Palms" section against the "Old Man" section in his novel.

Perhaps the most perplexing incident in Carpenter's affair with Faulkner is also the most telling example of the "counterpull" of his character. He wanted his lover and his wife to meet and enlisted Ben Wasson's help, asking his friend to pose as Meta's suitor. Neither Wasson in *Flashbacks to Faulkner* nor Carpenter in *A Loving Gentleman* pretend to fathom Faulkner's motivations in arranging this awkward and damaging collocation, although both assumed he wanted to punish his wife. Clearly, Estelle could not be at her best in Hollywood. She had no time to decorate their home, Wasson remembered, and Carpenter recalled a rather pathetic spouse trying to ingratiate herself with her husband's friends.

Understandably, Carpenter fixes her memory on Faulkner and speculates that he was feeling a "morbidity in his nature that even he did not fully understand"; he was comparing the two women; he was experiencing a "sexual thrill by playing a dangerous game." None of these reasons is especially convincing, and she does not explore them. Rather, she is so taken with Estelle's obvious debilitation and so certain of Faulkner's ironic, pitying view of his wife that Carpenter's predominant impression is that her lover was contemptuous of his mate. Wasson came away from the Meta-Estelle meeting convinced that Faulkner would divorce Estelle and make good his desire to marry Meta.

Yet Faulkner held back. Why? It seems that because of certain unresolved elements in his attitude toward women he was able to see Meta and Estelle only as opposing archetypes in the allegory of his love life. Indeed, setting up their encounter in his Hollywood residence virtually assured a conflict he was not prepared to settle. It may have been his way of dramatizing for Meta

48 FAULKNER AND BIOGRAPHY

what he had been saying all along: his home ground was divided, and he did not know how to present himself in any way other than as a disjunctive personality. It is difficult to believe, moreover, that Faulkner really expected to fool Estelle, the childhood sweetheart who had to have been sensitively attuned to her husband's moods—as she proved by calling Wasson the next morning to denounce him for bringing "Billy's girl" into her home.[10]

So why did Faulkner risk his wife's anger—which at one point prompted her to attack him physically—and jeopardize Meta's place in his Hollywood life? Earlier in *Flashbacks to Faulkner*, while speaking of their college days together, Wasson notes that his friend "liked to stage a scene." This is Wasson's way of saying Faulkner had to be in charge, had to set the conditions in which he could be observed. More is involved here than playing a role, for as Meta Carpenter observed, he was extremely sensitive to place, and in subtle ways he became different people in Hollywood, New York, and, surely, Oxford. In this scene with Ben, Meta, and Estelle, he was giving full play to the "counter-pull" of his character. He was bringing together his childhood sweetheart and wife, his Hollywood mistress who was, in a way, his protégé, and his college confidant, who had also served as his New York agent and Hollywood buddy. Finally, there was Jill, the daughter as offstage presence. In one compact scene he had managed to gather together the significant elements of his life. In such a scene Faulkner could expect Estelle to assert her privileges as a wife. He knew she was more comfortable with men than with women and that she thrived on being the center of attention. Meta, then, would be met as a challenge. For her part, Estelle would play both the generous hostess and the protective wife—and Faulkner needed protection from Meta, whether he admitted it to himself or not. As his daughter Jill told Judith Sensibar, Faulkner seemed to specialize in courting women who were unattainable and was always shocked when they suddenly became available. Meta was ready, no doubt, to marry him, and he seems to have employed Estelle as a buffer.

The dialogue Wasson gives Meta and Estelle during a "half-hearted toast" vividly enacts the divisions in Faulkner's character:

"To Hollywood," Estelle said. She was twitching nervously.
"No, to Mississippi," Meta said.

Each woman is portrayed as making a gesture toward the other, although Estelle comes off as far less confident than Meta. On the other hand, note both the compliment and the condescension in Estelle's line to Wasson about Meta: "I hope you take this pretty child out a lot." From Estelle's point of view, Meta may have seemed like a neophyte in this lifelong battle for her husband's affection.

Estelle could be direct and brutal, as she was many years later with Joan Williams, confronting that young woman in Memphis and asking her outright if she intended to marry her husband. After the affair with Williams was over and "poor Joan" (as Estelle called her) was married, Estelle wrote to Saxe Commins in terms that are reminiscent of her superior attitude toward Meta: "Naturally I am glad that the child found a congenial, nice man to love and marry and wish her every happiness.["][11] In the earlier Hollywood episode, in her own home, Estelle chose to play her husband's game, but she made sure that Meta got the message about "my Billy." Indeed, Meta was shocked by Estelle's use of "Billy" and apparently felt that the diminutive demeaned her dignified lover.

No matter how enfeebled or neurasthenic Estelle might look, she worked diligently to get the better of Meta. By inviting Meta to his home, Faulkner, in effect, showed that he believed Meta would hold her own, for, in a way, she was her lover's stand-in, a woman whose sensibility, he felt, was akin to his own, as she recognized in *A Loving Gentleman*. Faulkner remained impassive throughout his evening with Meta and Estelle and thus could comfortably observe these two women act out the scene of his contriving. He shifted the pressure from himself by having them compete in front of him. He had once mentioned to Wasson his belief that relationships between women were somewhat like a contest, and Wasson in *Flashbacks to Faulkner* remembered his friend's remark when Estelle and Meta met: "[Estelle] and Meta, when I introduced them, gave one another the femininely characteristic once-over, and I was reminded of Bill's comment so many years before that even small girls, when they meet for the first time, looked one another over, and knew everything about each other."

If Estelle did not ultimately lose Faulkner, it was partly because she refused to give him up or relinquish her own rights. As Robert Hamblin points out, her writing style reflects "both an independence of will and a strong desire to call attention to herself."[12] At the same time, her vigorous use of dashes, underlining, exclamation marks, and emphatic adjectives suggests a tremendous insecurity she vehemently labored to overcome. With so many of her letters unconventionally punctuated and broken up and slashed (she rarely uses periods or commas) it is difficult not to conclude that her sense of self and of society was fragmented and that she never felt fully connected to others. She was gallantly combative, however, and Faulkner, with his admiration for similar characters in his fiction, may have secretly welcomed the battle she gave him—even magnifying her force as an adversary.

Judging from what Jill Faulkner Summers said to Judith Sensibar about her father's attitude toward women, and from similar comments by Ben

Wasson and Meta Carpenter, it seems fair to infer that Faulkner was keenly attracted to what he saw as the vulnerability of women even as he admired their strengths. The ideal woman for him would have had to combine indomitability and fragility in just the right proportions—as his daughter Jill gradually realized, learning to interpret the distinction her father made between appearing dependent while remaining, on a deep and inconspicuous level, autonomous. In her own case, she remembered that "although he encouraged me to be independent he still wanted me to go through the motions of being helpless and female. . . . He seemed to feel that frailty was a virtue and liked the idea of little girls in pinafores."[13] A similar attitude sometimes prevailed in his treatment of a puzzled Meta Carpenter who could not reconcile his deft handling of her as a woman coming of age with his occasional desire to dress her up as a little girl. In speaking of Faulkner's "sexual key" she evokes in *A Loving Gentleman* "the image of a young woman . . . tremblingly responsive to his desire." Not only a woman weak with passion but a woman just plain weak appealed to Faulkner's tenderest emotions. Jill remembered that he was most caring in periods when Estelle was not well and disliked any show of toughness in her: "[He] flatly refused to see the strengths she did have. My mother was very Southern in that she could make any man believe he was superman. She was also very manipulative for she was, like most Southern women, taught to obey implicitly, "so far as he is wise and she is able."[14]

Both mother and daughter, the passage above suggests, schooled themselves in reading and catering to Faulkner's moods while not really accepting his definition of femininity. As Judith Sensibar points out, Estelle was not a passive personality but took an energetic interest in life around her. And she did not withdraw from her husband even when he seemed to lose interest in her.

Estelle's letters to her husband's editor, Saxe Commins, reveal that she continued to be engaged with his work by learning to cultivate one of his closest friends and professional associates. She made sure that Commins and his wife Dorothy knew how much the Faulkner family appreciated their efforts to support and advise the head of their household. Her correspondence with them between 1951 and 1956 gradually grew more frank and intimate, for she counted on their sympathy in helping to repair the bond between herself and her husband, a bond that Faulkner seemed to take every opportunity to break, even claiming, absurdly, that his wife "never had any regard or respect for my work, has always looked on it as a hobby, like collecting stamps."[15] Writing just a few days after his letter to Commins on October 25, 1952, complaining about a wife who did not recognize that his first responsibility was to himself as an artist, Estelle wrote Saxe saying: "It is bad, I know, for an artist to undertake all Bill does—but how to circumvent it? I am at a loss—." In this astonishing collocation of letters, husband and wife present reverse mirror images of the other, each claiming the other as a dependent who works at cross purposes.

Naturally, Estelle was wooing Commins, telling him what she thought he wanted to hear and appealing to his sense of fair play and compassion. Commins, she had to know, was a decent man who anguished over both the literature and lives of the writers he edited, and Faulkner had warned him that "in ten minutes, she can have you believing that black is white. Of course, in eleven minutes you know better, but sometimes it is too late by then." He would say the same thing to Jean Stein.[16]

Estelle was also writing to Commins out of frustration that Faulkner would not acknowledge her true role, which was not simply one of a drunk he often had to nurse but of Mrs. William Faulkner (she was irritated when Commins addressed her as "Mrs. Estelle Faulkner") who had a loving and proprietary interest in his life and career. Without husband and child she admitted that "Estelle Faulkner . . . would be a total nonentity." She was very pleased on those occasions when her husband appeared "handsome and distinguished," and she was calmest when he tacitly consented to her presence as the consort of a great writer.[17]

Estelle sympathized with her husband's "divided mind and heart" to use the words Joseph Blotner finds appropriate to characterize her mixed feelings at the time of her marriage to Cornell Franklin. In the final years of her marriage to Faulkner, she seems to have become resigned to what Blotner calls Faulkner's "compulsion to be attached to some young woman at all times." Estelle understood the mania of compulsions, as late in life, she renounced her drinking and never resumed the alcoholic behavior Faulkner had deplored. By finding some peace in herself she also was able to forgive faults in her husband and to concede him the right to do as he pleased. After Faulkner's death, she worked on exquisite abstract paintings, reflecting an aesthetic sensibility her husband never truly acknowledged.

As Faulkner aged, the "counterpull" persisted as he was drawn back to his early years by identifying with Joan Williams's frustrating efforts to become a writer and an independent person. With his encouragement, she eventually fictionalized his memories of youth and his increasing reliance on her. Her novel, *The Wintering*, begins with Almoner's dreary account of his youth and desire to leave home, to lose his virginity, to become free of familial and societal standards, to become, in short, the autonomous artist. The young Almoner is still inarticulate, without the creative voice Williams herself hoped to find by associating with Faulkner. Almoner can seem boyish in

Amy Howard's presence; in life, Faulkner could appear almost childlike and as dependent as Estelle, confessing to Williams, "I don't know anything else to do with the rest of my life but put it into your hands."[18]

At twenty, Williams found it impossible to identify with the fifty-year-old Estelle whose life, unlike Faulkner's, seemed over. As Williams puts it: "But who, I wondered, would fall in love with a woman of fifty? I felt her full of delusions, and wished she were not so frail that she'd taken my arm for support on the way into the restaurant. I felt protective of her too."[19] At forty, after experiencing her oldest son's inability to empathize with her age, Williams could more easily commiserate with Estelle, who was neither too old nor too enervated to cope with her husband's lust for life. Notice the alacrity with which she could respond to Williams's sudden call to Rowan Oak in July 1962: "In Oxford Mrs. Faulkner answered the phone and said of course I must see Bill, and to come right away. After greeting me, and calling him, she ushered her mystified sister off the porch where they had been sitting and left us alone."

Estelle understood, better than any other woman, the "counterpull" of her husband's character. He was never of one mind or heart, and he attracted women of similar sensibilities. Meta Carpenter spoke to Panthea Broughton about Faulkner's unease in Hollywood, of the "sense of misplacement [that] troubled him sorely," so that he "clung" to her "as to the last of his own in a strange land." Joan Williams created out of her friendship with Faulkner a female character, Amy Howard, inspired with the same uneasy "counterpull": "It's as if some second presence is always with me making me want to run away from wherever I am and do something different from what I'm doing." Finally, Estelle managed to be both soft and tough. She exemplified the Faulknerian standard, the ideal he had worshipped in absentia, the woman full of faults who did not, in the end, run away or crumble. She stayed with him as his inspiration, his nemesis, and his first love.

"Sole Owner and Proprietor"

William Faulkner and Jean Stein

I never expected to write this essay. Jean Stein had provided limited cooperation with Joseph Blotner's biography, allowing him to use the bits of Faulkner's letters that related to his writing life.[1] But he wanted more from her, to make her love affair with Faulkner commensurate with his romantic feelings for Joan Williams. "I know you are a shy and sensitive person," he wrote to Stein on January 12, 1970: "this is one more reason why I have appreciated so much your taking me into your confidence and helping me as you have done. But it has occurred to me that I owe it to you that your relationship should not be presented at a lower level of intensity than it possessed, particularly by comparison with such another relationship as the one I mentioned." He suggested she might want to "pick out passages from any of WF's letters which seem to you to reveal the essence of what he felt for you." She did not.

No subsequent biographer was able to penetrate the barrier Stein maintained. As I was writing my two-volume biography of Faulkner, Stein died, and I sought access to her archive at the New York Public Library. An archivist told me that her collection was restricted, and my efforts to have one of her friends intercede with her family on my behalf, proved fruitless. Then, just recently, a friend of mine, Ellen Brown, told me she had gained access to the Stein papers for the purposes of doing a biography of Tennessee Williams. Ellen kindly scanned and sent to me one of the Faulkner folders. After reading just a few of his letters, I realized that awaiting me in two boxes of correspondence, was a Faulkner familiar to me and yet who had revealed to Stein parts of himself seen nowhere else.

They met at a party in St. Moritz on Christmas Eve 1953. Nineteen-year-old Jean Stein, daughter of Jules Stein, founder of MCA (Music Corporation of America), had asked Jean Feldman, wife of super agent Charles Feldman, to invite Faulkner to the party.[2] Like Joan Williams, Stein, saturated in Faulkner's work, wanted to know the man. Soon this attractive dark-haired beauty had aroused him out of his depression. He had never liked consorting with wealthy and privileged Americans abroad and had said so as early as 1925 in letters home to his mother, but Jean Stein captivated him.

In February 1954, in Cairo, Egypt, working with Howard Hawks on *Land of the Pharaohs*, Faulkner sent Stein several telegrams, including this one on February 17: "AM SICK FOR YOU STOP WRITE BILL." He wrote on Mena House Hotel stationery, March 1: "Each night when I turn out the light I have a last look into our [Hotel] Beaujolais mirror like the time I finally persuaded you to turn your head over your shoulder to see how pretty your pretty back was. Remember? Remember? Remember? May I say something confidentially? I love you."

Occasionally Stein preserved her handwritten notes to Faulkner—this one from March 7, 1954: "It was cruel of you to sound so near on the phone yesterday. And the worst of it is it all went so fast . . . this morning I can only faintly hear your voice." She had been desperate about not being able to get to Egypt. This was a time when a young woman felt vulnerable traveling alone: "I always feel that I can't arrive alone in a city without being slightly chaperoned. . . . Do you understand a little?" Even with a companion the arrangements to travel to Cairo immediately by air or boat seemed impossible. "I have been wondering about becoming more & more lost without you," she confessed. She signed herself Jean, saying "I trust you completely my love."[3]

Two weeks later he wrote: "Worked very hard all this past week, not to miss you so damned damned bad, finished script again, for the second time yesterday." Joseph Blotner evidently saw this letter, postmarked March 14, 1954, but used only the bits relating to Faulkner's scriptwriting, a job he hoped to finish by March 23, so he could return to Stein. Almost every other sentence was an "I love you," that crescendoed into "I want to look at you, touch you, talk of love to you and see your sweet dear face ducking into my shoulder and say, 'Stop it. Stop it. I cant stand it.'" He wanted to hear her say: "Yes Bill yes yes I belong to you. I belong to you." Other letters from Egypt reiterated his desire to continue seeing her—in Europe or America, whatever they could manage. He wrote a p.s. on April 19: "in case you dont know it, this is a love letter."

In May 1954, in Oxford, he wrote again about missing her: "being a sole owner and proprietor in absentia is very dull." He wrote her about his farming and his horses, including Lady Go-lightly, now 22, whose "jumping days are about over. She spends most of her time now sitting in a warm chimney corner knitting mufflers and socks for me." He had gotten good at fence building and would build one for her when they were together again: "Only I have already done that; love: completely around you, keeping you; you will never get out of it. Does that alarm you?" It shouldn't, he assured her, because it would be a "tender fence," and he would say nonsensical "little things" that would make her "glad of the fence." She wasn't just the "nicest thing" in his life but "all of it."

Although Faulkner welcomed trips abroad, pleased to do his duty on State Department assignments, he almost always viewed his arrival in foreign climes with dread—sometimes immobilizing himself with liquor, although he did not mention his dipsomania to Stein. Someone always had to take care of William Faulkner—Buzz Bezzerides in Hollywood, Saxe Commins in Princeton and New York, his stepson Malcolm in Oxford, Else Jonsson in Sweden, to name just some of the caretakers. In a rare admission of his invalidism, he wrote to Stein on July 24 about his trip to Brazil mentioning his expectation that someone from the State Department would be "nursing me on this expedition."

In August, on one of his State Department missions, he wrote her from Sao Paulo, saying it was hard to think of anything but her. Each time they met after intervals of several months it seemed to him she was, again, a virgin—a thought that obviously excited him, as it had always excited him when the thought, as a young man, was just that—only a thought. More perhaps than any other woman Jean Stein seemed the fulfillment of dreams that put him in a romantic realm of perpetually fresh creation.

Sometimes Stein stayed at the Barbizon Hotel in Manhattan, where one of Faulkner's many short notes reached her, postmarked September 2, 1954. This was the hotel that, in effect, chaperoned young women like Grace Kelly and Sylvia Plath, forbidding males to get beyond the lobby to penetrate the society of ambitious young women so astringently described in *The Bell Jar*. We don't have Stein's letters, but we know that like Plath and Kelly, she was ahead of her time, developing the kind of independence that Linda Snopes displays in *The Town* and *The Mansion*. In fact, Faulkner said so on May 4, 1956, telling Stein: "You're like Linda Snopes. I'm all in this world you can trust."

Even while Faulkner was drawn to Stein's boldness, he tried to effect a sort of soft-hearted suzerainty, realizing that his reign over her was bound to be brief. She was beyond him in the Barbizon and he was dreaming about her in Oxford. The Barbizon, seemingly impregnable, stood in for the very form of the female body that Faulkner wanted to open up, as if that was the only way he could fully experience himself. He was a "little sick" of waiting to see her: "each time I shut my eyes I see your pretty body again. Though come to think of it, they haven't seen much else, open or closed either, since that first time when you finally forgot to be shy about me seeing it, do you remember when that was? I bet you don't." He seemed to want to archive their affair, placing it between the covers of the book he made of their times together, as he imagined being between her thighs as he entered her.

As to Jean's parents, especially her mother, he knew what they wanted and it would not be him but a husband as a "a sort of continental, cosmopolitan thing." He drew back from this role as godfather or uncle. "Dammit"—he was not speaking "like your sweetheart, your owner and prop." He went to an Elizabeth Taylor movie and saw a resemblance to Jean: "the same dark vivid alive hair," no matter the features that set them apart. He was working out in the sun getting a burn but also "getting rid of some of the fat across my equator. You will like me better now." But he had to stay put in Oxford and be there for Jill's wedding in August. In the meantime, she was to address letters to him c/o Random House—the best way to prevent "interference with your letters," since those coming from his publisher would not arouse suspicion. He was talking to his heart saying: "I don't know, I don't know, I cant tell you, I don't know how we can do without her that long."

In an October 25, 1954 letter, he made a drawing of her standing naked, her head in profile, while the rest of her in high heels was his view of her rear end and began his letter: "Do you remember this? one night, you had taken off dress and bra and then you went into a sort of calm, doldrum, I think making faces at me around the curtain until I came in and slipped your pants and petticoat down myself until you stepped out of them and went prancing away without a stitch but two ear-drops and two slippers?" He wanted as much of her as she wanted of him: "Because of our age, some day you will find someone—you should, I want you to, to be happy—whom you would rather have in your life than me. But I don't think it is yet. Don't be afraid though to look, to try. Remember always that I know you are generous and brave, and that you know I am constant and I love you and I will never hurt you; I am always when and where you want me." In November 1954 he wrote to her: "Only one week and I shall walk again in the beauty of my proprietorship."

On January 26, 1955, Stein noted their discussion of her coming for a weekend in Oxford. She teased him about his servants. Wouldn't they be upset? He seemed almost angry when he said: "I wouldn't have any Nigras that I couldn't control."

In February 1, 1955, in Oxford, he was writing to her: "I just miss you so damned much." She was in his blood, in his dreams: "Dearest Beautiful Pretty Miss Stein being your sole owner & proprietor takes up all my time." Asleep or awake, it didn't matter: "I love you." He dreamed about her, but wanted to wake up, look at her, and then go back to sleep again.

In a handwritten account, dated March 1955, Stein described planning with Mary, her aunt's "negro cook," a "Mississippi dinner" for Faulkner. He wanted Mary to be his guest as well and to make her part of their conversation. Stein told Mary to dress up, and she appeared in a "black décolleté cocktail dress" with wonderful "toeless suggestive shoes." She put on an apron as she served dinner, including a fish resembling catfish (the genuine article could not be obtained in New York City markets, Stein said, "too snobbish to sell cat-fish,)" hush puppies, and a raspberry mousse Stein had made "a little too rich." The phone rang and Mary asked Faulkner if he would speak to her daughter Margaret. "Certainly, Mary." He later said that Margaret had been primed to tell him he was the "greatest writer in this world" and she wanted his autograph. Mary was "smiling all over" when he told her what had been said on the call, and a few days later he was telling the story to a few friends, signing a copy of *A Fable*: "To Margaret Shelby from her Mother's friend William Faulkner."

In a letter postmarked April 29, 1955, writing at midnight in the Algonquin Hotel in room 505, "full of ghosts," he had made her up as his "Bunberry," alluding to Algernon's definition of the term in *The Importance of Being Earnest*: "the practice of creating an elaborate deception that allows one to misbehave while seeming to uphold the very highest standards of duty and responsibility."[4] He described the scene of their tryst: "I knock on the hall door and you say 'Who is it?' then open it, and you have not got a stitch on. Remember?"

The coming of spring had him imagining her with him while he worked, so he could say "What makes you so pretty?" So that she could reply: "You do." It was already too long for them to be apart: "The only thing left for us to do is to make up your mind that we will never be apart again forever." The wording reflects a kind of confused projection of his desires—of I and we as he simultaneously imagined her as her own person and all his—much like one of his fictional characters—independent and yet all his own. Each time he started a letter it turned out to be to her. He would use the phrase, "sole owner and proprietor" throughout their correspondence, staking not only a claim but mapping out his emotions. Many of his letters are undated, although some can be pinned down with postmarks. The dates, however, don't matter so much, since he enclosed her in a kind of fictional world, in which what she gave him: "love, peace, happiness, passionate beauty" and made it seem as though "you belong to me, and why you will always have a little trouble getting loose—when and if you want to, dont want a sole own and prop. any longer."

In mid-May, Faulkner had dinner with Stein's aunt and uncle and talked about her "circumspectly." Her aunt "a fine woman, the best friend you—a young girl—could have or need" was worried about Jean mixing with the "'wrong' people—radicals, etc." It all sounded a little like Linda Snopes

58 FAULKNER AND BIOGRAPHY

radicalized, with Gavin Stevens substituting for the aunt whose worry about her was "very fine." Faulkner had to make it seem as though he was on the aunt's side, part of a rescue and recovery operation, even if it is doubtful that the aunt would have found his form of participation welcome. As he admitted: "I couldn't say what I wanted to—that since you had put yourself solely in my ownership and keeping, I was the one to do the worrying." Aunt and lover agreed that Jean was exceptional and not content to just to "except things . . . but you want to do something with yourself, make something new during your time in this world, and that you will find what it is."[5]

Then he vouchsafed his "stroke of genius," telling Jean's aunt: "whenever she worried the most about what you might get yourself into, what mistake you might make before you knew it, to remember always that you are a 'lady,' whether you like the idea of being one or not, and that you will never be able or permit yourself to do, at the last analysis, anything that a 'lady' will not and does not do." So said her knight-at-arms, joining with her aunt in a vow to "defend and protect you at any cost, all cost," declaring his love not only for Jean but her aunt, even though he could not correct the aunt who confided to him that Jean had not yet been "sexually stirred."

By June 6, he was planning to join her somewhere in Europe—Paris, Italy, England, or Scotland "or anywhere else you like. For me, anything, just so we are together." That she was his creation seemed evident in his insistence that "you are not California to me, you began at the age of 19 in our shabby title room above the Palais Royal, or reading McCavity the Cat[6] in the narrow little bed in Rome that was hardly big enough for one." He had written her earlier in May as though out of a romantic novel like *The Wild Palms*: "Think of it: sleeping together, walking together, all the day together, and tomorrow and tomorrow and tomorrow."

In a June 18, 1955 letter, he said his sloop—"her name is the Ringdove"—reminded him of "you, since she has the nicest soft full swell of white upperworks and a slim waist and the prettiest little round girl shaped bottom you ever caressed I mean saw." It would seem he felt the same way about horses, telling Stein that Tempy's full name was "Magnolia's Ridgefield Temptress." She was a frisky horse and could make a "tremendous racket" with her forelegs atop her stall door, ready for a jump, which she did as he opened the door. It was all of a piece: training horses, outfitting his sloop, teaching Jean "for going on two years now," he said as he praised her letters: "They make me very very proud and careful of you."

In early September, in one of only a few of her own notes to Faulkner preserved in her archive, Jean seemed ready to jump: "Dearest Angel, I'll see you soon in Paris and work hard and take care of yourself. Yours ever

Jean." On the card he sent back to her, he began "Dearest spinster prettiest spinster, prettiest love. I love you. I cant live without you." The plan was to meet her at Hotel Beaujolais.

He could no longer hunt and kill since seeing "anything timeless and passionate with motion, speed, life, being alive, I see your young passionate beautiful living shape." He drew her shape, as he did with Meta, and included himself in profile smoking his pipe, then said it wasn't really her: "I left the teeth-marks off, do you remember: on the left side of the pretty soft girl's behind?" As with Joan Williams, he had to work around the vigilant Estelle to arrange his trysts. He used intermediaries, like Random House editor Robert Linscott—to get messages to Jean. "I'm glad Mr. Linscott likes you. But then, who doesn't?" he wrote, out of tribute to her as a kind of cynosure of admirers who abetted their romance. He planned getaways from Oxford, meeting her in Greenville, Mississippi, where Elia Kazan was shooting a movie, or in New Orleans. It all depended on when Estelle might leave for Virginia to visit their daughter. When Jean phoned Rowan Oak, Estelle picked up the receiver and handed it to him, but he couldn't talk because she stood behind him and could hear Jean's loud voice.

It wasn't just Estelle that made Faulkner wary of talking to Jean on the phone: "I dont call you too much because of a little town, small exchange, same operator who knows me, name, voice, etc., will take notice I am calling young girl in NY quite often; she may even listen to us to pass the time." Jean had no idea of how careful he had to be, he told her tactfully, not mentioning that he had run a similar stealthy romance operation with Joan Williams.

So after Jean's call, he set out "two pretty good precepts": "Never take counsel of your fears, and (2) Never let your enemy catch you in a lie." He explained that Estelle had been his enemy for about twenty years and would be Jean's enemy as soon as Estelle figured out the connection between them. It did Jean no good to lie about her background—to use an assumed name or other lies that Estelle could well "catch you in." Tell Estelle as little as possible so that she could not contact Jean's family, for example. Jean could say Faulkner was a friend of her family, which was true, and otherwise say no more than necessary to appease Estelle. He cautioned Jean: "She may, if she tries, get more out of you than you think." The Machiavellian Estelle could "in five minutes . . . make you believe black is white. Of course in six minutes you know better, but it is too late then." The duplicitous husband said of his wife: "She has practised deception so much herself that she has an affinity for it. . . . She divines it." Jean should stick to the line that she was simply an admirer of Faulkner's work. He never seems to have thought of Estelle, and the early poetry about her, when he anticipated his next meeting with Jean: "Then together, the breast points, the sweet soft girl thighs, the immortal inviolable virginity."

That meeting Faulkner had arranged between Estelle and Meta with Ben Wasson in attendance, at which Faulkner had affected a disinterested manner,[7] had its analogue in his projection of a scene that might occur if Estelle went with him to Greenville, where Jean had accompanied Elia Kazan and his crew making the movie, *Baby Doll*. Faulkner cautioned: "I will seem cold and dull, but remember, that is my way of telling her nothing: I will be talking to her and Kazans and Ben [Wasson], not to you." She shouldn't misinterpret his reserve: "Don't you ever again tell me I dont love you anymore."

He reminded her about how careful he had been not to make her pregnant. He was referring to his practice of withdrawal "when the man does want to do what he wants to do, no matter who suffers . . . in physical terms, that is the highest act of unselfishness I can do is to leave you at that moment, in time." He never wanted her to feel "any grain of regret or unpleasantness or trouble because of me." In effect, he was telling her why he had been so cautious about their meetings and that his unwillingness to risk more had nothing to do with his loving her less. He declared his love and his protectiveness in increasingly explicit words: "I dont want to come inside your girl's belly—for your sake; am afraid to chance leaving seed in you—for your sake."

Inevitably, Faulkner reported to Stein, word got through to Estelle. An old friend of hers from Shanghai said: "a girl named Jean Stein could wreck Jill's wedding." Questioned by Estelle, Faulkner feigned ignorance: "I dont place her," although he conceded he might have met her. He burned Stein's letters, but Estelle found a charred scrap of stationery with Jean Stein's name embossed in red. It brought back to him the way Estelle had handled Joan Williams who called Rowan Oak and Estelle, who almost always answered the phone, handed the receiver to him saying: "Here's your Memphis whore again." Later, Faulkner told Stein, Estelle called Joan's father to "warn him to save his daughter." This was the risk Stein would take if she ever visited Rowan Oak.

Faulkner did not press his suit—insofar as demanding more of Stein's time than she wished to give him: "I wont let you take an irrevocable step until I am convinced you are ready and want that more than you dont want it." The "stink" of gossip was not worth it so long as she wanted to enjoy her "young free years." He waited and worked: "I have just started on another novel, the second Snopes volume: some boredom and unhappiness and longing for you is good for me: I work to keep from grieving and missing you all the time. I save that for night. I dreamed last night, had to get up and change. Do you understand?" In *The Town* Faulkner's pent-up desire for Stein had its correlative in Gavin Stevens's yearning for Eula Varner and his restrained intimacy with her daughter, Linda. Only in his letters to Stein, could he let loose what was only incipient on his novel's pages. Yet like Stevens he held back his seed—if not quite everything else that Stevens held in suspension.

Gavin Stevens could buy Linda Snopes a banana split or an ice cream soda, but Faulkner feared even calling Jean Stein: "I love you," he wrote early June 1956: "No, I won't telephone you. If I heard your voice, I would miss you too much. I would be tempted to throw away the salvation of America and follow you at once."

In *The Town*, Gavin's meetings with Linda Snopes cause some gossip about what they could possibly have in common, and those moments are akin to what Faulkner sometimes felt in Stein's company: "The way you talk about your friends & their relationships with other men, I feel left out as if I were the only one who did own a bicycle on the block."[8]

It was chafing to be away from her as he spent time trying to turn his horse Tempy into a jumper, regretfully concluding she was "too light in the bone" to bear the pounding of his 150-pound weight. He worried that he might ruin her. And what about Jean Stein?: "I am never satisfied," he confessed, "when you are out from under my hand" and he could not "participate in beauty with you." He could sail, though, in his own sloop, which he kept well "fitted and varnished" in a sort of conditioning of perfection not so different from the way he thought of her as he signed off a mid-July 1956 letter: "God bless God keep pretty sweet soft girl bottomed." Such tag lines are reminiscent of his earliest erotic poetry.

Into late July, he continued to work away at *The Town*. After the trials of preparing *Requiem for a Nun* for the stage, and the decade long struggle with *A Fable*, *The Town* surprised him: "Book is going splendidly, too easy. Each time I begin to hope I am written out and can quit, I discover I am not at all cured and the sickness will probably kill me." Although the book was "going pretty well," it was not the same as in New York where he could say to himself: "Write me a few pages that will please me, and I will take you to call on, dine with, sleep with an extremely pretty and exciting girl." He confided in Jean about his writing and wanted her candid reactions: "I want to know how you liked Linda and Eula. You can tell me," he wrote in early November 1956. Did she see in his plea the same kind of chivalric code that galvanized Gavin Stevens? "I am a lot more than just the one you loved the most," Faulkner wrote to Stein: "I was the one that you knew you could always depend on and trust, and you knew you knew it."

He always said that he took the writer-in-residence post at Virginia to be near Jill, but his letter of July 26 suggests he would be close enough to Jean that he could "come up" to New York "every two or 3 weeks." By August 22, he thought it important to put her right where his writing was: "We will talk this fall. We will love each other for always, that's what we will do. Details will be settled later. Just finishing the book. I thought it was just a funny book but I was wrong. Not long now until we are au mieux. I love you. Bill."

He could get quite graphic with Jean, as he did with Meta Carpenter,[9] writing to her during his summer in Japan about her "pretty little vagina," wondering if it got wet remembering him. In late October 1956: "I need very much to spend a great deal of time with a great big virgin I am acquainted with, you know: the one with the soft pretty bottom with a wee wet little hole in it? that one." As his daughter Jill had observed, her father admired and wanted his women to mature and yet to preserve the very virginity he violated. As with his writer-in-residence position in Virginia, he used his work as chairman of President Eisenhower's "People to People" program committee, putting American writers in touch with their Cold War counterparts in Communist countries, as a cover for times with Stein. At the end of the year, he mentioned: "On committee business, tu comprends, that is, if you dont mind me referring to your pretty soft sweet girl parts as a committee."

He posed as a Stein family friend, even responding to her mother's "nice letter" about family difficulties—"not about you of course . . . the sort of letter she would only have written to someone she considered worthy of that much confidence, I mean, one who loved her family also, even if she doesn't know the true reason why." He liked the clandestine complications of romance, including his fantasy about Stein carrying one of his letters inside "your left brassiere, over the heart, or maybe inside you little pale blue pants. Though that might make walking a little difficult, distracting your attention from where you were going." That kind of playful fantasy made its way, as well, into his letters to Leslie Aldridge, whom he had dallied with in Princeton.[10] Although this sort of playful eroticism would not make its way into a Faulkner novel, don't forget the rivalry between Gavin Stevens and Major de Spain over Eula Varner, and Gavin's sophomoric use of a rake-head to blow a tire in de Spain's red roadster, and de Spain's revenge, as observed by Gowan, Gavin's nephew:

> the rake-head, with two flowers like a bouquet, all bound together with a band or strip of something that Gowan knew was thin rubber but it was another year or two until he was a good deal bigger and older that he knew what the thing was; and at the same time he realised what it was, he said he knew it had already been used; and at the same time he knew at least how Uncle Gavin was supposed to believe it had been

used, which was the reason Mr de Spain sent it to him: that whether Uncle Gavin was right or not about how it had been used, he would never be sure and so forever afterward would have no peace about it.

It's the "no peace about it" that seems in sync with Faulkner's letters to Jean Stein that reflect a level of erotic fantasy that Gavin never articulates, or perhaps we should say is never allowed to articulate, given not only his author's sense of literary propriety but also his keen understanding that what actually dissipates the impact of pornography—at least as literature—is its explicitness. That high literary standard Faulkner did not have in mind as he wrote repeatedly and respectively to his "prettiest love" with her "soft sweet girl's bottom."

As he planned his itinerary for State Department trips in 1955 and 1956, a lecture in Oregon, events in New York City, he looked for ways to meet her at various places around New York or in Europe—wherever he might have a stopover. In the meantime, he enjoined her: "Keep my locket and keep my heart." Such expressions were like what he told Joan Williams—that she had his life in her hands because he did not know what else to do with it. The difference in Stein's case, is that—judging by his letters—she was more importunate and impatient than Joan and much more ready to engage in the sex play that Faulkner craved.

At home in the spring of 1956, nursing what he thought was a bleeding ulcer, swearing off liquor and drinking milk, he counted on Jean's letters to cheer him up: "Your letter sounds happy, busy anyway. That's the way I want you to sound and be: to miss me a little, but not too much until I come back and all you need when you miss me is just to reach your hand out. Prettiest love sweet love sweetest prettiest sweet soft" he typed, and then wrote "so maybe I had better stop." What set Jean Stein apart from every other woman, except perhaps Meta Carpenter, was her utter abandonment to his fantasies of himself as lover and selfless protector.

By the end of spring 1956, Faulkner seems to have caught up with himself, so to speak, realizing that his physical illnesses and doldrums made him seem like the "champion long distance whiner"—a sure sign that he was feeling better, storing up his energy and anticipating a rendezvous with Stein in the fall. He aimed to be "more like I used to be when you had more fun being with me." By June he was telling her he "felt pretty well."

In February 1957, Stein wrote a note to herself: "for the first time awakening & waiting to be free of him (becoming less & less alive the longer I am with him each period) couldn't be with him anymore." For the first time she mentioned a "drunken spell from Tuesday till today Friday." She felt "horrible" about his asking her to accompany him to Athens, and then "hideous": "but I'm a human being too . . . can't only live, exist for him, even if I'm worthless. Then I said I miss you & he a little shocked said 'We poor lovers.'"

She would marry for the first time in 1958. For a time, Faulkner seemed inconsolable.[11]

Coda

Stein took notes on Faulkner's talk, some of which would be incorporated in her famous *Paris Review* interview with him, but other comments—what might be called Faulkner's table talk—never reached print and provide a side of him he never otherwise revealed, like telling Stein about the women he dated when he lived in Paris. He spoke to her about Estelle, that they had married "because we had liked each other as children. But her ambitious family married her off and then she returned to Oxford "like the lady guarded by dragons." But that was about as far as he would go by way of explanation: marrying Estelle to help her out.

Here are some examples, dated and undated of Faulkner's casual comments that Stein scrawled on various pieces of stationery and note paper as records of the raw data of their lives together:

December 29, 1953: "Sometimes I feel like disgracing the human race & being outlawed by it."

J: "Where are you?" (Meaning what are you thinking about?)

F: "With you my attention never wanders, it just prowls . . ."

J: "On my return to Paris from St. Moritz I suddenly realized I could not remember how you laughed & I then when I spoke to you on the phone to St. Moritz I heard your laugh & how I loved it."

F: "I had forgotten that I had a laugh, but I must have one."

J: "Then guess of whom I am jealous? . . . I am jealous of Yoknapatawpha county because you are sole owner &I proprietor of it too."

F: "Then I will give it to you (to be sole owner & proprietor)—no, I will sublease it to you. I don't know the legal terms—depending on your good behavior."

April 1954: Me: "I have been very upset recently discovering we are not free in life nor ever can be."

Faulkner: "One must not be upset but resigned—it is saddening."

December 11, 1954: "Longchamps (restaurant) looks like the inside of a hangover."

December 16, 1954: "When I'm working (on something) I do not like to be distracted by reading which demands concentration. I like to read simple books like mystery stories because I'm plotting and planning what I'm going to say at the same time."

Faulkner pointed out that he never had sex, was involved with a "negro" as a young man. Most of the young men in the South had been.

"Some day to have negro blood in one's family will mean the same as belonging to the Mayflower families."

January 1, 1955: Stein: "I admit to him that I had stolen off with the remains of the vodka the other night before because 'you seemed unhappy & depressed & I was worried for you.'"
    Faulkner on liquor: It "raised the civilization of man above that of animals—until then man had only made a few scratches on walls. Pouring out liquor is like destroying a work of art—like destroying a sculpture or burning books."

January 6, 1955: "(Faulkner describing the wine Chateau neuf du Pape): 'This wine comes from further south than the Burgundy wines—from the Rhône. It has a gusty taste coming from the stronger rays of sunshine.'"

January 7, 1955: Faulkner: "My insides sure must be surprised—they've been expecting a drink since 7 o'clock tonight, and all they're getting now (11:30 after theatre at Hamburger Heaven) is milk & a hamburger."
    Me: "At least I've completely corrupted you."

Most of this interview took place in my bed at 2 Sutton Place South, but please don't tell Truman Capote.[12]

"My speaking voice does improve depending on money (on the fee I am paid.")

Phyllis Cerf, wife of Random House publisher Bennett Cerf: "she is a kitten with steel claws underneath."

Estelle: "She used to have Jill to blackmail me with—but now that Jill is married she has no power over me anymore."

"Faulkner said John O'Hara is a Rutgers Scott Fitzgerald."

"Mr. Commins reminds me of molasses. Mr. Linscott of the feeling/sensation you have after diving through cold water & coming up on the other side of the pond."

"No, I can't remember quotations, phrases anymore, & I always used to remember them perfectly."

Jill: "Pappy, when you make your speech tomorrow [at her Pine Manor College graduation], please don't say ain't."

To Stein: "You are like the wind in the spring flowing through the violets & mint."

To Stein: "every time we need a little money, you can go out & sell one of my letters. You have the only collection of Faulkner letters in existence."

April 1956: "Carl Van Vechten looks like he came from under a stone."

June 15, 1956: "Jean reminds me of a virgin witch, all fresh & rosy from the cauldron."

Later he says: "I think I'll put you in my next book."

"I couldn't have written it without you." (That's after I tell him how worthless I feel next to him, one of the main reasons why I ended relationship, because [?] ego vanishing."

"F claims that he has never read the Life article on him; but last early spring in Rome, I saw them in his suitcase held together by a paper clip (having been removed from the magazine). However, I never saw him reading them, but he definitely had them with him. It is a good defense for him that he claims never to have read them. And I do not want to ask him, because I understand the reason, etc."

She worked hard on the *Paris Review* interview with him, sent him progress reports, and was proud of the result. She echoed his sentiments: "I love you belong to you miss you terribly."

In September 1959, he wrote to thank Jean for her "tender and gentle letter." He could not have imagined her writing any other way. He knew the man she had chosen to love had to be a "fine one, because you would not choose any other kind." He wished he had been younger, but he realized that would have made him a different man—not the one who had actually come to her, so that "we would not have loved one another." He then said, in effect, what he had imparted to Meta Carpenter when she married Wolfgang Rebner: "If he makes you happy, I will be the best friend he ever had." He wrote in an October 29, 1959 note: "Dearest Jean: I am so happy you have a daughter. I am partial to girl children; I hope that when she is 19 she will be pretty too, like you." With such sentiments, he could treasure his memories and also the fiction of what Jean Stein had made possible for him to imagine.

Addendum, found in Jean Stein's papers:

Prologue

I caught Mr. Faulkner as he was climbing past my window to peep in that of Miss Marilyn Monroe who also lives in the same apartment house. He was dressed in an Alpine hat and bombazine bolero jacket. With his climbing spurs he wore cloth topped buttoned shoes. I quickly signaled him by tapping on the glass. He was generous enough to interrupt his busy morning and devote a moment to a few questions.

Epilogue

"By the way Mr. Faulkner," I said." You are too high. Miss Monroe is on the 14th floor."

"Oh, shoot," exclaimed Mr. Faulkner. "Is my face red!!!!"

Another version has him wearing roller skates and "gracious enough to take time from his busy morning to devote a moment to a few questions."

Reminiscing about William Faulkner at the University of Virginia

A Biographer's Outtakes

On August 20, 2017, I delivered the inaugural William and Rosemary MacIlwaine Lecture at the University of Virginia. Afterwards several audience members approached me to share their memories of William Faulkner. This was all off the cuff, and I regret I did not write down the names of everyone who spoke to me as I intently listened to what they had to say.

1. Faulkner was walking along Rugby Road and one of the faculty wives saw him and said, "Oh, Mr. Faulkner, I wish you could write nicer things about the South." He muttered while he was walking, "wish I could, wish I could."
2. Mr. Faulkner was sitting on his horse and woman came up and said, "Oh, Mr. Faulkner, I just saw a movie based on one of your books. Now what was it?" She went through five or six titles, as he sat in silence, unwilling to help her out.
3. He wrote a letter to my parents on the back of a letter from a bank and had also repurposed the envelope.
4. One day my mother was riding with him at the Keswick Hunt Club. He said, "Madam, you remind me of my mother."
5. Out riding he saw people approaching looking like they wanted to smell the hem of his garment, and he took off.
6. He came to my Little League games. He'd be there, always in uniform: tweed coat and pipe, perfectly trimmed, mustache and hair. We always expected a book about Little League but that never came.

REMINISCING ABOUT FAULKNER AT THE UNIVERSITY OF VIRGINIA   69

7. I ran track when I was sixteen. The coach said: "That's William Faulkner, the timer, but don't bother him. My friend who was reading *The Bear*, said, "I'm going to go over and talk to him." He said, "Mr. Faulkner, we read *The Bear* this year." And he said, "Well, good." And then he said, "What did you think?" John said: "We really didn't understand it." Mr. Faulkner said, "It was just a bear." We liked to see him in his London Fog raincoat.

8. He was with us in a car on the way to ride horses. I was eight years old. I didn't know who he was. He knew I was scared about riding a pony. It was obvious. He said I would be all right and he told me a story. He was not a funny person, but what he said was funny. I can't explain it. Very dry humor.

9. I tried to talk with Jill about her father, but she would never talk about him.

10. Estelle would drive a Volkswagen bus, and she would go by the mailbox and toot.

11. Did you hear about the English department dinner party? The Faulkners arrived. Mr. Faulkner did not utter one word the entire night.

12. We had a reception after Dos Passos's talk to the Jefferson Society and invited Faulkner. They were not talkative. They exchanged pleasantries, but somehow we were expecting great pearls of wisdom.

Part Two

Faulkner, Politics, and History

Faulkner's Conservatism

In 1966, during my sophomore year at Michigan State University, I began to read William Faulkner. At the same time, I read Russell Kirk's *The Conservative Mind*. I still don't understand why it took me nearly fifty years to make a connection between Kirk and Faulkner, which I did while researching and writing my biography of William Faulkner.

Russell Kirk's Ten Conservative Principles reflect the way William Faulkner wrote, acted, and organized his life. As a property owner with notions of limited government, he brought that orientation to his fiction, to his work in Hollywood, to his commentary on civil rights, and to his everyday relationships with his family and community. His conservatism was not that of a party or movement but rather expressed what Kirk calls "a state of mind, a type of character, a way of looking at the civil social order."[1]

Faulkner believed in the "enduring moral order," that Kirk put first in his list of principles, and in Kirk's tenth tenet: reconciling permanence and change. Faulkner's famous Nobel Prize speech affirmed that only the "old universal truths" counted: "love and honor and pity and pride and compassion and sacrifice."[2] These words about human persistence can be found in his letters as well as in his World War II epic screenplay, the unproduced *Battle Cry*,[3] and in his Nobel speech as he evoked an image right out of his great novel *Absalom, Absalom!*, saying that after "last ding-dong of doom has clanged and faded from the last worthless rock hanging tideless in the last red and dying evening, that even then there will still be one more sound: that of his puny inexhaustible voice, still talking." He could have been thinking of the French architect, escaping his patron, the megalomaniacal Thomas Sutpen, obsessed with establishing himself in a mansion based on notions of a landed aristocracy. The architect, cornered by Sutpen and seemingly defeated, goes on talking, and with a gesture that seems to fling away the failure of his own puny resistance, overcoming his own defeat.

Faulkner revealed his conservative vision in novels like *Absalom, Absalom!* and *Requiem for a Nun* espousing the eternal verities of civilization. In

Requiem, the architect is reintroduced as Sutpen's "tame Parisian architect—or captive rather." But the community of Jefferson, Mississippi "had only to see him once to know that he was no dociler than his captor." The architect speaks to a frontier community's desire to build an edifice of itself: "You do not need advice. You are too poor. You have only your hands, and clay to make good brick. You dont have any money. You dont even have anything to copy: how can you go wrong?" Jefferson takes its shape from his molds and kilns. Even the destructiveness of the Civil War fails to disturb "one hair even out of the Paris architect's almost forgotten plumb." The architect's imprint remains, more than a hundred years later, "not on just the courthouse and the jail, but on the whole town," for he has built and made possible the community's own drive to preserve and perpetuate itself, a drive more narrowly conceived in *Absalom, Absalom!* in relation to Sutpen's ambitions. In *Requiem*, even after the community apparently loses much of its historical identity—"gone now from the fronts of the stores are the old brick made of native clay in Sutpen's architect's old molds"—still there is a surviving remnant of memory and of place found in the "thin durable continuity" of the jail itself and what it stands for.

Faulkner's emphasis on continuity, however fragile, is reminiscent of Kirk's second principle: "Continuity is the means of linking generation to generation; it matters as much for society as it does for the individual; without it, life is meaningless." When in *Go Down, Moses* Ike McCaslin renounces his birthright, his inheritance of the land and plantation his forebears have built on slavery, his seemingly righteous declaration deprives him of an influence in his community to change it for the better. Without his own stake in land, he is a powerless man, having forsaken, in Kirk's words, a third principle, "the chief sanction" of antiquity, "including rights to property." Faulkner emphasizes the irony of Ike's renunciation by having Lucas Beauchamp, an African American descended from the McCaslin family line, draw his strength from the example of old Carothers McCaslin, the founder of the plantation and the ancestral line. *Go Down, Moses* holds no brief for slavery or for white hegemony, but the novel insists that all of one's history must be carried forth into the present and ameliorated, not repudiated.

Faulkner's great novels about property and continuity followed his purchase in 1930 of a dilapidated antebellum home, known as the old Bailey place, originally built by one of Oxford, Mississippi's slave-owning merchant princes, a sinking structure that Faulkner shored up with supports of his own making. In recently discovered letters,[4] Faulkner, descended himself from a slave-owning family but also shunned by his own community as a shiftless itinerant, remade himself and his house, calling it Rowan Oak. This derelict house that he had played in as a child, sat on the edge of town, situated in exactly the right spot, just off Old Taylor Road, for an observer of the action, secluded, and yet within a short walk to the Oxford square. As one town resident testifies, walking along the Rowan Oak lane sided by towering cedars toward the Greek revival house, "one has a feeling of walking back in time, into a different world." Then, as now, the shift from present to past, from the modern neighborhood on the boundary of Rowan Oak to that cedar-lined lane occurs as quickly as the time shifts in Faulkner's fiction.

Faulkner's neighbors had called him "count no count" because of his paradoxical behavior—the aloof scion of one of Oxford's first families but also a bedraggled vagabond figure with no steady occupation. And yet he appealed to the owner of the old Bailey place, Will Bryant, a well-established farmer and businessman who shared with Faulkner an intense interest in their community's history. They became good friends. Bryant never foreclosed on Faulkner who sometimes had to delay making mortgage payments. Faulkner addressed Bryant as "Mr. Will," observing the deference he believed he owed to an older authority figure whose understanding of business far exceeded Faulkner's own. Their letters reenact the manners of a traditional society that Faulkner depicted in his fiction even as he realized that old world was undergoing tremendous change. Bryant applauded Faulkner's decision to name his house Rowan Oak, "persuaded by their chat about the religious connections of the Rowan tree," a Bryant descendent reported, noting "the sturdiness and long, sheltering life of the oak tree. A piece of Rowan wood over the door was to bring peace and happiness therein."

As Faulkner settled into Rowan Oak, he went further into debt, acquiring from Will Bryant the land surrounding his house, including the woods that he did not want to see despoiled in subdivided jerrybuilt projects he would disparage in *Requiem for a Nun*. After an $1,800 windfall from Hollywood he wrote to Bryant: "My credit is good now, and I want to keep it so. Also, I want to use it, judiciously of course, as I believe a certain amount of debt is good for a young man. But I also know that credit, in the hands of one young in business as I am, can also be dynamite." The novelist wrote as though he were addressing a tribal elder—and, in fact, at this time he had written stories about plantation-owning Mississippi Indians that he knew Bryant, a connoisseur of folklore, would appreciate.

But Faulkner was no reactionary, retreating into nostalgic sentiments. The country was undergoing massive changes in the 1930s even as he wrote about the momentous changes brought on by the Civil War in stories for *The Saturday Evening Post*. He collected this fiction in an episodic novel, *The Unvanquished* (1938), which confronted the mass migration of African Americans northward.

76 FAULKNER, POLITICS, AND HISTORY

Two boys, Bayard (white) and Ringo (Black) witness the disruption of the plantation-centered civilization both have taken for granted. Bayard, in retrospect, realizes the boys were caught up in a mass movement that overwhelmed their own efforts to keep their family's domain intact:

> the motion, the impulse to move which had already seethed to a head among his [Ringo's] people, darker than themselves, reasonless, following and seeking a delusion, a dream, a bright shape which they could not know since there was nothing in their heritage, nothing in the memory even of the old men to tell the others, 'This is what we will find'; he nor they could not have known what it was yet it was there—one of those impulses inexplicable yet invincible which appear among races of people at intervals and drive them to pick up and leave all security and familiarity of earth and home and start out, they dont know where, empty handed, blind to everything but a hope and a doom.

Bayard never thinks to ask: How much security could slaves count on? Are these migrating Black people "blind to everything" anymore deluded than Bayard and Ringo, grounded in their own mythology? In retrospect, Bayard seems quite aware of—if not exactly attuned to—the changes that are about to transform his native land. Ike McCaslin has his own negative assessment of Blacks transplanted to the North, but his isolation in *Go Down, Moses* hardly makes him the spokesman for Faulkner, a writer tied to the North and specifically to publishers in New York City and to producers in Hollywood in ways that Ike could not have imagined.

Bayard treats mass migration as problematic, and certainly beyond his ken, and perhaps, in certain respects, beyond Faulkner's, who remained in Mississippi, still very much a part of the past that made him, surrounded by African American family retainers who observed, in attenuated forms, the master-slave dynamic. When Faulkner first went North in 1918—to New Haven, where his mentor, Phil Stone, studied law at Yale, the budding writer believed Black people were better off in the South. As Hubert Starr, one of Faulkner's new northern friends noted, Bill was still an unreconstructed southerner.[5] But what did better off mean to Faulkner? Like Russell Kirk, Faulkner believed in the principles of precedent and prescription, which in his case entailed the traditional mutual dependence of whites and Blacks, which Faulkner believed benefited both races. He accepted the conventions of a paternalistic society, even with its racist and retrograde prerogatives because of his own family history, which included the devotion of the African American servants with whom he often felt closer than to his own father and mother. As a property owner, he employed these same servants at Rowan Oak, took care of their health, and provided them with housing. The prospect of overturning this quasi-aristocratic regime troubled him, although he realized that sooner or later this southern establishment would disintegrate under the pressures of a new generation, of the young people he embodied in the character of Chick Mallison in *Intruder in the Dust* (1948), *The Town* (1957), and *The Mansion* (1959).

Faulkner wanted the changes in his society to be gradual—a matter of one generation preserving the best of the past, and a new generation absorbing those enduring values even as it opened itself to a new world that would create its own traditions, expanding the notion of what it meant to be a decent and moral citizen. His last novel, *The Reivers* (1962), begins: "Grandfather said." The grandfather recollects his childhood in a tale that honors his past even as that past is giving way to the present. Like Kirk quoting Burke, Faulkner believed that healthy "change is the means of our preservation." But even healthy change was fraught with peril. Faulkner wrote about the human heart in conflict with itself, and that conflict persisted in his own encounter with the Civil Rights movement of the 1950s—for him a cataclysm in human relations that led to clashes with his own family.

Faulkner's first reactions to *Brown v. Board of Education* were entirely positive. The decision to strike down separate but equal did not surprise him. Indeed, his friend, the dean of the Ole Miss law school, had been predicting the Supreme Court decision for quite some time, and Faulkner had welcomed its inevitability. He knew that segregation had disadvantaged both whites and Blacks by creating an inferior school system for everyone, so that Mississippians, like his friend Phil Stone, went North to get prestigious degrees, and characters like Quentin Compson attended Harvard, his family having sold part of its land to support the prospects of its scion.

Faulkner's first prointegration public statements resulted in outrage in his community and in his family. The Falkners (the family's spelling of the name) were staunch segregationists and believed wholeheartedly in the Dunning school of history that taught Reconstruction as an unmitigated disaster for the South as unprepared and corrupt African Americans took over state governments and flouted their new authority over whites until whites were once again able to restore their hegemony. That view of Reconstruction, featured prominently in *Birth of a Nation* and *Gone with the Wind* has no place in Faulkner's fiction, although you can see the remnants of the Dunning thesis in a speech Faulkner delivered in Japan. At one point in *The Unvanquished*, Colonel Sartoris murders carpetbaggers registering African Americans for the vote, which becomes a legacy of violence that

Sartoris regrets and that his son, Bayard, refuses to perpetuate. What is more, Sartoris even invokes Lincoln as the peacemaker who would have kept Federal troops in the South to maintain order.

Faulkner did not explicitly support integration until the Supreme Court decision, delivered four years after the awarding of the Nobel Prize. Taking a stand on civil rights became unavoidable. Faulkner had agreed to take State Department sponsored trips abroad, and he knew the whole world was watching and expecting America to fulfill its promise of equal rights for all. In the South, in Mississippi, in Oxford, at home, his call for an integrated public-school system angered whites who called him "Weeping Willie" and baffled his own family. Nothing in his own personal code of behavior presaged his public stance of toleration. He lived the same way other Falkners did, observing his stratified society's code of manners. He routinely called African Americans "[n----rs]," and yet behind the scenes he paid for an African American's college education, supported a liberal newspaper on the Ole Miss campus, and befriended radicals like Ole Miss professor James Silver, who agitated for integration. None of Faulkner's quiet and even surreptitious efforts to reform his society, however, made much of an impression until he began to speak out and pen pieces in national magazines, including the African American *Ebony*, about the need not only for the South to change but for the South to lead the way at its own gradual pace.

This notion that the South had to rectify its injustices without northern intervention leads us back to Kirk. Faulkner believed that the North could not enforce integration—that change had to come from within. He distrusted organizations like the NAACP, believing its goals were worthy but could not be accomplished without a profound understanding of the nature of southern society, an understanding that, again, meant only the South could redeem itself. The North and civil rights organizations could pressure the South to change—nothing wrong with that, he said—but at crucial points, he argued that the process of change had to be slowed so as to allow moderates like himself to do their work in gradually resolving racial problems.

If Faulkner did not dispute the need for public protests, their timing disturbed him. Radical action riled his sensibilities as he reacted to the disruption of the customary behavior of southerners. He would have agreed with Kirk: "Sudden and slashing reforms are as perilous as sudden and slashing surgery." Forcing racial equality would tear apart families—his own included—as he had foreseen in *Absalom, Absalom!* In that novel, Charles Bon, the product of miscegenation, is pictured as confronting his white father, Thomas Sutpen, who cannot find a place in his heart or on his property for his own son who is murdered by a half brother, Henry Sutpen, even though Henry, by all accounts, loved Charles and yet could not break through the racial barriers between brothers. In all likelihood, as historian Joel Williamson revealed in his persuasive research, Faulkner's great-grandfather had sired a family of Black Falkners that his white progeny never acknowledged.

Faulkner's brother, John, declared he would fight—even resorting to violence—to defend segregation. Faulkner, unable to confront his brother, resorted to drinking to calm his anxiety, but the result impaired his judgment. In a controversial interview, which Faulkner repudiated as soon as it was published, he declared that if it "came to fighting I'd fight for Mississippi against the United States even if it means going out into the street and shooting Negroes." Faulkner's own heart was in conflict with itself. Like Henry Sutpen, he knew better than to accept the injustice that denied the respect and love of one's fellow man, and yet, like Henry as well, Faulkner could not reject his own society, however flawed and sinful. In some of his speeches, Faulkner spoke of how African Americans would have to prove themselves worthy of equality—an unsettling position to take since it seemed to ratify the encrusted belief, inculcated in his primary school education, that Reconstruction had proven African Americans were not ready for the full responsibility of citizenship, perpetuating a libel that Eric Foner and a generation of historians have refuted in their studies of Reconstruction governments and the positive role African Americans played in them.

Faulkner never enunciated a set of conservative principles, so that his responses to immediate events derived more from a sensibility than a reasoned argument. But it is not difficult to conclude, given Faulkner's inclinations, that he harbored convictions similar to Kirk's description of the conservative "affection for the proliferating intricacy of long-established social institutions and modes of life, as distinguished from the narrowing uniformity and deadening egalitarianism of radical systems. For the preservation of a healthy diversity in any civilization, there must survive orders and classes, differences in material condition, and many sorts of inequality." Faulkner, an arch opponent of the New Deal, distrusted what he considered to be the leveling uniformity of Roosevelt's policies.

In sum, Faulkner believed in the Kirkian conception of a voluntary community in which individuals could not be coerced to do right. To think otherwise, was to invite the collectivism of ideologies like Communism that Faulkner spent several years opposing in his State Department trips abroad. He believed in local control and showed what he meant by it in his script for *Drums Along the Mohawk* (1938), in which the colonists of upstate New York oppose not only British tyranny but also the dictates of centralization enforced by the Continental Congress.[6]

Perhaps Kirk and Faulkner are nowhere nearer to one another in principle than in understanding society through the metaphor of the body, in which any change must harmonize with "the form and nature of that body." When those two college roommates, Quentin, the southerner, and Shreve, the Canadian, come together to figure out the tragedy of the Sutpen family, they are bound together, in the words of Faulkner's narrator, by the umbilical of the Mississippi River, which runs through the continent and connects them like the story they have to tell, which is their bond that informs their understanding of how Henry Sutpen and Charles Bon, so clearly meant to love one another, are driven apart as the polar opposites of a society not yet able accept the color of all of its members. Faulkner worried that his society would enact that tragedy once again. There was no solution other than love—a word that Kirk does not employ in his ten principles of conservatism, but a word that hovers over his concluding belief in "people who recognize an enduring moral order in the universe, a constant human nature, and high duties toward the order spiritual and the order temporal."

Faulkner the Antifascist

In August 1925, twenty-eight-year-old William Faulkner, on his first sojourn in Europe, had a career-altering confrontation with fascism. In "Mistral," a story probably written right after his continental *Wanderjahr*, Don and an unnamed narrator—two Americans visiting an Italian mountain village—suspect that a young woman's suitor has been murdered in a plot to wed her to a fascist soldier. Don has this exchange with a waiter: "You have military in town." The waiter concedes "One." Don replies: "Well, one is enough." The waiter pointedly remarks: "Too many, some say."

In the story, the two Americans have a refrain, "I love Italy. I love Mussolini." What they dare not say is hinted at in their parody of what the villagers say to them: "No spika. I love Mussolini." "No spika" has become code for not wishing to speak the unspeakable: the likelihood that a fascist murder has been committed. The pressure against speaking out is so great that we cannot be sure that the murder has taken place—a measure of how closed-up Mussolini's Italy has become. The details of what actually happened can never be successfully determined—any more than what, precisely, happened in the Nelse Patton lynching that occurred during Faulkner's boyhood in his hometown of Oxford, Mississippi.[1] Both episodes occur in societies where the truth cannot be publicly spoken for fear of violent reprisal.

Hitler admired the American South for its racist, authoritarian rule. It's a quality that certain Faulkner characters exemplify and that the novelist exposes in *The Sound and the Fury*. "I give every man his due, regardless of religion or anything else. I have nothing against jews as an individual," Jason Compson tells a traveling salesman. "It's just the race. You'll admit that they produce nothing. They follow the pioneers into a new country and sell them clothes." To which the salesman says, "You're thinking of Armenians. . . . A pioneer wouldn't have any use for new clothes." Even Jason's more sensitive brother Quentin laments the "land of the kike and home of the wop." Similarly, Clarence Snopes, the sleazy politician in *Sanctuary*, opines: The "lowest, cheapest thing on this earth aint a [n----r]: it's a jew. We need laws against

81

them. Drastic laws. When a durn lowlife jew can come to a free country like this and just because he's got a law degree, it's time to put a stop to things. A jew is the lowest thing on this creation." No one escapes Faulkner's scorn in a novel full of sarcastic references to white Baptists; indeed, Snopes declares himself a decent Baptist before going on his anti-Semitic tirade.

Faulkner's antifascist politics have not received much comment. He grew up in Oxford, Mississippi, surrounded by racists, but so far as is known he had no contacts with Jews. He did not join political movements, but at an early age he became extremely sensitive to the treatment of aliens and foreigners, perhaps stimulated by his voracious reading of literature.

Faulkner's experiences with Jews began in New Orleans as a young writer in 1925, shortly before he set off for Europe. There, he relied on several Jewish friends, including Harold Levy, a Harvard graduate and musician, and Margery Gumbel, the wife of a securities broker, who backed the magazine *The Double Dealer*, which published Faulkner's sketches. His work then, and later, would not indulge in stereotypes like F. Scott Fitzgerald's Meyer Wolfsheim in *The Great Gatsby*, and Faulkner's letters lack the slurs against Jews that Hemingway favored, although in a pique after Horace Liveright had turned down Faulkner's third novel, *Flags in the Dust*, the writer announced to his aunt that he had a new publisher, Harrison Smith, so now he would be published by "white folks." (Liveright had never warmed to Faulkner, and the author did write to his mother on December 2, 1925: "O *damn that Jew*.")[2]

Six years later, in New York City, he dated the Jewish writer Leane Zugsmith, who was active in social justice and Communist causes, and formed warm lifelong friendships with Lillian Hellman and Dorothy Parker, also outspoken Jewish antifascists.

Faulkner's work has not been widely recognized as antifascist but knowing his views makes it possible to trace clear antifascist themes in his work, long before such views became widespread in the United States. In *The Sound and the Fury*, Jason Compson conceives of society as a fascist state in which the rule of law does not pertain to him: "I'm Jason Compson. See if you can stop me. See if you can elect a man to office that can stop me." He imagines himself as entering a courthouse with "a file of soldiers and dragging the sheriff out." That notion of a white supremacist militia becomes a reality Faulkner portrays directly in *Light in August* (1932).

German fascists mistook *Light in August* as a novel condemning race mixing. Faulkner's novels, unlike Ernest Hemingway's, were never banned or burned. But Faulkner later observed in an interview that in *Light in August* in the character Percy Grimm he had created a fascist before Hitler came to power. Percy Grimm organizes the lynching of Joe Christmas (presumed to be a Black man and to have murdered a white woman). He is a fascist, although the novel never uses the term: "He was indefatigable, restrained yet forceful; there was something about him irresistible and prophetlike." Grimm is an example of the blood and soil type that fascinated fascists; Faulkner declared in an interview that figures like Percy Grimm were "everywhere, in all countries, in all people."[3]

What is fascist about Grimm is not just his racial prejudice but also his militarism. When he organizes the lynching, the military is a godsend to him, relieving him of responsibility for his own actions as he subsumes himself in soldierly display and a sense of authority that is all-consuming:

> He could now see his life opening before him, uncomplex and ines-capable as a barren corridor, completely freed now of ever again having to think or decide, the burden which he now assumed and carried as bright and weightless and martial as his insignatory brass: a sublime and implicit faith in physical courage and blind obedience, and a belief that the white race is superior to any and all other races and that the American is superior to all other white races and that the American uniform is superior to all men, and that all that would ever be required of him in payment for this belief, this privilege, would be his own life.

Grimm ignores the American Legion commander and the sheriff, who each say they do not need his help. He clothes his vigilante mission in the uniforms of legionnaires whom he manipulates into believing they have been called up to protect the community and defend its honor. "What does your legion stand for, if not for the protection of America and Americans?" Grimm asks.

What is often overlooked in Faulkner's novel is the way it shows fascism as an endemic threat, not merely an evil outside of society itself. For all their differences, both Percy Grimm and Joe Christmas have associated their mas-culinity with the power and the desire to dominate. Joe Christmas (whose racial identity is unclear) attacks subservient women, white and Black; for Grimm, the target is the "Negro," upon whom Grimm will prove himself to his father and community.

Faulkner brought his antifascism to Hollywood, where he met many exiles from Nazi Germany. Here his political views became more explicit. In May 1938, in a rare public statement, he joined more than four hundred other writers in reacting to the Spanish Civil War: "I most sincerely wish to go on record as being unalterably opposed to Franco and fascism, to all violations of the legal government and outrages against the people of Republican Spain."

Those views also show up unmistakably in his film work. In the screenplay of *To Have and Have Not* (1944), Faulkner's adaptation of Ernest Hemingway's novel, Harry Morgan (played by Humphrey Bogart) has a fascistlike client, Mr. Johnson, who wonders why Harry keeps Eddie, a "rummy," as a crew member. Harry responds that Eddie thinks he is taking care of Harry. And more than Harry is ever willing to acknowledge, Eddie does just that. Eddie is *always there* when Harry needs him. Fascists do not understand—such is the message of *To Have and Have Not* in Faulkner's rendition—that the world is not divided between the strong and the weak. Rather, there is an interdependency in human affairs that cannot be summed up in an ideology of the survival of the fittest. The strong are strong only inasmuch as they take everyone on board—not just those who don't drink or have no disabilities. Eddie helps Harry do the right thing, which is to fight the fascists.

The Eddie whom Faulkner creates is not in Hemingway's novel, which devotes only a few sentences to the character, nor in the versions of the script and the character of Eddie worked on by other writers. Faulkner also wrote an unproduced antifascist screenplay, *Battle Cry* (1943), seemingly inspired by antifascist themes he saw in Hemingway's *For Whom the Bell Tolls*. In it, a French resistance fighter invokes the heroic example of the novel's protagonist, Robert Jordan, who sacrifices himself for the cause of the Spanish republic.

A Fable (1954), which won both the Pulitzer Prize and the National Book Award in 1955, can also be read as a fable of fascism. It centers on the encounter between father and son, the marshal and the corporal. The corporal is offered absolute power—in effect, inheriting his father's role—but he renounces the bequest and is buried as the unknown soldier. In all likelihood, the novel implies, another soldier will confront the same fascist temptation. Faulkner recognized that recurring temptation in the advent of the McCarthyism he opposed, and in the perennial return of demagoguery, which had been so much a part of the southern politics that governed his life. The story affirms that the issues of human rights fought over in World War II and the American Civil War, issues Faulkner also explored in *Battle Cry*, remain to be decided.

Faulkner's personal stake in opposing fascism is revealed in an anecdote told by one of his neighbors, when a couple of boys playing near his home in the 1950s told him that people said he was a "[n----r] lover." Faulkner replied that it was better than being a fascist.[4] Similar incidents were incorporated in *The Mansion* (1959), the last volume of the Snopes trilogy, in which Linda Snopes, an antifascist who has lost her hearing during her participation in the Spanish Civil War, returns home to rile her community by working for the education of African Americans. Her husband, Barton Kohl, a Jewish sculptor, dies in the war, and she comes home determined not to lose to the fascists again. She is met with blazing crosses and signs that call her a Jew Communist. Her father, Flem, is a homegrown fascist, ineffectively opposed by Faulkner's upholders of decency like Gavin Stevens, Chick Mallison, and V. K. Ratliff. In effect, Linda engineers Flem's murder, by arranging the release of Mink Snopes, Flem's nemesis, from prison to commit the crime. Linda chooses the radical option, to root out evil. Viewed by male characters, including Mink, as a disabled, weaker vessel—another Eddie—she drives away from home in a Jaguar, fully in command of herself and what she has done.

In Hollywood, Faulkner observed what his lover, Meta Carpenter, called "Jew haters" on movie sets. Watching the sons of his Jewish friends die in World War II, Faulkner wrote, "I just hope I dont [sic] run into some hundred percent American Legionnaire until I feel better."[5] In Hollywood, a Jewish writer accused him of not liking Jews. "You're right," Faulkner said, "but I don't like gentiles either."[6] That he identified with Jews nonetheless is reflected in his statement during the 1950s, when he received death threats for his pro-integration statements. "I am doing what I can," he wrote to a European friend. "I can see a possible time when I shall have to leave my native state, something as the Jews had to flee from Germany during Hitler."[7] The unsentimental creation of Linda Snopes, who departs her native South after the murder of Flem Snopes, and after Faulkner had explored the bigotry of characters like Jason Compson and Clarence Snopes, is the culmination of an evolving vision of Jews, fascism, and the totalitarian history that we are still reckoning with today.

Faulkner as Futurist

"The past is never dead. It's not even past." Hardly a day goes by without Google Alerts informing me that someone has appropriated that statement—usually prefaced with "Faulkner said." Well, he never said it. Gavin Stevens does, in *Requiem for a Nun*, and like every statement of a fictional character, this aphorism cannot simply be attributed to the author. "The past is never dead" pursued to its logical conclusion is an absurdity, obliterating both present and future.

This idea of Faulkner as fixated on the past has a long pedigree, perhaps beginning with "On *The Sound and the Fury*: Time in the Work of Faulkner," a much-read 1939 essay by Jean-Paul Sartre.[1] "In Faulkner's work," Sartre contends, "there is never any progression, never anything which comes from the future." But what he describes in his quotations from the novel are Quentin Compson's ruminations about time, not Faulkner's. Sartre says that "Faulkner's vision of the world can be compared to that of a man sitting in an open car and looking backwards." But Sartre does not consider that in order for that vision to travel backwards the car has to move forward, and in that progress is change, which Warren Beck characterized as "man in motion" in his classic 1961 study, so titled, of the Snopes trilogy. Sartre—not the first philosopher to pursue an idea that overwhelms and distorts reality—argues that the past "takes on a sort of super-reality, its contours are hard and clear, unchangeable." Tell that to any close reader of the 1936 novel *Absalom, Absalom!*, in which the past changes virtually moment by moment depending on who is talking.

Sartre asserts that Faulkner's characters "never look ahead." That would come as a surprise to Lena Grove in *Light in August* (1932), whose road trip is nothing but looking ahead, or to Bayard Sartoris in *The Unvanquished* (1938), who refuses to perpetuate his father's cycle of violence, not to mention Linda Snopes in *The Mansion* (1959), who puts an end to Flem Snopes's patriarchal fascism. Characters like Ike McCaslin in *Go Down, Moses* (1942) are doomed because they cannot relinquish their fealty to the past. In Faulkner's greatest novel, *Absalom, Absalom!*, a Canadian, Shreve McCannon, announces to his Harvard roommate, the diehard southerner Quentin Compson, "In a few thousand years, I who regard you will also have sprung from the loins of African kings." This astonishing prediction comes after Shreve and Quentin have spent hours and hours putting together the fraught trajectory of Thomas Sutpen and his progeny: the fable of a father who rejects his mixed-blood son, of a white brother who murders his Black brother, with racial division at the heart of this family tragedy occurring during the Civil War. Nearly forty-five years after that war, Shreve tries to wrench Quentin out of his fixation with the past by asking, "Why do you hate the South?" Quentin's last words are also the novel's conclusion: *I dont. I dont! I dont hate it! I dont hate it!* Quentin is stalemated because he cannot move beyond the past.

Shreve's point is that ultimately what the past means is what the future makes of it. And the future in Faulkner, notwithstanding Sartre's conclusion, is not "closed." Shreve believes that the story of the Sutpens that he has helped Quentin to construct will take on a transformative meaning in later ages. The Sutpens' story is that Thomas Sutpen rejected his Black son Charles Bon, Thomas's child by his first wife, after Charles came calling at Sutpen's Hundred to secure some sort of acknowledgment from his white father even as he courted his half-sister Judith and seduced his half-brother Henry, who would eventually murder Bon rather than accept him as a member of the family. In Shreve's expansive view, miscegenation will become a meaningless concept. Naturally, this is an easier tack for Shreve than for Quentin, who is at Harvard precisely because he is the Compson scion, expected to carry on the family line. Although Quentin never makes a racist comment about Charles, he obviously cannot get beyond the barriers between the races that have brought to the South, and to Quentin personally, an unbearable grief that results in Quentin's suicide.

But what is it, exactly, that propels Shreve into the future that Quentin cannot bear to contemplate? How do we get from the suave Charles Bon, an irresistible figure to all who meet him, to Charles Etienne, his angry son by an octoroon mistress, to his slack-jawed, howling grandson, Jim Bond, and finally to African kings and a lineage that will outlast Quentin's? Some first readers of *Absalom, Absalom!* supposed that in the figure of Jim Bond, Faulkner was deploring the degenerate results of race mixing. But how can that be when Shreve asserts that his typical descendant a few millennia hence will have "sprung from the loins of African kings"? How can that be when Jim Bond is outnumbered in Faulkner's fiction by white idiots like Benjy Compson and Ike Snopes? Jim Bond, unaware of his troubled heritage, seems to Shreve a harbinger not of a degenerate future but of a time when race will

88 FAULKNER, POLITICS, AND HISTORY

not matter. There will be no Miss Rosa, who tells her part of the Sutpen saga to Quentin, and calls Jim Bond a "[n----r]."

Race, it seems to Shreve, is a construct that in some distant epoch will be dispositive of nothing—neither intelligence, character, nor conviction. It is the individual who will be sovereign, and not his color, since Jim Bond and his kind, Shreve predicts, will "conquer the western hemisphere," their skin bleached out, the better to blend in. At the end of the novel, Jim Bond disappears and his whereabouts remain unknown. He fades into humanity, as will the story of Thomas Sutpen and his brood.

And isn't this the import of Charles Bon's actions? This sophisticated New Orleans denizen, the product of a multicultural society, refuses to act like a Black man. He is an ironic figure in the provincial society of northern Mississippi, with a nonchalant air coupled with a quiet determination to assert his rights. To the town of Jefferson he is an attractive yet suspect stranger, welcomed, at first, into the Sutpen home. His exotic entrance into this society is met with a fascination verging on idolatry and loathing, the latter because he cannot be neatly categorized.

The advent of Charles Bon is like that of no other character in the American literature leading up to Faulkner's work. Bon is a herald of the future, of an America that would elect a biracial president who blithely and without any apparent embarrassment called himself a "mongrel"—in one confident statement overturning more than a century of malarkey about tragic mulattos who could not reconcile themselves to their mixed blood. Barack Obama went further, saying on ABC's *The View* in 2010, "We are sort of a mongrel people.... I mean we're all kinds of mixed up.... That's actually true of white people as well, but we just know more about it." He was so right, Faulkner might have said. For Charles Bon has no qualms about race mixing—whether in his marriage to an octoroon or his courting of his white half-sister Judith.

Mixing and matching—which is what Quentin and Shreve are doing in composing the story of Charles Bon—has implications that Shreve accepts and Quentin evades. The fascist idea of blood and soil that Thomas Sutpen adopts is utterly irrelevant to Bon—and to Faulkner, who parodied racist language in his sendup of the educated Gavin Stevens's pontifications (in *Light in August*) about what the conflicted Joe Christmas's white and Black blood made him do.

Charles Bon's expansive sense of time and place is the equivalent of Faulkner's, as Bon demonstrates in his letter to Judith Sutpen, written while he is fighting in the Civil War:

> if I were a philosopher I should deduce and derive a curious and apt commentary on the times and augur of the future from this letter

which you now hold in your hands—a sheet of notepaper with, as
you can see, the best of French watermarks dated seventy years ago,
salvaged (stolen if you will) from the gutted mansion of a ruined aristocrat; and written upon in the best of stove polish manufactured not
twelve months ago in a New England factory.

The past, present, and future exist all at once in the old paper and new ink

because within this sheet of paper you now hold the best of the old
South which is dead, and the words you read were written upon it
with the best (each box said, the very best) of the new North which
has conquered and which therefore, whether it likes it or not, will
have to survive, I now believe that you and I are, strangely enough,
included among those who are doomed to live.

Bon is not right about his own survival, although in this letter he lives with
a vision of the future that emerges from *Absalom, Absalom!* in the question
Shreve puts to Quentin as the novel ends.

For Faulkner, all of time existed as a moment, during which all could be
changed: past, present, and future. He said as much to a French interviewer,
acknowledging the importance of Henri Bergson's view of "lived" time (as
opposed to "mechanistic" time).[2] Nothing Faulkner ever did, nothing his
characters ever did, was irremediable. His own novels he subjected to revision, telling his editor that the discrepancies in the Snopes trilogy proved
that he now knew more about his characters than when he first put them
on the page. In short, he resisted the idea of making the last two volumes of
the Snopes trilogy conform to the first. The past held no sway over the present or what Faulkner might yet write. He was not bound by his own books.

In Hollywood, Faulkner reworked a World War I memoir, *War Birds*,
into a screenplay, introducing the Sartoris brothers, Bayard and John, and
in the process making Bayard—so reckless and self-destructive in the post-
humously published *Flags in the Dust*—into the steady, reliable Sartoris.
Faulkner dramatizes this transformation by having Bayard bring home
the pilot who shot down John's plane, as well as the French woman who
remains loyal to her lost beloved. If the film had been produced, the canon
of Faulkner's work would have been shifted ever so slightly—just as it would
have been if his screen adaptation of *Absalom, Absalom!* (titled *Revolt in the
Earth*) had been filmed. In that script he explored the future of Clytie and
Judith, Sutpens of a Manichaean bent who are fixated on the past but are
also, especially in Judith's case, struggling to create a future free from her

father's racism. Judith lives abroad, in England, seeking the new perspective that Quentin cannot achieve, just as Linda Snopes in *The Mansion* forsakes Yoknapatawpha, Faulkner's mythical county, for the hazards of fighting on the Republican side in the Spanish Civil War, but returns home to agitate on behalf of civil rights and other social justice causes.

Judith and Linda and all of Faulkner's characters have to contend with the pull of the past, but they are not doomed by it, unless, like Quentin, they can measure the present only by the past. Faulkner, too, was susceptible to such backward thinking—at one moment of extremity saying he would fight another civil war to preserve his Southern heritage. But he quickly repudiated this lapse, which, as he acknowledged, had been prompted by drink. He understood the tendency to wallow in the past, but that wallowing was itself a sign of defeat that he could not abide.

Traveling the world during the 1950s as an ambassador of American culture and values, Faulkner came to believe even more strongly that the South and the rest of the nation would have to change, above all by abolishing the racial divisions that his greatest novel so palpably portrays. He knew that, like Shreve, who will not let Quentin sulk unchallenged, the world would not wait for the South to change, and his characters and his fellow Southerners had better get a move on. The future awaited them. The past is never dead because its meaning is forever changing.

War No More

The Revolt of the Masses in *A Fable*

So much of Faulkner's value as a modernist writer has been associated
with his searching exploration and innovative expression of individual
consciousness and conscience, that we may undervalue his turn in a
book like *A Fable* toward large-scale social phenomena
that affected whole populations.
—JOHN T. MATTHEWS

But there is one curious thing about mobs. Like our juries,
they have a way of being right.
—WILLIAM FAULKNER TO MEMPHIS *COMMERCIAL APPEAL*, FEBRUARY 15, 1931

A change will come out of this war. If it doesn't, if the politicians and the
people who run the country are not forced to make good the shibboleth
they glibly talk about freedom, liberty, human rights, then you men who
live through it will have wasted your precious time, and those who dont
live through it will have died in vain.
—WILLIAM FAULKNER WRITING TO HIS STEPSON, MALCOLM FRANKLIN, JULY 4, 1943[1]

Still too young to be unmoved by the old insidious succubae of trumpets,
too old either to make one among them or to be impervious.
—WILLIAM FAULKNER TO HIS AGENT HAROLD OBER, APRIL 22, 1944[2]

If the book can be accepted as a fable, which it is to me,
the locale and contents wont matter.
—WILLIAM FAULKNER TO ROBERT K. HAAS AT RANDOM HOUSE, MARCH 24, 1947[3]

In *A Fable* (1954), William Faulkner declared his war on authority. Before the beginning of the novel, he wrote a note that he perhaps meant for the book jacket, if not a preface, declaring "man may finally have to mobilize himself and arm himself with the implements of war to put an end to war." He began the novel near the end of World War II, and it would take him almost ten years to complete the most subversive work he ever published—a surprising turn for a man who had served in the RAF, loved to wear his uniform and lingered lovingly on uniforms in *A Fable*, was proud of his nephew Jimmy's Air Force service in World War II, evoked the military glories of the South in his fiction, and would have worn the US uniform again if he had not been too old to serve a second time. On May 27, 1940, he wrote to his publisher: "I got my uniform out the other day. I can button it, even after twenty-two years; the wings look as brave as they ever did. I swore then when I took it off in '19, that I would never wear another, no how, nowhere, for no one. But now I don't know." He worked on air defenses in his hometown of Oxford and walked his beat as an air raid warden. Faulkner spent 1943–1944 in Hollywood writing scripts (*The De Gaulle Story, Battle Cry, To Have and Have Not*) that promoted the fight against fascism. He was no pacifist, he insisted in his prefatory note to *A Fable*. And yet in the very moment of victory over the Axis forces, he began to write a novel that he knew might be unpopular because it questions the very authorities he had served and that had produced the war.

A Fable is a warning about the prospects of the future in a postcolonial world. In the late 1940s, writing an undated and unfinished letter to his son-in-law Faulkner expected that by 1952 or 1953 the "3rd and last world war will begin, which will completely exhaust the earth like Napoleon did in 1800; that when the last shell has been fired through the last barrel and they have fought a little longer with sticks and stones, exhaustion will bring hundreds years of (comparative) peace like the 100 years between Waterloo in 1814 and the first Marne battle of 1914." War to Faulkner was a production. It had to be engineered and, in the end, was about the preservation not of peace, not of justice, but of power and office. Part of his unusual delay in publishing the book that he kept announcing would be ready, and then wasn't, had to do with, as he said, ridding himself of the Hollywood hyperbole he had readily succumbed to in his prowar screenplays. Now he was bucking the triumphalism of victory that would ensure a postwar reassertion of authority and office, and reactionary regimes that other, younger contemporaries like Norman Mailer also forecast in the portrait of General Cummings in *The Naked and the Dead* (1948). Faulkner had no certainty that democratic individualism would endure even as he announced in his Nobel speech that humankind would prevail. Prevail on what terms? That is the question he puts in *A Fable*.

WAR NO MORE: THE REVOLT OF THE MASSES IN *A FABLE*   93

Faulkner's postwar anxieties about war and peace were not some kind of later in life misgivings. A younger Faulkner, the author of "Turnabout," published in *The Saturday Evening Post* (March 5, 1932), ends his World War I story with this broadside against authority, delivered by a bomber pilot on a mission: "God! God! If they were all there—all the generals, the admirals, the presidents and the kings—theirs, ours—all of them." What made Faulkner turnabout in the midst of World War II, a "good war," and herald a future that threatened to overturn the established order? What made him later say, at West Point in 1962: "War is a shabby, really impractical thing"?[4]

He made part of that turn against authority in Hollywood from his writer's cubicle wondering when mogul Jack Warner would fire him as others were fired at the studio during the war while Warner himself got his commission as a Lieutenant Colonel. Warner had wanted to be named a General, but the military brass had balked at such a blatant and so Hollywoodlike claim to a bogus authority. Perhaps that is why Faulkner, Warner's underling, responded so eagerly when director Henry Hathaway pitched the idea of a modern retelling of the Christ story, which Faulkner made into the story— first as a script and then as a novel—of a military recruit who rejects his role in war and whose example rouses the crowd that moves as one against the organization of a society mobilized for war: "Only it was the people advancing on the cavalry. The mass made no sound. It was almost orderly, merely irresistible in the concord of its frail components like a wave in its drops." It is a sentence that anticipates Elias Canetti's prophetic *Crowds and Power* (1960): "A foreboding of threatening disintegration is always alive in the crowd." Faulkner knows as much: The uprising is organic, spontaneous, and also vulnerable, the work of individuals. The crowd behaves like a force of nature, but with elements susceptible to dissolution even as it gathers momentum as a wave of protest, overtaking the cavalry sent out to subdue it: the "crowd had already underswept the military, irresistible in that passive and invincible humility, carrying its fragile bones and flesh into the iron orbit of the hooves and sabres with an almost inattentive, a humbly and passively contemptuous disregard, like martyrs entering an arena of lions." When called mobs, crowds are portrayed as cowardly disrupters of public order, but when crowds are regarded as the agents of change, as they are in *A Fable*, then their portrayal is positive.

The crowd confronts the infantry, "debouching from the Place de Ville on the crowd's rear." Then the traditional, ancient apparatus of the state as organized in the military chain of command asserts itself, beginning with the cavalry officer reporting to the "officer of the day, who would have dispatched the orderly, who would have summonsed the batman, who would have interrupted at his ablutions and shaving the adjutant, who would have waked the town-major in his nightcap, who would have telephoned or sent a runner to the infantry commander in the citadel." It takes time to control crowds because of the complicated ranking on which authority depends. The cumbersome working of society through individuals bound together in the service of the state is challenged by the velocity of the countervailing collusion of an individually populated crowd that coalesces and disperses, as it "poured into the boulevard" and flung the "cavalry aside and poured on, blotting the intersecting streets as it passed them as a river in flood blots up its tributary creeks, until at last that boulevard too was one dense seething voiceless lake."

Faulkner understood the tremendous power of crowds, of the mass that could overwhelm the institutions of society on which the making of war and social control depend. Paradoxically such crowd power depends on its weakest links, the individuals who would have to reject their role in the chain of command, which is also their claim to status inside the stratified state. The overwhelming fear that crowds can arouse is the power they have to shake the status quo, to instantaneously exert an authority they have not acquired through subservience to the hierarchy of control. Faulkner experienced this hierarchy of control, not only through his own experience of the military during flight training in Toronto but also through his plight as a writer at Warner Bros. when, in effect, he served as a private under Lieutenant Colonel Warner, whose absolute power meant that his subalterns—the producers and other adjutants who kept the studio running—could never deliver on the promises to Faulkner that he would be released from his onerous seven-year contract or, failing that, would be awarded the significant increases in salary that he merited. "I've been told that if I behave myself, stay sober, turn out the work, cause 'em not one scintilla of trouble, they'll tear up the contract and give me a new one," Faulkner wrote to his lover Meta Carpenter. In short, he simply had to follow orders. Passed over for promotion, so to speak, Faulkner would eventually revolt, go home, declaring his separate peace with Hollywood and bugger the consequences of defying his enlistment.[5]

In Hollywood and at home, work on *A Fable* became a kind of long running war with himself and the world as he worked out his salvation by ridding himself of his studio style while writing about the individuals and crowds renouncing the power of the state over them. Opposed to crowd power is the Generalissimo: the "slight gray man with a face wise, intelligent, and unbelieving, who no longer believed in anything but his disillusion and his intelligence and his limitless power." He commands all the allied forces and must put down the mutiny, initiated by a French regiment of three

WAR NO MORE: THE REVOLT OF THE MASSES IN *A FABLE* 95

thousand soldiers, that has resulted in stopping the war, since the Germans also cease fighting. The aroused crowd, many of whom have family members in the mutinous regiment, portends the dissolution of the authority that all leaders of the war—it will be shown—seek to maintain. The war has worn down its soldiers who appear in the novel's opening scenes "dazed and spent," while the thirteen mutineers (their leader, the corporal and his twelve disciples) are "grave, attentive, watchful."

There are instants in history, Faulkner seems to say, when a nation coalesces and finds its collective voice, as in the crowd scenes in Carlyle's *French Revolution* that Faulkner may have absorbed through his perpetual reading of Dickens and *A Tale of Two Cities*. The corporal, not yet named, appears in a lorry with his twelve, like Christ among his disciples, at a remove from the turmoil of the moment: "interested, attentive, and calm, with something else in it which none of the others had: a comprehension, understanding, utterly free of compassion, as if he had already anticipated without censure or pity the uproar which rose and paced and followed the lorry as it sped on." "Utterly free of compassion" is a show stopper, a signal that although the corporal is in some respects a peasant prince of peace, he is not the Christian Christ come again to minister to humankind.[6] He delivers no Sermon on the Mount; he speaks no parables. He hardly speaks at all but leads by example and by his utter devotion to humanity, to what individuals, bonded together as they are in military service, can accomplish in abolishing the very military they serve. Discussions of the novel have been led astray by taking the parallels between Christ and corporal too seriously instead of seeing the crucifixion as a starting point for a perennial struggle against authority. Faulkner believed that Christ spoke to us at individuals, and only as individuals could we unite to complete his story. Faulkner did not like the institutions of Christianity any more than he liked the institutions of the state and put up with both in so far as they ministered to individuals.

That the corporal anticipates the mass reaction against authority is a result of the impact he has already had on his regiment, which is ready to abjure war. The regiment's repudiation of their duty is replicated in the uproar of the purposeful crowd, shaping the moment as history—the opposite of the chaos that is so often attributed to mass upheavals. The shackled peasant-faced corporal and the beribboned and braided Generalissimo stare at one another "across the fleeting instant" as the lorry carrying the mutineers speeds on. Like the camera set-ups in the films Faulkner wrote, this scene is a time-shot we are privileged to capture in a close-up as the Generalissimo's "confreres" flank him "in rigid protocol," intent on imposing the order that the crowd threatens to overturn. The crowd moves on, creating its own protocols.

So does the slight, but determined woman who comes at the tail-end of this crowd scene, famished yet spitting out the bread she is offered by a sergeant, another sign that like the crowd she is on a kind of mission baffling to the soldier who offers her sustenance. She is famished for more than food. Her "urgency," it is said, is even greater than the crowd's. In a portent of a world about to come to an end, she reaches the Place de Ville after the crowd has vacated it, so that the site seems like a stage on which "all mankind seemed to have drained away and vanished, bequeathing, relicting to her the broad, once-more empty boulevard and the Place and even, for that moment, the city and the earth itself." It is as if the world is returning to its origins, to a primal state and abolishing history, which is perhaps what Faulkner had in mind in choosing the word "relicting." She is, as we later learn, the corporal's intended, come to claim a human right of self-determination that governments and armies abrogate. She also embodies a feminine imperative that is opposed to war in the novel, and a feminine authority, as Noel Polk points out, that men seek to abolish by excluding women from war.[7] It is why, in *A Fable*'s first section, the corporal's intended annoys the sergeant who feeds her the bread but is exasperated because she is in the way. He is "impatient at the stupidly complicating ineptitude of civilians at all times," but that she is a woman prompts another question: "Who does she belong to?" A woman can be no more than an appendage in the male world of war, which is an end in itself. Later we learn she has been a whore, one of those outside of the lawful perimeters of the state, who has forsaken her profession for a life on the corporal's farm. Her resistance to authority makes her one of the "emergent voices of submerged populations," as Barbara Ladd puts it, who "surge up" in *A Fable*.

Charles Gragnon, the commander of the regiment that has mutinied, is told by his superior, the corps commander: "The boche doesn't want to destroy us, any more than we would want, could afford, to destroy him. Cant you understand? either of us, without the other, couldn't exist?" The war, and the governments that make war, are mutually dependent, and Gragnon has to realize he counts for nothing other than to carry out orders. Sounding like Mailer's General Cummings, the corps commander declares: "'It is man who is our enemy: the vast seething moiling spiritless mass of him. Once to each period of his inglorious history, one of us appears with the stature of a giant, suddenly and without warning in the middle of a nation as a dairymaid enters a buttery, and with his sword for paddle he heaps and pounds and stiffens the malleable mass and even holds it cohered and purposeful for a time." We know that such a man, or the parody of such a man, steps forward and declaims: "I alone can do it." The mutiny, the corps commander explains, is an "occupational hazard. . . . We hauled them up out of their ignominious mud by their bootstraps; in one more little instant they might have changed the world's face. But they never do. They collapse, as yours did this morning. They always will. But not us. We will even drag them willy-nilly up again, in time, and they will collapse again. But not us. It wont be us." The authorities, in other words, will prevail.

Faulkner is said to have had little interest in politics, even though he lived in a culture rife with it. For him politics claimed a factitious authority, a sovereignty that only the individual can assert. At best, governments are tolerable, even if politicians are not, so long as some mutual support pertains among the governors and the governed. Gragnon believes he has served himself by serving in the army, as Faulkner did when he wore his RFC uniform, which simultaneously made him stand out and identified him as part of a cause. But the corps commander tells Gragnon that he is expendable. He serves a purpose, but he cannot, in the end, be considered purposeful in his own right. The military ribbons on display in *A Fable* honor individuals, but in fact the ribbons—like so many memorials and statues—exist to honor the armies and authorities that bestow the awards, which is why Faulkner himself reluctantly played along in his ambivalent attitude toward the Nobel Prize, his Gold Medal for fiction, and the other awards offered to him. Occasionally, as in his refusal to attend President Kennedy's White House dinner for Nobel laureates, he rebelled and turned down the invitation to prop up a politician and his party.

To go to that presidential dinner, Faulkner would have to dress in black tie, the uniform of awards ceremonies, which he had done in Sweden and even joked about as apparel he would put on display in Rowan Oak, his Oxford home. He liked the trappings of office and of award ceremonies and performed quite an outstanding hunt ceremony in full regalia at Rowan Oak. So it is no surprise that after the opening crowd scene, we get a gathering of military chiefs whose uniforms and tailoring are described in such loving detail that it is possible Faulkner missed a calling as a haberdasher. What matters to the generals is to keep the war going, whereas Gragnon remains fixated on his own sense of honor that can be satisfied only by having his mutinous regiment executed. The orphaned Gragnon, adopted by the army, the source of his identity, now reeling from his exposure to the politics of war drives out to the front to feel the "solitude and pride of command," that the mutiny has taken from him. The war is at a standstill, an aide informs Gragnon: "It's the men . . . the ranks. Not just that regiment, nor even our division, but all the private soldiers in our whole front, the boche too." What is at stake is not simply losing the war but the collective action of soldiers: "Defying, revolting, not against the enemy, but against us, the officers."

Faulkner never made it far in the military, serving as an enthusiastic cadet, a pilot-in-training, treating flying as the cavalry of the air. He never got off the ground because the war ended before he could seat himself in a plane. He identified with the officer class, wanting the glory that his great grandfather, the old Colonel, had won, even in Civil War defeat. In *Soldiers' Pay* (1926), Cadet Lowe wishes he had suffered aviator Donald Mahon's death wound. Faulkner returned home from Toronto pretending to have been marked by war with a limp. War fascinated but also repelled him not only because of the slaughter but because it shot to hell his own hopes of glory. Learning to fly in the early 1930s, he sought a barnstorming antidote to the misery of knowing he had lost out. That lost opportunity makes a fugitive appearance in *A Fable* in a curious scene in which Gragnon recalls an aide who also laments his missed opportunity to be heroic. The aide confesses that in peacetime he had been a couturier desperately wanting "to be better some day. But that wasn't what I wanted. I wanted to be brave." He decided to be an actor, play Cyrano, one of Faulkner's favorites that got him to New York to see Jose Ferrer in the role. But acting is not enough for the aide: "Then I knew what to do. Write it," the aide tells a perplexed Gragnon:

> "Myself write the plays, rather than just act out somebody else's idea of what is brave. Invent myself the glorious deeds and situations, create myself the people brave enough to perform and face and endure them."
> "And that wouldn't have been make-believe too?" the general said.
> "It would have been me that wrote them, invented them, created them."

Writing to publisher Robert Haas about his sonnets commemorating his son's loss in World War II, Faulkner wrote: "The only difference between you and the sonless grief less natural poet is, the poet is capable in his imagination alone of all grief and degradation and valor and sacrifice."[8] In effect, the power of writing, of the word, becomes the heroic deed, which for Faulkner became all the more precious and perhaps the reason why he has this aide, such a lover of fine clothes, die in a botched effort to flag down a war bound vehicle that is as futile as the self-defeating cavalry charges of the Civil War that Faulkner glorifies and mocks in *Flags in the Dust*.

Faulkner would write himself in and out of war for most of his life, setting up a duality that Joseph Urgo pursues in a chapter on *A Fable* in *Faulkner's Apocrypha*. Writing to his stepson Malcolm Franklin on December 5, 1942, Faulkner detected the "the same old stink . . . rising from this one as has risen from every war yet: vide Churchill's speech about having no part in

WAR NO MORE: THE REVOLT OF THE MASSES IN *A FABLE*   99

dismembering the Br. Empire. But it is the biggest thing that will happen in your lifetime. All your contemporaries will be in it before it is over, and if you are not one of them, you will always regret it."[9] *A Fable* gives full play to both sides of war—not only to the adversaries but to the men who fight the war and the men who lead them. "Let the whole vast moil and seethe of man confederate in stopping wars if they wish, so long as we can prevent them learning that they have done so," the group commander exhorts Gragnon. We have it in our power to stop war, Faulkner's novel argues, if only we knew it. The mutiny that spreads to both sides of the front has already proven as much: "Yes, let them believe they can stop it, so long as they dont suspect that they have," the group commander reiterates: "Let them believe that tomorrow they will end it; then they wont begin to ponder if perhaps today they can." Isn't that always the hope of those in power? That the crowds will disperse, the demonstrations, so full of hope, will, in time, disintegrate into the status quo?

Faulkner turns over the ramifications of the mutiny again and again, introducing new characters, and repositioning the story as if part of some mad group of Hollywood rewrite men. That Hollywood is on his mind is evident in his account of a battalion runner, a demoted officer deprived of his authority in "in a plot whose meretricity and shabbiness only American moving pictures were to match." The battalion runner makes sure he is caught with a woman, "taken in delicto so outrageously flagrant and public, so completely unequivocal and incapable of other than one interpretation" that the military has to strip him of his pips. It is not war per se the runner abhors so much as the power to wage it by a "ruthless and all-powerful and unchallengeable Authority" that he imagines "would be impotent before that massed unresisting undemanding passivity. He thought: They could execute only so many of us before they will have worn out the last rifle and pistol and expended the last live shell."

Out of his old Hollywood script, Faulkner resurrected in *A Fable* a character played by Lionel Barrymore in *The Road to Glory* (1936). In the film, the old man shows up at his officer's son's outpost, with a bugle and tries to lead the kind of heroic charge common in the nineteenth century but is undone by the immense firepower of modern war. But in *A Fable*, still looking for his son, the old man announces the "one," the return of Christ who will end all wars. Faulkner was no true Christian believer in a second coming, but he did believe in "the one," the individual who can change history, as he reiterated in a speech to his daughter's high school class, urging the graduates to

raise your voice for honesty and truth and compassion, against injustice and lying and greed. If you . . . will do this . . . as individuals

... you will change the earth. In one generation all the Napoleons and Hitlers and Caesars and Mussolinis and Stalins and all the other tyrants who want power and aggrandisement ... will have vanished from the face of it.[10]

The battalion runner does not believe in Christ, but he does believe in the power of one, exemplified by the mutinous corporal. The rebellious runner so outrages a sentry, determined to hold rank and do his duty, that he strikes the runner with his boot as his sergeant says, "Kick his . . . ing teeth in."

The very idea of insubordination, of taking up history by yourself, is a revolting idea not merely to authorities but to those whose identity and sense of order is entirely predicated on a hierarchy of control. William Faulkner opposed the New Deal, at least in part, because it created a greater bureaucratic authority that made it more difficult, he believed, for individuals to assert themselves. When he had an opportunity to observe the machinery of the state close up on one of his State Department tours, he wrote that "the people in our State Department in Europe are intelligent people. They have learned by sad experience that the enemy, the opponent, is not the foreigner, it's in the State Department in Washington, the bureaucrats in Washington."

Asked about student riots and protests, Faulkner said they demonstrated a "perfectly normal impulse to revolt." And he did not qualify that statement or feel an urge to condemn crowd violence. He was no revolutionary, to be sure, but he was a subversive. Not until many years later did his niece discover that he had funded her underground newspaper attacking white supremacists.[11] His dim view of the FBI, as portrayed in *The Mansion* (1959) expresses his dissent and wariness of the national security state. And don't forget he created one of the great subversives: Linda Snopes, who not only fights fascists in the Spanish Civil War but back at home brings down a fascist patriarch.

And yet Faulkner yearned to be part of a nation that exists, Noel Polk argues in *Faulkner and War*, for war.[12] That Faulkner never actually engaged in combat was an everlasting psychic wound. He returns to it repeatedly in *A Fable*, with Levine who is grounded before he ever gets into the air. Like Faulkner, Levine knows his aircraft, watching a German general in bomber biplane, called a Harry Tate after a music hall comedian. The plane appears overhead like the star in a film, dominating Levine's imagination, like those aircraft Faulkner's drew so meticulously in flight school. Modern war was so disturbing to him because it had become so bureaucratic, so corporate. But his attraction to military service, to the uniform, is on display in *A Fable* as Levine laments the change in the aviator's tunic: "his was the new RAF thing not only unmartial but even a little epicene, with its cloth belt and no shoulder-straps like the coat of the adult leader of a neo-Christian boys' club and the narrow pale blue ring around each cuff and the hat-badge like a field marshal's until you saw, remarked, noticed the little modest dull gold pin on either side of it like lingerie-clips or say the christening's gift-choice by godfathers whose good taste had had to match their pocket-books." Faulkner as martial couturier made sure to return home rigged up in a Royal Flying Corps uniform, fulfilling his idea of how a wounded warrior should look. The switch from the RFC to the RAF outfit in April 1918 while he was in Toronto became yet another way to thwart William Faulkner's fitness for battle.

Levine is frustrated because he waits a whole year to enlist in deference to his mother's worries about losing her son in war. Faulkner did much the same, deciding not to make good on his plan to join an ambulance corps because his mother objected. Levine watches the sky and repeats the catalogue of the hero aviators he has wanted to emulate. Now grounded, a "door had closed on glory," he cannot belong to "the brotherhood of heroes." Like Faulkner in flight school, Levine writes letters home to his mother. The German general Levine spots in the Harry Tate coming in for a landing also brings Levine back to earth, mourning that he will never confront death "in the closed select one of flying." Stuck writing *A Fable* for ten years Faulkner had to relive, again and again, the humiliation of inaction. Levine is told, in effect, not to move, to initiate nothing: "Levine. You've been here three weeks. Not long enough to have learned that this squadron is run by people especially appointed and even qualified for it. In fact, when they gave you those badges, they gave you a book of rules to go with them, to prevent you needing ever to rack your brains like this. Perhaps you haven't yet had time to glance through it." Every soldier is the same and unknown, except for those heroes and generals in planes. He is told to "sit somewhere and be quiet." But as Levine listens to his superiors, their panic is palpable. What to do if the war has permanently stopped? Everything has been organized around the military mission, and no alternative seems conceivable. With the war halted, Levine cannot finish the letter to his mother: "because the cessation of the guns yesterday had not only deleted all meaning from the words but effaced the very foundation of their purpose and aim." What is there to measure a man by, if not by war? Without that war, Faulkner's characters, like Faulkner himself, lack fulfillment.

No wonder then that the mutiny of three thousand men captured Faulkner's imagination: "the entire three thousand spread one-man deep across a whole regimental front, acting without intercommunication as one man." Such can be the case with crowd psychology, Canetti writes, "Suddenly it is as though everything were happening in one and the same body." This powerful coalescence, *A Fable* allows, exerts an authority that threatens to overturn and overwhelm not merely the military code of conduct but the very organization of a society on which war depends. Late into his life, Faulkner like to execute the military drills he had learned in Toronto for the pleasure of his University of Virginia hosts, Joseph Blotner and Frederick Gwynn, both World War II combat veterans.[13] He wanted to share the very soldierly solidarity that *A Fable* glorifies and guts. And no wonder the book took him a decade since he was challenging his own proclivities, understanding how the quest for glory degenerates into vainglory, into the actions of martinets, and into regimes that count on the sacrifices of the Levines who are not supposed to question military protocol but to accept, for example, a German general shooting his pilot. "By the book," Captain Bridesman tells the shocked Levine, "a German pilot who lands an undamaged German aeroplane containing a German lieutenant general on an enemy aerodrome, is either a traitor or a coward, and he must die for it"—just as by the book, Gragnon wants the mutineers executed. In Levine's case, his conception of war as an honorable mission is blasted because the allies collude with the Germans to perpetuate the war that the mutiny has halted. For Levine, collaboration with the enemy is the "death of England," and his own death, which he accomplishes with a pistol. Levine is like another Faulkner suicide Quentin Compson in *The Sound and the Fury*, who cannot abide the defeat of the South that has nurtured him and his own defeat in not being able to defend it.

But the book—the rules of warfare—become nugatory to the bafflement of everyone—the crowd and the military hierarchy—when it is learned that thirteen men, only nine of whom are French, with the rest apparently representative of a French Foreign Legion internationality, have somehow brought about a mutiny that has put the war on pause under the leadership of a corporal whose name is not known. How can a leader not be named? How can a movement that suspends the war proceed without publicity and the perquisites of fame on which the historic is built? How can a group of men, not all of whom speak the same language, lead a mutiny? These men are virtually a postcolonial threat to the French authorities, and frightening in their inspiration of the overflowing crowd streaming through the city and toward the compound where the thirteen will be (so everyone thinks) shot. Then the crowd takes flight back toward the city, like, we are told, a flock of birds but purposeful as though in a Hitchcock thriller, to watch the generals arrive to "preside with all the impunity and authority of civilised usage over the formal orderly shooting of one set of men by another wearing the same uniform." Yet the crowd's expectations are thwarted as the day ends without an execution, prompting the exodus of people toward home in further expectation of returning to the same point after their repasts.

WAR NO MORE: THE REVOLT OF THE MASSES IN *A FABLE*   103

Then Faulkner divagates, fulfilling the purpose of a book that deviates from the demands of conventional plots and realism just as the mutiny disrupts the war. The battalion runner who has renounced all the perks of office and wants nothing to do with the military establishment is confronted with an unaccountable "blackamoor minister," "an old Negro in a worn brushed top hat, with the serene and noble face of an idealized Roman consul" looking for a bow-legged Cockney soldier who used to be a horse groom and is now running a kind of insurance operation in which he doles out ten bob to men who pay him back six pence at a time as long as they survive the war. The scheme, of course, inverts the point of insurance companies, which is to profit at the expense of the customer. The horse groom, on the contrary, is counting on his soldier-customers living as long as possible. In a book-length study of the novel, Keen Butterworth sees him as a negative character profiting from men's fear of dying. But he is also setting up a counterculture, so to speak, to the war machine that expends lives lavishly to win what will benefit none of these soldiers. To fortify the point, Faulkner has the exgroom, now a sentry, induct his customers into a Masonic association, another private order of society that the army cannot penetrate.[14]

The soldier's improbable scheme is at the heart of this improbable novel, which is why the story of the horse groom and his cohort comes close to the dead center of Faulkner's far-fetched fable. Not only does the preacher show up in a motor car supplied by the French state, he has a powerful female French backer. He has changed his name from the Reverend Tobe Sutterfield to Tooleyman, a corruption of *tout le monde*. He is everybody, and history personified, from an old Black man to a Roman consul. He is also, as Barbara Ladd points out in *Resisting History*, deliberately implausible: "Tooleyman's mere presence in France is amazing—that a seemingly uneducated and impoverished black southerner could, in such a short period of time, get to Paris, meet up with a wealthy American woman, and end up presiding over a charitable organization of such reach is clearly improbable. What connections! Beneath the radar. Never revealed."

This calculated implausibility began in Hollywood, where the idea of *A Fable* germinated in Faulkner's discussions with William Bacher, a producer, and Henry Hathaway, a director but also resulted from the novelist's work on *Battle Cry*, an ambitious World War II film, written in collaboration with Howard Hawks. The film proved too expensive for Warner Bros. to produce, but it may also have seemed unprofitable because of Faulkner's determination to overthrow studio conventions, to introduce a Black character named America, who is wounded and cared for by a good old boy, an unreconstructed Southerner who nonetheless becomes the Black's caretaker. This is one of the "implausible alliances" that Ladd notes in the novel that welcomes the "implausibility that realism would foreclose." Realism, she observes, is the narrative choice of empire, since realism ratifies what is rather than what, as *A Fable* has it, might be. She calls Tooleyman the "irruption into European history of an African-southern figure . . . an irruption of Everyman in a novel in which Everyman is no longer a universalized European subject but instead a figure representing 'All the World' in its complex multiplicity, in its unassimilable difference, and in its indifference."

Tooleyman is the crowd personified in search of the fiercely individualistic horse groom who does not want to be found. History and humanity have a claim on the groom that Tooleyman presents, telling the battalion runner of the three-legged horse who two years before the war began won all the races in the American South, a horse that ran in order to run—not for any ulterior purpose, and not with the backing of an owner, from whom the horse groom had stolen the horse, although Tooleyman insists no stealing is involved because "It was the world's horse. The champion. No, that's wrong too. Things belonged to it, not it to things. Things and people both. He did. I did. All three of us did before it was over." The idea of ownership and what it did to an animal or person hit home with Faulkner who disliked the way Jack Warner bragged about owning and, in a sense, racing Faulkner. When an editor at Random House proposed that Ernest Hemingway do a preface to a Modern Library edition of *The Sound and the Fury* and *As I Lay Dying*, Faulkner wrote on March 22, 1946, that it was tantamount to making him one of those "eunuch-capon pampered creatures in some spiritual Vanderbilt stables, mindless, possessing nothing save the ability and willingness to run their hearts out at the drop of Vanderbilt's hat."[15]

The third party in the Tooleyman-horse groom enterprise is a young Black boy, Tooleyman's grandson, who rides the horse to perpetual victory flaunting all efforts by the state, including local law enforcement officials, prosecutors, and the FBI to capture the reivers in a plot that Faulkner would return to in his last novel. The incredible threesome are abetted by a society that values the pluck of this outlaw threesome and does not want them to be caught. The horse groom is inducted into the Masons, a telling development, since this secret society, thought of as conspiratorial, represents the alternative to a publicly established civil society.

It has to be understood that Faulkner grew up in his father's stable among Black hostlers. There he became part of a kind of secret society that depended on the expert handling of horses. Among horses, all men were equal, and all men entitled to their own alternative to authority, an entitlement Faulkner exerted when he was forced to forsake the stable for another family business:

WAR NO MORE: THE REVOLT OF THE MASSES IN *A FABLE*   105

"Quit school and went to work in Grandfather's bank. Learned the medicinal value of his liquor. Grandfather thought it was the janitor. Hard on janitor." Faulkner wrote this fanciful biographical note when asked for an author's biography and burnished his credentials as a duplicitous misfit but also his behavior as a man not beholden to any institution. He absorbed in the stable what he attributes to the horse groom:

> It was because there had developed apparently on sight between the man and the animal something which was no *mere* rapport but an affinity, not from understanding to understanding but from heart to heart and glands to glands, so that unless the man was present or at least nearby, the horse was not even less than a horse: it was no longer a horse at all: not at all intractable and anything but unpredictable, because it was quite predictable in fact; not only dangerous, but in effect, for all its dedicated and consecrated end and purpose—the long careful breeding and selecting which finally produced it to be sold for the price it brought to perform the one rite for which it had been shaped—worthless, letting none save the one man enter the same walls or fence with it to groom or feed it, no jockey or exercise boy to approach and mount it until the man bade it; and even then, with the rider actually up, not even running until—whatever the communication was: voice, touch, whatever—the man had set it free.

In *A Fable*, the notion of freedom has to be embodied in the tale of a Black man who can evade and also manipulate public institutions in defiance of their precepts and yet in conformity with their craving to acknowledge the very authority that Tooleyman exhibits and thwarts. It is Tooleyman, like Ned McCaslin, the Black descendent of a white slave-owning family, in Faulkner's last novel, *The Reivers* (1962), who puts together the team that runs the horse that runs them, a team that the horse groom would rather not acknowledge in his self-contained isolation, which is as distrustful of any authority, including Tooleyman, as the battalion runner who becomes obsessed with the freedom the threesome represent, who run away with a horse so that it could not be put out to stud, using "its bullocks to geld its heart."

When cornered the threesome are protected by the "curious, watching attitude of the town," which a lawyer calls "a mob," which his client, the horse's owner, realizes is just people watching and waiting—very much like the crowds at the beginning of *A Fable* who await the outcome of the mutineers' fate. What the mutiny and the reiving represent is the pageantry of freedom, and Faulkner's recall of a "battered yet indomitably virgin continent, where nothing save the vast unmoral sky limited what a man could try to do, nor even the sky limit his success and the adulation of his fellow man." Faulkner often liked to explain Mississippi as a frontier society, the two words together almost a contradiction in terms, which in later life he countered with his other inclination, which was toward Virginia and what he called its snobs, who worshipped the protocol of the hunt and the ceremonial garb he delighted in showing off for the camera.

The three-legged horse, by the way, is never saddled but raced with a bellyband, the very epitome of a virtually bareback world without the straps and cinches that nevertheless could not prevent Faulkner from frequently falling off his horses. That he continued mounting and remained part of the fox hunt, no matter the bruises and breaks that were the agony of his last days, are foretold in the running of the disabled yet triumphant horse. In one scene the crowd closes in on the turnkey charged with holding Tooleyman. The turnkey is an office holder—a jailer who has obtained his job through family connections. The crowd in the "same voice" tells him to step aside. Present also is an attorney, another spurious figure of authority—as Faulkner explained to his agent, Harold Ober: "The lawyer begins a political speech, the sort of thing which has held American crowds for a hundred years, full of rhetoric and meaning nothing. But as soon as the crowd realizes what it is, they rise up . . . just push him out of the way and overtake the turnkey and the Negro and set the Negro free."[16]

The crowd thwarts the law, provoking one of Faulkner's extended historical passages that derives from his obsession with jurisprudence—its power and limitations that he would probe so often in the character of Gavin Stevens, the cynosure of civilization in several novels and stories. Faulkner, as a young man tutored by a literature-loving lawyer, Phil Stone, never got out of the habit of visiting his friend's law office and arguing points of law. You can almost see Faulkner looking over Stone's law books in the scene when the crowd "poured on into the auditorium," practically inundating history and the "ghosts upon Littleton upon Blackstone upon Napoleon upon Julius Caesar—the progenitors of laws and codes." The lawyer, recognizing the limitations of the law to quell the crowd, extricates the turnkey and the threesome from the moil (one of Faulkner's favorite words) of the masses, who are not a mob but "Man pouring steadily into the tabernacle [the courtroom], the shrine itself, of his last tribal mysteries, entering without temerity or challenge, because why not?" The courtroom and apparatus of the state ultimately owe their life to "Man," now in the shape of the crowd, which is the exact opposite of every mob encountered in Faulkner's earlier fiction. As the turnkey declares: "Because this thing is all wrong. It's backwards. The law spirits a [n----r] prisoner out of jail and out of town, to protect him from a mob that wants to take him out and burn him. All these folks want to do is to set this one free."

Over and against the crowd, the corporal, and every other challenge to authority, stands the Generalissimo, the "old general," and his fellow generals, including the Germans. The old general faces a formidable force because the crowd has not merely coalesced but creeps "cityward at the pace of the smallest and weakest," which is what every fascist abhors who believes in the survival of the fittest. But the Generalissimo has an authority based in lore that makes him seem at one with his army, with "all who knew the old marshal's name" and believed the "old man remembered the name and face of every man in uniform whom he had ever seen." This improbable myth nonetheless makes it seem as though the Generalissimo values every individual regardless of rank. He is, in fact, the scion of a family that recognizes no bounds to its ambition and is the very epitome of the rapacity—another of Faulkner's favorite words—that drives human beings forward. But the Generalissimo has not taken the obvious route of the privileged—instead beginning his career in a remote African outpost, lost to history for years, before emerging to claim his prerogatives. The Generalissimo has acted like the unnamed corporal who emerges out of obscurity to stop the war. Indeed, the Generalissimo's "harsh high mountain face . . . might have been a twin of the corporal's except for the difference in age." In fact, the Generalissimo is the corporal's father, who has engendered a son in a "youthful folly" he has abandoned but will in the course of events have to acknowledge and annihilate as offspring unsuitable to his design (the word the corporal's wife uses for the Generalissimo's actions) much as Thomas Sutpen in *Absalom, Absalom!* rejects and disowns his Black son as a defect in his white design. The corporal is an heir as wayward as William Faulkner himself, the eldest son who disappointed his own father and grandfather because of a failure to take up the position of authority on which the family had built its fortunes.

The corporal's intended, the same unnamed woman who had spit out the sergeant's offer of bread, confronts the Generalissimo with the claims of humanity and of family that he cannot countenance without relinquishing his command of the war, which means, more war to come, as the German general predicts when speaking to the English general alongside the Generalissimo and his American counterpart. Only the German general is willing to make explicit what the other generals prefer to remain tacit: They have met to preserve the world for war, and they—generals on all sides—will train their fire on their own mutinous men, as the battalion runner learns when his own gathering of rebels is annihilated in two barrages and flames engulf half his body "neatly from heel through navel through chin." The shocked runner screams, "They cant kill us! They cant! Not dare not: they cant!" The desperate Quartermaster General tells the Generalissimo the barrages are meant to "prevent naked and weaponless hand touching opposite naked and weaponless hand" in order to preserve "our tight close unchallengeable hierarchy."

The Generalissimo confronting the corporal, his son, gains no advantage by revealing that Polchek, one of the twelve, has betrayed the corporal. How long before others do as well? the Generalissimo asks the corporal, who stubbornly avows his faith in his disciples. "Then take the world," the Generalissimo responds, "I will acknowledge you as my son; together we will close the window on this aberration and lock it forever." The corporal, in short, is offered the very power he has opposed—which would not be the first time a rebel has become his opposite number. Remember this is the old general first portrayed as no longer believing in principles divorced from power. He offers his son "all the world to work on and the heritage I can give you to work with." A family dynasty awaits: "I am an old man, you a young one; I will be dead in a few years and you can use your inheritance to win the trick tomorrow which today my deuce finessed you of." Turning the corporal's argument for martyrdom against him, the old general claims "it's not I but you who are afraid of man; not I but you who believe that nothing but a death can save him." But the corporal knows that his authority cannot be transferred to the state, which is what the old general commands.

But without the state's power, without institutional support, how can the corporal succeed? This is what the priest assigned to change the corporal's mind asks by his invocation of St. Paul: "a Roman first and then a man and only then a dreamer and so all of them was able to read the dream correctly and to realize that, to endure, it could not be a nebulous and airy faith but instead it must be a *church, an establishment.*" And did not Paul, who knew how to deal with Rome, in the end destroy Rome while the church flourished? Paul, the priest maintains, "required no martyrdom." But for the corporal, such a surrender to the state, results in the death of principle, the demolition of permanent peace.

Reasons of state take precedence over individual lives, even lives of its faithful servants. Three soldiers are assigned to execute Gragnon: Buchwald, a Brooklyn Jew, an Iowan, and a Mississippi Black, whom Buchwald calls "Sambo," and who proudly announces his lineage: "Philip Manigault Beauchamp." These three names conjure European royalty, a Yoknapatawpha heritage, and a spirit of independence exemplified in the figure of Lucas Beauchamp in *Go Down Moses* (1942) and *Intruder in the Dust* (1948). The Iowan tells the inquisitive Beauchamp: "In the army, you dont ask what you are going to do: you just do it." But in fact the three men argue about what

WAR NO MORE: THE REVOLT OF THE MASSES IN *A FABLE*

they are about to do and how to do it in the kind of spirited individuality that Faulkner valued and that emerged in dire circumstances. They argue about protocol, about how to shoot a French general in a kind of mockery of the very idea of protocol. All this takes place in the bowels of the Hôtel de Ville: "empty of any life or sound save that of their boots, the white-washed stone sweating in furious immobility beneath the whole concentrated weight of history, stratum upon stratum of dead tradition impounded by the Hôtel above them—monarchy revolution empire and republic, duke farmer-general and sans culotte, levee tribunal and guillotine, liberty fraternity equality and death and the people the People always to endure and prevail." Dead tradition is what the corporal has defied and what the execution of Gragnon represents. The People are sovereign in *A Fable*, which is why the corporal cannot accept the old general's, the old world's offer. Faulkner believed history could not go on in the same way again and again, and he hoped *A Fable* would stand as his declaration for a new kind of history, fulfilling the notion of the People that his nation had promulgated but also impeded.

The concluding chapters of *A Fable* are an agonizing, sometimes bathetic denouement. After the low comedy routine of Gragnon's three executioners, who have botched the killing and have to plug a hole in the back of the head since protocol demands the shot be to the front, the next day shines on "the gaudy uniforms and arms and jangling accoutrements and even the ebon faces too of the Senegalese regiment." Faulkner's obsession with haberdashery always has a point—in this case an obsessive one as he refers to "the gaudy arras of the Senegalese," "rigid palisade of Senegalese heads," who represent, in Barbara Ladd's telling, "the sense of constraint and danger, but also the sense of hope, one feels in the novel. Their gaudy unassimilability is a trope for resistance even though they purportedly serve the interests of empire." These French colonial subjects, 130,000 of them strong, served in World War I Europe and would later win their independence in 1960. They are a sort of nationalized foreigners that bemuse Faulkner who, I take it, understood how they fit into his back home tradition of faithful Black family retainers who served him and yet expressed distinctive personalities and signs of independence that were never strictly under his command. Earlier in the novel the Senegalese guard the mutinous regiment in a compound: "lounging haughtily overhead along the catwalks and lending a gaudy, theatrical insouciance to the raffish shabbiness of their uniforms like that of an American blackface minstrel troupe dressed hurriedly out of pawnshops." Blackface is associated with subservience to white power that has to be entertained, but hark to that "theatrical insouciance," the hint of a subversive attitude that would erupt in the demise of colonial Africa as Faulkner anticipated in his public speeches. From the vantage point of post-World War II, such passages as this one transform World War I into another front against colonialism: "another front, manned by all the troops in the three forces who cant speak the language belonging to the coast they came up from under the equator and half around the world to die in, in the cold and the wet—Senegalese and Moroccans and Kurds and Chinese and Malays and Indians—Polynesian Melanesian Mongol and Negro."

To put it another way, *A Fable* is about tomorrow, which is the title of the last chapter. The corporal is, of course, executed and becomes through more low comedy the occupant of the tomb of the unknown soldier, a counterpoint to the grand state funeral of the old general. But the irony, naturally, is that the corporal is unknown, but then as his name suggests, he represents the body of war, and his role is assumed by the battalion runner, half blasted to death by his futile effort to continue the mutiny. He is the walking wounded: "one half of his visible flesh was one furious saffron scar beginning at the ruined homburg hat and dividing his face exactly down the bridge of the nose, across the mouth and chin, to the collar of his shirt." He is the ruined land of France that includes the corporal's farm. But the runner, like the three-legged horse moves forward. He shows up at the old General's state funeral and pitches his medal at the old General's caisson. While the old general is lauded for his achievements, the runner disrupts the ceremony, scornfully repeating pious patriotic sentiments: "'You too helped carry the torch of man into that twilight where he shall be no more; these are his epitaphs: They shall not pass. My country right or wrong. Here is a spot which is forever England." The runner is dismissed as a crank, who insulted his own country (England) and France. Maybe he will die this time, a voice in the crowd ventures—to which the runner, speaking in French says, "Tremble. I'm not going to die. Never." It is a bitter but hopeful ending. The story, the resistance, however wounded, goes on.

Faulkner was no pessimist, or cynic, or idealist, or realist. He had the power to suppose and to present *A Fable* as a supposition. We, the unknown, the crowd, he insists, have the power to change the world, one individual at a time, if only we knew it.

Part Three
Faulkner and Hollywood

Recreating
Absalom, Absalom!

Revolt in the Earth

After so many books and articles about Faulkner in Hollywood, what is left to say? Just this: I have yet to read a book or article that shows just how remarkable his works and days in the American film capital were compared to any other major writer who spent time there. He worked in Hollywood intermittently for two decades and for all the major studios (on and off the books) and contributed to something like fifty film projects. Although he was often quoted exhibiting his disdain for Hollywood, and his own capacities as a scenarist, in fact he was as fascinated with Southern California and its most famous industry as he was repelled by it. That his scripts needed to be rewritten is hardly significant since just about every writer's scripts were worked over by other writers. That he was often uncredited is also pretty much par for the course—even for the best screenwriters like Ben Hecht. Except for Hecht, I wonder if any other screenwriter was as versatile or as pliable as Faulkner when it came to working on a script with collaborators. Jerry Wald at Warner Bros. counted on Faulkner for fast rewrites, and even after Faulkner stopped writing for Hollywood in the mid-1950s, Wald was on the phone seeking his advice.[1]

What is perhaps most striking about Faulkner is that he treated film as an entirely independent medium—no matter if he was working on an adaptation of his work or that of others. While he certainly regarded his novels as superior to anything he produced on screen, those novels and the characters in them were fair play when he worked as scenarist. The Sartoris twins of his fiction are given quite different roles to play in his screenplay, *Warbirds*. In short, what he wrote in a novel or story was fair game for the screen. He learned this early when Howard Hawks told him they would have to create a part for Joan Crawford in Faulkner's adaptation of his story, "Turnabout," which became *Today We Live*. Whatever disappointment Faulkner may have expressed, especially since he had been told that his original script (all male characters) was excellent, he nonetheless got down to work in writing a script far more ambitious than just including a role for Crawford. That script, available in Bruce Kawin's edition of Faulkner's MGM screenplays, includes opening children's scenes that resemble those in the first section of *The Sound and the Fury*. Hawks found those scenes unfilmable—partly because they would have added significantly to the length of the picture and because he could not find the right child actors—but it was typical of Faulkner to reimagine his own work rather than grouse, as F. Scott Fitzgerald did, for example, about the interference of producers and directors who wanted to reshape what he wrote. In the employment of others, Faulkner did his best to suit their tastes and requirements, while importing, when he could, his own sensibility and original material.

There was nothing haughty about Faulkner in Hollywood. He could be reticent, aloof, and stubborn, sometimes, but seemed to appreciate how his scripts changed when Hawks and his actors got hold of them. He said as much about the improvisations and rewriting that went on daily on the set of *To Have and Have Not*. He thought the actors and director made his work better. A writer like Hemingway, who never dared to do Faulkner's kind of work in Hollywood, could not have conceived of such a situation in which he was not the star. So disposed was Faulkner to learning from and taking aboard criticisms of his work that at Warner Bros. in the 1940s he was highly regarded by producers even as he quietly exuded an air of independence that no amount of submission to studio dictates shattered. Producers looked out for him, covered for him when he got drunk, and in general wished he had been given better material to work with.[2]

Sometimes Faulkner seems to have deliberately written scenes or dialogue that he had to know could not be used. In the script for the Twentieth Century-Fox production of *Drums Along the Mohawk*, he had the Henry Fonda character rape his wife, played by Claudette Colbert.[3] But he turned his work in on time and, in the main, wrote according to studio conventions. He kept to himself his interest in what film might become—released from its Hollywood restraints. Only in one instance, in July 1937, did he write an unHollywoodlike screenplay, *Revolt in the Earth*, in collaboration with an independent filmmaker, Dudley Murphy. Faulkner did not show the script to Warner Bros. producer Robert Buckner until 1943. The two men got along well and had enjoyed a mutual respect, as Faulkner made clear in letters home to his family. But Buckner was so appalled by the *Revolt in the Earth* that he advised Faulkner not to show it to anyone else. Buckner did not make his objections explicit, perhaps because he found the script unredeemable. No evidence so far has been discovered that Faulkner, or Murphy, showed the script to others, and it is a mystery as to what happened to the script between 1937 and 1943. Why did Faulkner try to revive interest in *Revolt in the Earth*? What made him, in the first place, turn to Murphy?

Murphy's biographer, Susan Delson, who had access to Murphy's private papers is no help. He evidently said nothing about the collaboration with Faulkner. In fact, she relies on Tom Dardis's statement that the Faulkner-Murphy collaboration occurred in 1943. But Faulkner scholar, Stefan Solomon, was the first to find a *New York Times* article on July 18, 1937, announcing the existence of *Revolt in the Earth* "an original screen story by William Faulkner about Mississippi swampland folk."[4]

So what prompted William Faulkner to work with Dudley Murphy? On June 16, 1937, Faulkner put in his last day's work on *Drums Along the Mohawk*. His script had gone through several drafts—by him and others. For the rest of June, Faulkner seems to have waited, in some distress, for more studio work. His French translator, Maurice Coindreau, saw him on June 20 and noticed he was constantly drinking. On June 30, Fox distributed Faulkner's 238-page dialogued treatment of *Drums Along the Mohawk*, but by this time the film would go on without him and his script. On July 21, he wrote home that his contract with Fox would not be renewed and that he expected to be home "sometime between Aug 22-Sept 1." In late August he returned to Oxford, and by September 1 he was in Memphis to take a forty-five-minute flight on his Waco C biplane.

So the work with Murphy probably occurred toward the end of June and perhaps extended through much of August—enough time certainly for Faulkner, who wrote quickly, to complete a screenplay. Released from his Fox contract, he could do business with Associated Artists, a cooperative artist's enterprise, the *New York Times* reported, that with Murphy's assistance had enlisted Faulkner, Dashiell Hammett, and others, to create screenplays outside of studio-driven system. Like many of Murphy's in-and-out of Hollywood career moves, this film never materialized. Perhaps that is why the screenplay languished.[5] Meant for an independent production company, it had no future until five years later when Faulkner began working closely with Buckner at Warner Bros. on several projects, including *The De Gaulle Story* and *Battle Cry*.

Murphy brought a good deal of interesting experience to the work on *Revolt in the Earth*. The director, son of a well-known painter, came from a family background that would have made him receptive to Faulkner. Murphy's mother was from the South, and her grandfather, while in Kansas, served with African Americans in the Civil War. Murphy had served in World War I as a pilot and billed himself as a bit of a daredevil—perfecting just the kind of persona that Faulkner had tried on with his tall tales of aerial combat exploits.

By the time Murphy met Faulkner, he had befriended Algonquin Round Table members, as had Faulkner, and had worked with Sergei Eisenstein, whose script for *Sutter's Gold* Faulkner had rewritten in 1932. In Paris, Murphy had consorted with Hemingway, Ford Maddox Ford, James Joyce, Ezra Pound, and in New York, with novelist/photographer Carl Van Vechten, who had shown Faulkner Harlem and would later photograph the novelist. Van Vechten had made it his mission to explore the burgeoning of African American art, and why many whites were so fascinated with what was called "[n----r] heaven," which he used as the title of a controversial novel, published in 1926. The term originally referred to the balconies in movie theaters where Blacks in the Jim Crow era were relegated. But the term had been transformed into a celebration of a culture in Harlem so unique and attractive that whites wanted to experience it for themselves with Van Vechten serving as their ambassador. Murphy had directed films like *St. Louis Blues* (1926), the only film in which Bessie Smith performed, singing one of Faulkner's favorite lines, "I like to see that evening sun go down," and *The Emperor Jones* (1933), with Paul Robeson in the starring part. Later, there was a projected role for Robeson in Faulkner's screenplay of *Battle Cry*, and Eugene O'Neill's fascination with African American life—also reflected in *All God's Chillun Got Wings* (1922). Through O'Neill and Van Vechten, the vector of African American culture enters the stage and screen of white consciousness. Van Vechten-O'Neill-Murphy converged, as I suggest, in the making of *Revolt in the Earth*.

Nigger Heaven, like other novels of the time, explored the complexities of color, including the success of some Blacks "passing" as white, but also of some ofays (a slang term for "whites") trying to pass into African American culture. One of the characters in *Nigger Heaven* observes: "You know as well as I do that practically every other ofay in the South has a colored half-brother and you know how many successful intermarriages there have been, especially in the West Indies." This half knowledge—or at least half way curiosity about Black/white consanguinity—filtered into Faulkner's novels like *Absalom, Absalom!* that, in turn, may have fascinated the Van Vechtens of the North, seeking inspiration in the African American creative revival known as the Harlem Renaissance. What Van Vechten and Faulkner might have said to one another is lost to history, and perhaps they said nothing at all about ofays, but some kind of communion may have occurred between two ofays who recognized, as Kathleen Pfeiffer puts it in her excellent introduction to

Nigger Heaven, "that insatiable appetite in the 1920s—for anything black and primitive." For Faulkner that appetite continued into the 1930s, with the references in *Absalom, Absalom!* to Thomas Sutpen and his "wild negroes," "wild [n----rs]," "wild blacks," repeated seventeen times like a refrain that refers to some aboriginal energy that will become the focal point of *Revolt in the Earth*.

Eugene O'Neill, whom Faulkner reviewed in 1918, may well have stimulated not only an interest in the so-called "black and primitive," but in what made, in Faulkner's words, "'Emperor Jones' rise up and swagger in his egoism and cruelty, and die at last through his own hereditary fears."[6] Jones runs amuck in the primeval forest haunted by the legacy of slavery that he thinks he has overcome. In *Revolt in the Earth*, Whites go amuck, only half-recognizing their consanguinity with Blacks, and succumb to their "hereditary fear."

Although Faulkner had worked on the film that became *Slave Ship* (1937), Fox had excised the speech written for the slaver, Captain Lovett: "I went into it when I was a boy. All it meant to me then was excitement. Boys have no sense. Then it was just life . . . I never thought any more of it than that—and then I was older, before I knew it . . . what I was, and what I was doing."[7] In Faulkner's version of *Slave Ship* (originally titled *The Last Slaver*, an adaptation of a novel) Lovett goes down with his burning, sinking ship in a conflagration reminiscent of Sutpen's burning mansion whereas in the released film Lovett successfully quells the mutiny of his slave-running crew, frees the slaves from the hold of his ship, and lives happily ever after with his beloved on a Jamaica plantation. Just who is working that Jamaican earth is a question the film never asks.[8] In short, Hollywood was not prepared to explore the consequences of slave trading and holding, which Dudley Murphy, the outsider, might help Faulkner do, as well as reaching a national audience through an independently produced film, as the director had done with O'Neill's *The Emperor Jones*, a play that had a significant impact on Faulkner's psyche.

While Dudley Murphy's film adaptation of *The Emperor Jones* had not enjoyed a huge Hollywood success, it premiered on September 19, 1933 in New York City at the Rivoli theater to sold-out crowds for two weeks, with the same success in Los Angeles in November, although after that it became difficult to extend the film's distribution, especially in the South where theaters would not show a film that starred an African American. Faulkner was not in New York City or Los Angeles during the film's run, although Murphy could have screened it for him.

The flamboyant Murphy enjoyed collaborating with artists and writers, including Eugene O'Neill, who had praised Dubose Heyward's scenario of *Emperor Jones*, written for Murphy. The play had a significant impact on Faulkner's handling of race, beginning most significantly with a sketch,

"Sunset," in the *Times Picayune*, published close to ten years before Faulkner began work on *Absalom, Absalom!*[9] That sketch and *The Emperor Jones*, explore an atavistic treatment of the African American character, criticized at the time by certain Blacks and whites alike, and yet also welcomed by many critics of every color as the beginning of an effort to explore Black consciousness in ways that contradicted the sentimental and stereotypical *Gone with the Wind* school of race depiction, perpetuated both in fiction and film.

"Sunset" opens with a newspaper item supposedly from the Jackson, Mississippi *Clarion-Eagle*, as if to explain what had provoked the creation of the sketch:

Black Desperado Slain

The negro who has terrorized this locality for two days, killing three men, two whites and a negro, was killed last night with machine gun fire by a detachment of the -th Regiment, State National Guard. The troopers set up their guns before the copse in which the black was hiding and when there was no reply to their fire, Captain Wallace entered the place and found the negro dead. No reason has been ascertained for the black's running amuck, though it is believed he was insane. He has not been identified.

No reason, unidentified, and presumably crazy—there must be a story there! The newspaper one would expect to be identified is the Jackson, Mississippi *Clarion-Ledger*. The "-th" is the kind of made-up designation common in nineteenth-century fiction. Items like this one certainly appeared in southern newspapers, often portraying African Americans as going berserk and committing crimes, like Nelse Patton raping a white woman, and lynched not far from where Faulkner lived.[10] At any rate, the function of the faux newspaper item is to contrast the detached account in the public prints to what the sketch has to tell.[11]

A deluded, unnamed Black countryman, dazed by the New Orleans traffic, tries to board a boat that he thinks is bound for Africa. He "wants to go back home, what de preacher say us come fum." He is hustled and shoved and met with scorn. He is given a job that he thinks will help him on his way to Africa. He is conned out of four dollars from a white man who says he can take him to Africa. Dropped off near Natchez and told Africa is a just a mile across the fields, the Black man loads his gun, thinking to protect himself from jungle animals. When he hears voices he thinks they are savages, "folks that eat you." He shoots defending himself in the dark and is pursued, escaping but now resolved to return to his country home. Delirious for a day, he is then shot at again and is wounded for a second time, and the next day set upon and killed: "His black, kind, dull, once-cheerful face was turned up to the sky and the cold, cold stars. Africa or Louisiana: what care they?"

The cheerful, deluded, and doomed figure is no Emperor Jones. He has neither the ambition nor the cunning of O'Neill's character, yet "Sunset" speaks to at least the white notion of African Americans as a diaspora, with a shifting sense of home and yearning for lost origins. The displaced Black man, searching for his identity, fascinated Faulkner, but not until he proved capable of creating Thomas Sutpen, a lost white soul, bewildered by the mischancing of his design, could Faulkner be susceptible to situating a white protagonist in *Revolt in the Earth*, who is as lost in the Black world as the Black in "Sunset" has been lost in the white one: cursed, pushed and shoved by whites who cannot comprehend the "Black Desperado's" quest.

Who knows what kind of pitch Murphy made to Faulkner? If he showed *The Emperor Jones* to Faulkner, perhaps the parallels between Sutpen and Jones stood out. Perhaps Faulkner did not even have to see the film, since he knew the play. How much did Murphy tell Faulkner about his struggle to become a mainstream director and how he could not find his niche and had opted to spurn Hollywood studios and venture out on his own, securing Faulkner's attention, who had in common with Murphy a fascination with characters who struck out for themselves, even when they came to grief against the very powers of environment they had sought to overcome.

The main character in Murphy's adaptation, played powerfully by Paul Robeson, has a lordly ambition worthy of Thomas Sutpen, and like Sutpen, Jones is twice displaced: first from the America of his origin and then from his reign on a Caribbean island. To begin with, though, Jones is the pride of his Black community. He is given a send-off in his church with the song "fly away," a salute to his new job and journey as a Pullman porter. A man of some dignity, he comes from a congregation far removed from the dangerous big world he is about to confront and best—much as Thomas Sutpen, in his West Virginia redoubt is shocked into his ambitious quest motivated by his humiliation at the front door of a white planter when he is told by a slave to use the back door. Both Jones and Sutpen believe in their own worth, whatever the world says—so much so that Jones imagines a scene for his beloved in which the President of the United States, accompanied by marching bands in front and back of him, congratulates Jones on obtaining such a fine job.

Jones lives the high life, frequenting night clubs. with the money he has earned as a Pullman porter but fights for his life after he catches a gambler shooting crooked dice and stabs him in self-defense. Next Jones is seen in

120 FAULKNER AND HOLLYWOOD

a chain gang pounding rock singing "Water Boy" a lyric Faulkner enjoyed performing many times.[12] It is a mournful yet exhilarating expression of human endurance, sung in Robeson's, powerful, stately style:

> There ain't no sweat boy
> That's on a this mountain
> That run like mine boy
> That run like mine

In the sweat of his labor, Jones is whipped by a white guard, but he overpowers him, escapes, and is then seen aboard a ship shoveling coal. Almost immediately he dives into the waters near a "[n----r] island," where he is purchased by a white trader, Smithers, who is outdone by his slave, the superior trader, and becomes Jones's lackey, serving Jones much like Wash Jones serves Sutpen—except that the white serves the Black, who deposes the island's Black "king" and names himself emperor. This Napoleonic rise happens in a swift fablelike plot that results in a domain for Jones that is akin to Sutpen's Hundred.

Like Sutpen in the West Indies accumulating his fortune as a slave driver and then a Mississippi planter, Jones accumulates wealth by taxing his subjects, so that in six months, he figures, he can depart with his fortune—again like, Sutpen imagining his successes in yet in a more lucrative land. The scope of Jones's ambition is just as unbounded as any white man's. Jones dismisses lynching and Jim Crow as part of the world he has abandoned. He orders Smithers to light his cigarette and throttles the white man when he suggests Jones is vulnerable not only in the White Man's world but also in the realm of Black people he has so far cowed and treated with contempt. The parallel with *Absalom, Absalom!* is apposite, since Sutpen's betrayal of Wash Jones, his white acolyte who scythes down Sutpen, is reversed in *Emperor Jones* when the subjugated Blacks rise up against their Black master, leaving Smithers to announce to the "Emperor" that his subjects have deserted him.

The arrogant Jones, scornful of the beating drums and voodoo rites, thinks his upbringing in the Baptist Church will steel him against a superstitious people and Smithers, who warns the Emperor about what he will find in the primeval forest through which Jones must travel to escape the insurrectionary subjects who pursue him. "Listen to that roll call," Jones says, as the drums sound. He is still a man as confident of his design as Sutpen is of his. In his Napoleonic uniform Jones thinks that his destiny will triumph over any untoward circumstance—even a revolution—certain that he can reconstitute the kingdom of his will as surely as Sutpen supposes he will be

RECREATING *ABSALOM, ABSALOM!: REVOLT IN THE EARTH*   121

able to do after the Civil War. As Jones leaves his palace, Smithers calls after him: "Give my regards to any ghosts you meet." The casual joke, in fact, presages the deadly visitations awaiting Jones. The woods he thinks he knows begin to close in on him as the drums become louder, mimicking the loud beating of a tell-tale heart, as his fears begin to overcome his braggadocio.

Like Sutpen, Jones believes he has considered all the factors, and yet he cannot find the food he has stored in the forest. He begins to speak the language of what he has called "bush [n----rs]," as he associates the drumming with the coming of hants (ghosts). Jones begins scolding himself, as if he is talking to one of his subjects, the very Blacks he believes he has conquered. He hallucinates scenes from his past, dwelling on their meaning in a querulous voice not so different from Sutpen's effort to reckon with his past in his monologue with General Compson meticulously going over the events that have led to the imperilment of his design.

Jones deviates from the Sutpen story as another hallucination drives him back to his Baptist upbringing, as he crawls and then kneels, asking for forgiveness for his wrongs. It is the kind of submission that angered certain Black viewers and that has no parallel in Sutpen's quest for greatness. But Jones's act of repentance is nugatory as he is tormented by a forest spirit and grovels in atavistic fear, no longer articulate but merely a stumbling, mumbling, whimpering creature. But his demise, surrounded by the subjects he has exploited, is the result of a hubris that has made him suppose his design can surmount all, and places him right next to Sutpen, who is done in by a Wash Jones who realizes, too late, that Sutpen's design includes neither Jones nor his granddaughter, rejected because she has not produced a male heir in her coupling with Sutpen. But *Absalom, Absalom!*, as perhaps Faulkner realized, left open questions about race and white and Black identity that could be explored in the quite different medium of film.

To call the script, titled *Revolt in the Earth*, an adaptation of *Absalom, Absalom!* is misleading. It contains many of the same characters, and new ones as well, that is such a departure from the novel that "adaptation" does not seem to be the right word. The world in *Revolt in the Earth* has an ambiance, a structure, and a style foreign to the novel but similar to Murphy's film adaptation of *The Emperor Jones*. Anyone thinking of *Revolt in the Earth*, as an adaptation of Faulkner's novel is bound to be disappointed, just as anyone thinking of the script in Hollywood terms is bound to disgusted. Murphy and Faulkner seem to have set out to create a film in which Black idioms and beliefs overturn the white, patriarchal language and thought of white supremacy.

The film opens on a marble statue of Sutpen striking a grandiloquent pose not so different from Faulkner's great-grandfather's in the Ripley, Mississippi, cemetery. Clytie, aged twelve, is shown gazing raptly at the statue, calling to mind, at least in a biographer's mind, those Black Falkners in the Ridley, Mississippi, graveyard that historian Joel Williamson discovered and that the white family did not acknowledge. In *Revolt in the Earth*, Sutpen appears in the first scene as a "wraith," capitalizing on film's ability to superimpose past and present with a directness that supersedes prose.

The film periodically returns to Clytie at the statue as the cynosure of the story. The sound of galloping horses dissolves into a shot of a cabin of a Black family. *Absalom, Absalom!* never ventures inside Black domiciles or confronts characters like an "old negro woman" smoking a pipe. She has a "cold, brooding, inscrutable expression" a suggestion of an enigmatic, elusive awareness that the "hale, swaggering, proud Sutpen" does not acknowledge. From the very beginning this film foregrounds a Black consciousness against white obliviousness. The old woman "cold and still and a little fatal, almost a little contemptuous," watches Sutpen and he hesitates, "in mid stride," as if momentarily checked. He looks at the newborn, calling it a "heifer," and asks "What scrub is this?" The woman answers: "It's the devil's scrub." A curious choice of words, meaning? Scrub, in Sutpen's vocabulary probably means an insignificant thing, but it could also mean, literally, to the woman the scrubbing or cleansing of the devil. Sutpen, taken aback, looks at the woman "sharply" and asks her what she means. She replies "I means what I know. What dey tole me." Who told her what, Sutpen wants to know. "I never said it," the woman replies: "It been said on dis place for my time." Pressed by Sutpen she reveals the prophecy: "When de devil spawn on Sutpen land / dey'll be a revolt in the earth till / Sutpen land has swallowed Sutpen birth." In short, the land will have its revenge against this rapacious white man. "The sourceless laughter" becomes louder and sustained suggesting mockery of his pretensions, which he dismisses as "[n----r] mumbo jumbo." As the laughter becomes even louder, Sutpen seems about to dash to the earth the child he has taken from its mother, but he lowers the child, scorning the "displeasure of [n----r] witch doctors," saying he will give them a "a little Sutpen help," he will call the child Clytemnestra.

As the sound of his galloping is heard, the old woman foresees that "one [Charles Bon] will die and one [Henry Sutpen] will ride away. The film, in short, makes an understanding of the Sutpen story not one that Quentin and Shreve work out in the novel after listening to Mr. Compson and Rosa Coldfield, but a saga that is the property of the generations of slaves represented by the elderly Black woman. Sutpen is indeed a "wraith," his dreams of dominance a phantom of his imagination while the woman is "unwinking," imperturbably puffing on her pipe.

RECREATING *ABSALOM, ABSALOM!: REVOLT IN THE EARTH* 123

Clytie's attachment to the statue recalls Rosa Coldfield's evocation of her in the novel, which occurs after the Civil War is over, after Sutpen is dead, after Charles Bon has been murdered by Henry, and Henry has disappeared. In this context Clytie seems to Rosa "free, yet incapable of freedom who had never once called herself a slave." Rosa calls Clytie "wild," a product of "half-untamed black, half Sutpen blood," with a fidelity "only to the prime fixed principle of its own savageness." Even though Clytie is part of the new dispensation in the post-Civil War South she is still a Sutpen who can "cut a cord of wood or run a furrow better (or at least quicker)" than Wash Jones can, according to Rosa Coldfield.

Rosa's italicized chapter in *Absalom, Absalom!* reads like a meditation on past and present that is extended in *Revolt in the Earth*. Sutpen's savagery, his wrestling with his slaves in *Absalom, Absalom!*, is not merely a part of his biography but an expression of currents in contemporary thought that Carl Van Vechten explores in *Nigger Heaven*. Sutpen's intimate contact with his slaves seems both a concerted effort to exert mastery but also to come in contact with the very savagery he professes to scorn, especially in *Revolt in the Earth*. In Van Vechten's novel, Mary Love, a light-skinned African American librarian, who is proud of her exhibit of African sculpture, thinks: she has "lost or forfeited her primitive birthright which was so valuable and important an asset, a birthright that all the civilized races were struggling to get back to—the fact explained in the art of a Picasso or Stravinsky." It is the African beat, she muses, that still drives civilization forward, even as her African American contemporaries deplore the "primitive" subject matter of the very art she extols. So it is with Sutpen whose dynamism entrances everyone—even those like Rosa Coldfield who profess to find him repellent. But in the film his dynamism is associated with the beating of African drums. Mary Love seems to presage Sutpen's attraction to savagery even as he claims to abjure it. Mary laments: "If she could only let herself go, revel in colour and noise and rhythm and physical emotion, throw herself into the ring with the others, figuratively shouting and hurling their assegais!" These slender, iron-tipped, hardwood spears are beautifully made weapons, deadly masculine and yet so feminine in their shape. They appeal to Mary's aesthetic and sexual sensibility. The weapons wound but also arouse.

Stefan Solomon has noted the sophisticated use of sound in *Revolt in the Earth* that marked an advance over the soundtracks of Hollywood films in the 1930s. The galloping hooves that signal Sutpen's hegemony are countermanded by the drumming and laughter, but also by his treatment of Milly, Wash Jones's granddaughter, who has also produced a "heifer," and, to Sutpen's disappointment, another girl. The irony of his rejection of both white and Black daughters is emphasized when Wash joins in the Black laughter, then stops laughing as he apparently realizes that his fidelity to Sutpen has put him on the same level as the slaves. In *Absalom, Absalom!* Wash murders Sutpen with a scythe, but in *Revolt in the Earth*, Sutpen strikes away the jug Wash had aimed at him and lashes him with a crop. The script notes Sutpen's departure signaled by his horse's hooves, which carries "through the dissolve" to the first scene with Clytie at the statue, except that Sutpen, even as wraith, is absent. Visually and aurally, Sutpen's power has faded and is overtaken by the "[n----r] laughter" that "emerges and continues through the dissolve." To contemporary ears the n word is hard to accept, but it has a specific function here, suggesting that the very sound of the inferiority that Sutpen derides, the laugher that can sound "idiotic," actually announces the impending demise of his megalomaniacal design.

Sutpen is now shown in conference with Henry as they watch Charles Bon in the garden courting Judith—without permission Sutpen notes. Henry assures his father that Bon is a gentleman and will do the right thing, but Sutpen counters: "How well do you know him?" Sutpen tells his son he has been duped into admiring those urbane qualities in Bon that Henry lacks. Judith is called and told that Bon is a blackguard. She is defiant and seems to know more than either Sutpen or Henry do about Bon's intentions. Not simply white supremacy but male chauvinism seems an illusion in this screenplay.

As Bon enters Sutpen's library the sound of tom-toms erupts as in *Emperor Jones* along with an ambient laughter and drumming that grows ominously louder. Bon is as compelling as Paul Robeson in *The Emperor Jones*, overwhelming Sutpen's concerns as the film dissolves to Judith and Charles in an embrace as the drums, which he cannot hear, arouse her. She declares her wish to accompany him and Henry to New Orleans, a wish they do not honor. The men board a steamboat to the accompaniment of sensuous "negroid" music. In *Absalom, Absalom!*, the romantic and perhaps even homoerotic attraction between them is transformed into the pull of what is termed the "African beat" that "completely" arouses Mary Love in *Nigger Heaven*.

The scene dissolves to Judith and Clytie in a sewing room with Black women making Judith's trousseau, but out of a trunk an old woman retrieves a wedding dress and places the ill-fitting garment against Judith, asking if Judith remembers that "old Aunt Carry says she wouldn't marry nobody." The women laugh then become silent as Judith "flings the dress at Clytie," another sign that the white masters refuse to recognize what their Black slaves are trying to tell them.

In New Orleans, Henry and Charles attend a quadroon ball that is also engulfed in "negroid" music while women parade in masks that make it

RECREATING *ABSALOM, ABSALOM!: REVOLT IN THE EARTH*   125

impossible to know if they are Black or white. The music, in other words, overwhelms the distinctions of race and sweep up everyone in the primordial on which civilization is built. Journeying to Harlem, traveling back to Blackness, Carl Van Vechten suggested, was the equivalent of returning to the roots of whites as well—although whites and the librarian Mary Love are drawn to and yet resistant to fully acknowledging those roots.

The masquerade makes race nugatory. In Faulkner's great-grandfather's fiction, masking aboard a riverboat in *The White Rose of Memphis* is employed to hide the true identities of white people, with Blacks having no part in the game of storytelling. In William Faulkner, masking is a way of subverting racial categories. Just imagine how such a scene of Black-and-white in disguise would look on a Hollywood screen. Could Faulkner have been anything but exhilarated at this outage to his employers' prejudices and Hollywood conventions?

Henry is shocked at Bon's duel with the man who has escorted the beautiful octoroon Bon unmasks at the ball. She is Bon's wife and her escort is shot dead. When Henry is made to understand what has happened the sound of the tom-toms recommences. An outraged Henry is introduced to Bon's son by the octoroon as the background laughter rises. From that New Orleans room, and from a brief scene with Sutpen joking that it will take Judith two months to prepare for her wedding while Henry and Charles are in New Orleans, the film dissolves to the sewing room of Black women laughing about "no hurry about fixin' this dress." The implication is they already know the wedding cannot proceed just as Henry bursts into the room and rips the dress off Judith, refusing to give his reasons to Sutpen but looking at directly at Clytie. On screen, the looks exchanged between them, the secret knowledge that no white can penetrate would become palpable. And Sutpen does not see it! He declares the marriage will go on, and Henry departs to murder Bon, returning to announce that now Judith cannot marry him. On Bon's body Judith finds the locket that she presumes holds her daguerreotype but is, in fact, one of the octoroon wife. Toinette, given a name only in the film, not in Faulkner's novel, thus providing a more specific identity and sense of Bon's own racial solidarity. His inscription, in French, says that Toinette will be his wife always. However deep are his feelings for the white Judith, he has not forsaken her Black counterpart. A whole identity for Bon, comprises both Black and white. Judith cries out for Henry. Why she does so is not explained, but perhaps it is what he had revealed in his killing Bon that has prompted her to call for him.

A "kaleidoscope of scenes of the Civil War" includes a shot of Henry falling dead and Sutpen taking his son in his arms as shells explode "beating a savage rhythm all around . . . similar to the tom-toms" in a scene that dissolves into a jungle enveloping the Sutpen house during a voodoo ceremony where the Black women talk about how the prophecy of doom, in the film's second scene has come true as Judith paces in the house to the beat of the drums that come to a "savage crescendo." She is then shown after a dissolve on a battlefield with her dead father, taken away by a northern soldier at her urging.

Clytie, in the next scene, stands at Sutpen's statue, a survivor of the war, embracing a Black man, and then is shown having given birth in a slave cabin, with a witch doctor putting an amulet on the infant's neck as a dissolve opens on a houseboat in the bayou with Wash, twenty years older, standing over a dead mother with a crying child and the sound of the drums, while in a New York City hospital delivery room Judith has given birth even as her head turns from side to side to the beat of drums only she can hear. A concerned doctor who cannot hear the drums she insists he must stop, advises her husband to take her out of the country to escape the past life her husband says she will not talk about. Aboard a liner she looks backward as the drums grow fainter.

Nothing like this postwar life of Clytie and Judith is imagined in *Absalom, Absalom!* Nothing like the past that is drummed into Judith and remains in Clytie as repository of her identity has any place in the novel. What takes all of *Absalom, Absalom!* to relate becomes the first act of the movie, which now flashes forward to a seventy-year-old Clytie staring at the statue which is overwhelmed by jungle growth, emphasizing once again Sutpen's own African sensibility.

The film cuts to a bayou where Charles and Henry had once traveled on a houseboat, which is now a wreck that Wash's son, also named Wash, occupies. The laughter of Black people segues to a scene set in 1910. The Sutpen house is now a ruin inhabited by Clytie who gazes at a photograph of Judith and her grandchild, Miriam. This memento, inscribed to Clytie, comes from another world, where Judith inhabits an English garden like a "grand lady" and is present at the wedding of Miriam to an English clergyman, Eric, who is writing a "treatise on primitive religions and their ceremonies." Judith is grateful that she has escaped the Sutpen curse, which her progeny will never know, although a dissolve to Clytie activates the drums that sound "sinister and sardonic" as the telegram from Judith announcing Miriam's marriage is read to her Black aunt as yet another dissolve segues to Black people singing spirituals in a performance on a London stage. The music excites Miriam as Judith assumes the same pose as Clytie hearing the drums and the announcement of Miriam's marriage. "Judith is almost savage as she grasps Miriam's arm," as if enacting the very savagery she believes she has escaped.

RECREATING *ABSALOM, ABSALOM!: REVOLT IN THE EARTH*   127

This sudden disruption of this modern, urban scene with savagery is reminiscent of *Nigger Heaven* when the college-educated African American Byron Kasson succumbs to the "wild music" of a "Black Mass" and "brazen claws of tone," the "shrieking torture music from the depths of hell," the reverberating tom-toms as a "pure black woman" performs "evil rites." Waiters appear in this Harlem club "with shields" as if enacting primitive rituals that suffuse the modern setting with ancient ceremonies akin to a scene in Dudley Murphy's film of *The Emperor Jones,* in which the circle song in a Baptist church segues to the dancers in the Caribbean island that Jones thinks he has conquered.

At Miriam's wedding Eric has heard about a white voodoo doctor in a New Orleans bayou, who is seen in a cut to a be a Kurtz-like figure who has gone native in a jungle drum scene, which, in turn, cuts back to a theater box where Eric and Miriam are entranced by a play about "A white man making himself a black king in a white country!" A fascinated Eric proposes they visit Judith's ancestral home, exactly what Judith has feared. Miriam exclaims: "No, no! It would kill Grandmama for me to go back. She won't even let me talk to her about it." Yet Miriam sways and pants in a movement that is "completely negroid." An aghast Eric is embarrassed as Miriam's "face is animal." As she writhes against him and the tom-toms beat, he capitulates to her plea that they go to the bayou. "Now! Tonight!" Miriam is experiencing what the white characters in *Nigger Heaven* seek: a return to roots. They want to be moved by the history that their culture has denied to them, much as Judith has tried to deny her granddaughter her heritage. "The tom-tom's are now beating savage and exultant and loud."

This attraction of white to Black—what else can you call it except primitivism?—is one of the most disturbing aspects of the screenplay. It has no parallel in *Absalom, Absalom!* The music of Black dance, which drew Carl Van Vechten to Harlem, and led to the creation of his novel, *Nigger Heaven* is the contemporary analogue to the drumming and dancing in *Revolt in the Earth.* The whites have, it seems, forgotten the elemental origins of humanity that make all human beings of the same family. Eric, like Van Vechten, senses this kinship.

The second act reveals the white witchdoctor to be Wash Jones's grandson in a voodoo sacrifice ceremony wearing cow horns and a Prince Albert coat. In the third generation, the Jones family has gone native, completely inverting the fealty that Wash once accorded Sutpen. Wash III cuts a woman's throat followed by several scenes of a terrified Judith aboard ship in pursuit of Miriam as she rides through a swampland frightened by snakes but urged on by Eric who does not seem to hear the tom-toms, evidently unaware of the past that Miriam's presence has aroused, including Clytie who awakes

128 FAULKNER AND HOLLYWOOD

and is silently aware of this convergence of the modern world with the past, as scenes switch between the voodoo ceremony to turning train wheels, as if the momentum of the past/present continuum has accelerated. Clytie awaits with her children and her childrens's children for Miriam to arrive, which they to the accompaniment of the drums heard in the voodoo ceremony.

Clytie and Miriam finally meet at the Sutpen house, recognizing one another instantly. Now everyone hears the drums from the voodoo ceremony. Miriam listens and is "restive." Eric spots the voodoo witchdoctor, now in overalls in the Sutpen garden as Miriam grows frightened and demands that they leave. But Eric is thrilled to see and hear the real thing, so much better than the stage show at the Albert Hall. The besotted Eric is willing to pay for a voodoo service just as Wash III shows up and Miriam, nearly hysterical, wants to leave. Clytie, refusing to indulge Eric's desire for a voodoo service, tells him "You go home." But Eric persists as Miriam shuts herself in the house. The second act ends as he plans his excursion, even though Miriam pleads with him not to leave her as Wash III in the garden watches her window, until Cyltie's presence makes him fade into the darkness. He represents, it seems, the very savagery of the past that Judith has sought to escape and that Miriam dreads without knowing why.

The third act opens with Eric, now a "tropic-exploring Briton" aboard a boat on the way to witness a baptism. Miriam tries to follow in the jungle and almost falls into quicksand, saved from death by Wash III who nonetheless frightens her because of his sinister "faun-like" expression. "You belong to this land," he tells her. Miriam runs back to the Sutpen house but in a frenzy dashes into the garden where an "inhuman" Wash III lurks. Cut to Miriam in Wash III's cabin, a prisoner saying to herself she must be "mad." And then she enjoins him: "I must go back. Let me out!" But to the increasing sound of the drums she sways next to Wash III who dances with abandon to the thudding drums.

Clytie has sent a message to Eric requesting his return to the Sutpen house. She tells a baffled Eric he must take Miriam away with him, that what is "here, it ain't for you." Against a chorus of rising and falling laughter, an outraged Eric declares he will discover what Clytie is hiding. Like Judith, Miriam is now tormented by the drums Eric cannot hear. She begs him to take her away before nightfall. He won't leave because he is determined to write a book about what he has seen from the point of view of the first white man who has discovered what has been kept from him. Out in the jungle, awaiting the start of another ceremony, Eric is accosted by Clytie who tells him he must take Miriam away by daybreak: "Ain't you know dis place done run her whole family out?" At one point, Clytie calls Eric "marster," as if he has put himself in the oblivious Sutpen's place, assuming a command over events that is not his to seize.

Miriam, evidently released from Wash III's cabin and unable to sleep, is shown again at the Sutpen house, calling for Eric, who is out in the jungle, crop in hand like a European explorer surrounded by Africans he is "trying to intimidate by his sheer lack of skin pigment." He rushes at them but they simply vanish into the jungle. Clytie confronts Wash III in the garden, the drums thudding loudly, raising a rib from a pig she has slaughtered, which terrifies him, and he strikes her down. As Miriam paces madly in her room, Eric is lost in the jungle. Cut to Wash picking up Clytie's rib and plunging into the jungle, followed by Miriam whose voice Eric hears crying out to him as she sinks into quicksand. Dissolve to Wash III beside the houseboat wreck wearing the white witch doctor's headdress as the scene dissolves into daylight with Clytie once again brooding before Sutpen's statue.

The laughing, chanting Black people are heard repeating the Sutpen curse. To them it sounds like a joke. "It do sound funny," one of them says. "Whut you reckon it mean?" Another says "I don't know dat. I do well to 'member how to say it." Amid laughter one says "Ain't dat a fack." Then a snake "writhes down from the statue and away into the jungle."

This horror movie version might well disappoint readers of the novel, and anger some with all the references to "[n----r] laughter." Clytie, who seems to have a knowledge never revealed in *Absalom, Absalom!* remains in *Revolt in the Earth* an enigmatic, inscrutable figure, the unknowable Sutpen, the survivor, the Clytemnestra whose role in the murder of Agamemnon (Sutpen) is occluded, as it is in different versions of her actions in Greek mythology and drama. She stands in *Revolt in the Earth* as a kind of medium, attuned to the forces that undo the whites, who are surrounded by Blacks they do not comprehend, notwithstanding white claims to superiority. The relentless laughter and drumming, like a Greek chorus, serve as an abiding mockery of white mastery. And though the script does little to develop the white witchdoctor, it is apparent that Wash III, who refers to himself as a poor white, has more in common with Black people—or fears he has more in common with them—than he allows himself to admit except when he dons the witchdoctor mask.

For all its melodramatics, *Revolt in the Earth*, Faulkner's only transformation into film of a major novel, powerfully presents the Black rebuke to white power in a work that is akin to Sherwood Anderson's *Dark Laughter*, set in New Orleans. Black sensuality, as depicted in Anderson's novel, and in Faulkner's script, may seem offensive—equating Blacks with animality—but African Americans also represent a life force, a closeness to nature that Sutpen is separated from and which he tries to defy by treating both his slaves and Wash's granddaughter as merely animals. Their animality is human and whites are in the sway of it as much as Blacks, but the whites seek to deny that truth by mastering Blacks. Even Judith, who tries to escape the family's fate cannot resist writing to Clytie and sending photographs of Miriam, acknowledging their bond even as she tries to attenuate it by staying away until Miriam's departure for America makes the English idyll impossible to sustain.

The juxtaposition of jungle and garden scenes, the cultivated and the elemental aspects of existence, overcome some of the limitations of the horror movie format, as do the scenes in England, on the stage, and other scenes in New Orleans at the octoroon ball, where Henry cannot function in a civilization built on a masquerade. In *Revolt in the Earth*, Charles Bon dies not because of his Black blood—at least not so as the censors would notice—but because of his easy commerce with color which so offends Henry's notion of a gentleman. Bon's unmasking of himself—showing to Henry that the courtesies and manners and ceremonies (including marriage) are so many masks that are the accoutrements of a gentleman—leads to his murder by the outraged Henry. And Miriam, never told about her family history, is bound to sink in the quicksand of its dodgy identity. In short, the Sutpen saga is a voodoo horror show, a curse of the Sutpen arrogance and inhumanity. Sutpen's statue is not crumbling like Shelley's Ozymandias, but the jungle (nature) reclaims it. The earth has revolted against those who have sought to dominate it. The futile history of white rule remains in the voices and laughter of the Black people chanting about the earth swallowing up the Sutpens.

That Hollywood in the late 1930s and early 1940s would film anything resembling *Revolt in the Earth* seems inconceivable. How it seemed to Faulkner is impossible to say. The fact is, however, that Dudley Murphy represented an alternative to the studio system, "smashing in on the consciousness of the screen world," as one reviewer put it.[13] Not averse to melodrama, Murphy always hoped he could give Hollywood enough of what it wanted even as he tried to change it. Did he seduce Faulkner in thinking the two of them just might crash through the production code?

On January 6, 1943, on Warner Bros. stationary, Bob Buckner reported his reaction to *Revolt in the Earth*: "a very badly conceived story with no possibilities whatever for a motion picture. Please forgive me if I seem too presumptuous about this, but I have such high a regard for you as a writer that I refuse to be disillusioned."[14] What Faulkner made of Buckner's rejection is not known. At any rate, along with Dudley Murphy,[15] he produced a Eugene O'Neill inspired script that is testimony to his desire to do more than just pick up his check.

Faulkner's Shadow

Hollywood, Hemingway, and *Pylon*

> If *Absalom* proves to be about the sins of the father, lines of descent, a
> society's decline, and the burden of the Southern past, *Pylon* takes up
> the irrelevance of sin (not to mention fathers), lines of ascent,
> a society's transformation, and a weightless future.
>
> —JOHN T. MATTHEWS

Published before *Absalom, Absalom!* (1936), and seemingly a deviation from the Yoknapatawpha saga, *Pylon*, usually considered a minor work, nevertheless has more in common with its esteemed successor than has been commonly supposed. Both novels are about deracination and displacement. Like Thomas Sutpen, *Pylon*'s rootless flyers swoop down on land that has been converted into property, into the possession of one man, the not-so-fine Colonel Feinman. *Pylon* has its Judith Sutpen in the figure of Laverne Shumann, who contends with love and power and holds her own in a male-dominated world, as does Ann, played by Joan Crawford in *Today We Live* (1933), the screen adaptation of Faulkner's World War I story, "Turnabout" (1932). Crawford, understanding perfectly the demands of her role, insisted on dialogue that was as clipped as that delivered by her male counterparts. She realized that she had to adopt the same taciturn style of the males who understate their emotions and prove themselves in action. Even on the ground, women such as Crawford embodies, are with their men in the air.[1] They are aerial bodies and, like their lovers, are alienated from their terrestrial contemporaries and the conventional obligations that women are supposed to fulfill.[2] Laverne is the most extreme example of these daring women, especially when she taunts her own son with "who's your father?"[3] That the boy can take his pick of two men, and that Laverne cannot assure her husband's father, Dr. Shumann, that the boy is Roger's, is far from the boundaries of Yoknapatawpha. Or is it? What do Charles Bon and Judith Sutpen ever really know about their consanguinity?

Laverne Shumann is not the nymph pursued in Faulkner's early poetry but is rather full-bodied—part of a life intensely lived, which means risking death. She is a woman possessed, the cynosure of male society, but also her own woman, dogged by a reporter, who is a descendent of Keats's frail knight, "alone and palely loitering"—in effect, a knight manqué. The war is mentioned only once in *Pylon*, when Jiggs, the air crew's mechanic buys "one of the pulp magazines of war stories in the air," which will give Laverne and her male companions "something to do on the train" that takes them to the air shows in which they will duel in the air with their competitors. If this is not the world of gentleman flyers, it remains, nevertheless, a kind of chivalric endeavor involving sacrifice and heroes, however corrupted for popular entertainment and profit.

By 1935, in several short stories, film scripts, and novels, Faulkner had already connected the world of Yoknapatawpha to the high flyers of World War I and the barnstormers of the postwar period in the figure of young Bayard Sartoris, bereft of his place in traditional southern culture and willing to risk all in the test piloting that results in his death. Young Bayard and his twin, John, belong to that reckless crew of aviators in "Death Drag" (1932), "Honor" (1930), and other short stories. They live in the moment, unsure of the future, even as they continue to engage in "mock heroic" actions.[4] On what terms, if any, can the world of the gentlemanly ideal, still in the sway of the Faulkner family and their community, prevail in the modern world of airports and circuses of the air? It is a question posed by Faulkner's own actions, when he encouraged all of his brothers to fly and to put on air shows. In New Orleans in 1925, he accompanied Hamilton Basso who was writing a feature story about "The Gates Flying Circus." Basso told Joseph Blotner that Faulkner seemed to relish the frightening flights in a rickety Wright Whirlwind two-seater: "Nobody *else* in our crowd had gone looping-the-loop in a bucket seat and open cockpit over the Mississippi River."

Faulkner's daredevil testing of himself is reminiscent of the Hemingway credo of grace under pressure. While Faulkner did not come under fire, as Hemingway did during the First World War, Faulkner nevertheless tested himself again and again, not only in the very same airplane in which his brother Dean crashed and died but much later in his persistent efforts to take his horses on jumps that resulted in repeated agonizing injuries and broken bones. Called Pappy by his family, Faulkner's hazarding of life-threatening situations places him closer to the bull-fighting, safari-hunting Papa than has been previously supposed. *Pylon*, an underestimated novel, is at the nexus of

FAULKNER'S SHADOW: HOLLYWOOD, HEMINGWAY, AND *PYLON*   133

major aspects of Faulkner's fiction and life including Hollywood, flight, and craft. The novel is also part of an important intersection with Hemingway in terms of the fiction Hemingway wanted to write while he felt forced to pursue a secondary publishing milieu (journalism) even as Faulkner bound himself to Hollywood scriptwriting.

Faulkner was writing in the era of Governor Huey Long, whose administration promoted the construction of high visibility projects that enhanced the profile of Louisiana and his own reputation as a politician who put people to work during the Depression while contributing to the progress that made modern life comfortable. Faulkner had little interest in Long, as he explained in a letter to Robert Penn Warren about *All the King's Men*. The governor's life could not be the basis of a great novel.[5] But the consequences of a regime that conjoined commerce and politics and cut corrupt deals, afterwards staging celebrations purported to be for the public good, agitated an author who had become part of a Hollywood no less self-promoting and venal than Long's Louisiana.

Long's Shushan Airport, named after the Levee Board president, had a layout that may have reminded Faulkner of a movie set. The airport had two large hangars not so different from sound stages and a tower with murals commemorating the history of flight in high relief depictions of airplanes and their daring pilots. And like a Hollywood studio emblazoning its logo, the airport had Shushan's name or his initials inserted in every available spot. In short, if you wanted to see the show, you had to put up with the advertising. And Faulkner was there for the show, indulging his keen interest in barnstorming pilots who had already appeared in "Death Drag" and "Honor." He had organized his own local air shows, and flying was a Faulkner business, taken up by his brothers Murry, John, and Dean. The very idea of flight had captivated all of them since the day Faulkner had convinced them they could make their own air machine. That their dreams had crashed into a ditch did not dissuade the boys from pursuing the lift that flying always offered. And crashing, after all, was part of the excitement.

Faulkner was invited to a Shushan air show, and it did not disappoint.[6] Milo Burcham defied the rainy weather and demonstrated why he was the world champion at upside down flying. The famous Michel de Troyat, on a calmer day, performed his air acrobatics, as did Clem Sohn, jumping from ten thousand feet with a flour sack he emptied to mark his descent. After some near miss collisions and a forced landing, a pilot and parachute jumper plunged to their deaths in Lake Pontchartrain. In one case, the body could not be found; in another, no relatives could be located for the nomadic airman.[7]

134 FAULKNER AND HOLLYWOOD

Faulkner first thought the show could be the basis for a popular story, "This Kind of Courage," which his agent, Morton Goldman, submitted to *Scribner's* on May 10, 1934. But by mid-October, Faulkner asked Goldman to send the story back to him because "I'm now writing a novel out of it."[8] Why not publish the story *and* write the novel? Faulkner did not say. It never troubled him to reuse and adapt published material, but perhaps he had no other copy to work with. At any rate, he had discovered more in the story and wrote it just about as quickly—in about two months—as *As I Lay Dying.* Why the urgency when he was already hard at work on *Absalom, Absalom!*?

Faulkner's own explanation is that *Absalom, Absalom!* had stalled, and he needed the relief that writing a different kind of novel provided.[9] But as Robert W. Hamblin suggests: "It seems significant that the novel Faulkner wrote 'to get away from' the high modernist *Absalom, Absalom!* is a book patterned to a degree after Hollywood criteria."[10] In fact, in July 1934, Howard Hawks suggested to the stalled novelist that he should write about flyers, and Faulkner told him about "This Kind of Courage," which Hawks liked, saying, "That sounds good."[11] By October, Faulkner had begun work on the novel, finishing a first draft on November 25, and sending a revised version to the publisher in mid-December.

With *Pylon*, he could dispense with the genealogy of his characters fraught with the intricacies of a narrative overwhelmed by the eruption of the past in the present. Faulkner's flyers—Roger, Laverne, and Jack—have, for most of the novel, no past. Their lives seem the work of happenstance. Their mechanic, Jiggs, is an unreliable alcoholic who is nevertheless devoted to them, which is all they seem to require. The novel's center of conscious-ness—always referred to as "the Reporter"—is not even given a name. He is drawn to the aviators because they are so alive in the air. On the ground, their lives seem rootless and sordid. Roger and Jack share Laverne, who is married to Roger because he won the roll of the dice with Jack. Laverne is, as Tom Dardis observes, like the tough-talking women—Hildy Johnson in *His Girl Friday* (1940) and "Feathers" in *Rio Bravo* (1959)—that populate Howard Hawks's later films.[12] She is also like Joan Crawford's character, Ann, in *Today We Live*, the female fulcrum of male triangles—first of a brother and a lover, then of two lovers, involved with her brother in the terse tension of war and romance.

Faulkner's treatment of the reporter is original and yet probably based on Hermann Deutsch, a thin, tall journalist with a shambling gait that Faulkner transformed into his shambolic, skeletal character. The two men first met in 1925 in New Orleans and were impressed with one another. Deutsch remem-bered Faulkner saying to him, "If somebody in the Yale Bowl was going to be

FAULKNER'S SHADOW: HOLLYWOOD, HEMINGWAY, AND *PYLON*   135

shot, you'd be standing next to him." It was a line Faulkner would elaborate on in *Pylon*, when the editor says as much to the reporter.[13]

At the air show, the novelist spent a good deal of time in Deutsch's company, watching the journalist carry around on his shoulders a little boy who belonged to one of the aviators. Out of this meager material, Faulkner conceived of the reporter who is increasingly involved in the lives of the flyers he comes almost to worship because they seem solely intent on their air missions, so to speak. They are, in Cleanth Brooks's words, "hooked on speed."[14] They are adventurers and likened to "immigrants walking down the steerage gangplank of a ship." They are refugees hazarding a trip into what was still then the new world of flight. They no longer have a secure place, a home to which they could return "even if it's just only to hate the damn place good and comfortable for a day or two"—as Faulkner seemed to do when he arrived in Oxford after his days in Hollywood.

It also looks as though Faulkner patterned the besotted, drunken reporter on himself, according to Howard Hawks. Faulkner could become voluble when it came to talking about flying, one of his friends told biographer Carvel Collins.[15] When Faulkner turned up in New Orleans after the air show, he looked as if he had slept in the gutter, according to one witness who said so to him. "Yes, ma'am, I have," he assured writer Roark Bradford's wife. Faulkner claimed to have become involved with the flyers, sleeping and fighting. It was a "disjointed, confused, nightmarish tale of having been offered a ride by a man and woman riding a motorcycle, or perhaps riding two motorcycles, with stops to visit bootleggers," said Roark Bradford's son, who also remembered that Faulkner never forsook his "elaborately polite and chivalrous" manners: "He was the only person over the age of twenty-one who was allowed to call my mother 'ma'am.'"[16] Faulkner had not eaten for several days. He certainly acted like the starved reporter when he devoured three eggs and bacon she had made for him. He talked about two women and three men living together indiscriminately,[17] which he compacted into the one woman and two flyers who become the reporter's obsession. At the same time, this was a Faulkner who was a kind of hanger-on in this world of high flyers. To Phoebe, the wife Vernon Omlie, Faulkner's flight instructor who accompanied him to the Shushan air show, Faulkner was very much like the reticent reporter who goes along for the ride and puts himself at the service of the flyers. She said Faulkner had "no real desire . . . to be a precision flyer," or make flying a business. It became, instead, "a mental and emotional release"—as it does for the reporter who liberates himself from the grimy and gloomy environs of the newspaper office. Phoebe observed a "rather shy man who wanted to be left alone." In a "pair of old coveralls," he would lose himself in a "group of mechanics, and help out by washing parts or doing what he would around the general aircraft operation rather than be out where people could see him and lionize him."[18] In short, Faulkner craved the anonymity he confers on his reporter.

The reporter appears like an allegorical figure, almost like a ghost in a medieval mystery play. In the popular imagination, especially as it was fed by movies like *I Cover the Waterfront* (1933), the journalist is usually self-sufficient and cynical, manipulating the woman he loves and willing to do whatever it takes to get the story, which often involves corruption and solving a crime or a criminal conspiracy. The journalist is like H. Joseph Miller (Ben Lyon) in *I Cover the Waterfront* or Hildy Johnson (Pat O'Brien) in *The Front Page* (1931). Both journalists are humanized and redeemed by beautiful women, who bring out the reporter's qualms about newspaper work. In fact, in Miller's case, he is a budding novelist—a sure sign that morally he is better than most crass reporters.

Faulkner forgoes the Hollywood sin and redemption scenario with characters who never do follow a conventional moral compass and are not bound by any community's standards of propriety. This air crew belongs nowhere and everywhere. It does not matter where they go so long as they can perform their show. By one definition, these are free spirits, not bound by any rules except those of the air races funded by capitalists like Colonel H. I. Feinman, Faulkner's version of Colonel A. L. Shushan. To emphasize the impurity of Feinman's power, he is identified as chairman of the Sewage Board. He is, in effect, the lord of a landfill, since the airport rests on reclaimed lake bottom. Ironically, the press treats Roger, Laverne, and Jack with fascination and scorn, while spending not a moment inquiring into how the airport got built or what purpose the air race show fulfills in Feinman's master plan that includes stamping F all over his property.

Only the reporter believes the story is the air crew itself, not just their antics in the air. He is fascinated with how they live apart from the society they entertain. They seem to find it enough to be with one another. They work together as one unit, although Jack has a temper he expresses by kicking Jiggs, and Roger—even more than the others—lives to fly. Even as he expects to survive, he never discounts the risks of death. The reporter alone sees these characters as admirable—in part because he is a Prufrock, afraid to bring the moment to its crisis, to confess his love for Laverne and for what the flyers represent to him. As the reporter, he is a passive observer. He is repeatedly described as a scarecrow and a cadaver, one of the walking dead in T. S. Eliot's unreal wasteland city, one of the poet's impotent hollow men. Using journalistic jargon like "dogwatches" evokes the environs of

FAULKNER'S SHADOW: HOLLYWOOD, HEMINGWAY, AND *PYLON*   137

journalism, but the novelist's compounded neologisms like "typesplattered" create a vocabulary that vitiates the reporter's profession. The stories journalists tell are a sensationalistic mess.

The factitious Feinman Airport opening, set in New Valois (New Orleans), is presided over by a disembodied amplified voice, "apocryphal, sourceless, inhuman." The newspaper office is similarly disquieting, a room right out of a film noir, with "down funneled light" from the editor's desk lamp. Journalism would not be depicted in such dim surroundings until the release of *Citizen Kane* (1941). In the hermetic "dusty gloom," the editor expresses a frustration with the reporter that many readers of the novel have also experienced:

> You have an instinct for events. . . . If you were turned into a room with a hundred people you never saw before and two of them were destined to enact a homicide, you would go straight to them as crow to carrion; you would be there from the very first: you would be the one to run out and borrow a pistol from the nearest policeman for them to use. Yet you never seem to bring back anything but information. Oh you have that, all right, because we seem to get everything that the other papers do and we haven't been sued yet and so doubtless it's all that anyone should expect for five cents and doubtless more than they deserve. But it's not the living breath of news. It's just information. It's dead before you even get back here with it.

Like the new journalists Tom Wolfe first touted in the 1960s, the reporter becomes part of the events and people he covers, latching on to just those characters that appeal to newspaper readers. But then he is unable to go beyond recording what they say to him. He cannot, in other words, turn his reports into stories, "the living breath of the news." But what the reporter wants to do cannot be contained within a newspaper article, any more than Faulkner felt his talent could be fully articulated in movie scripts or stories for popular magazines. As Jay Parini points out, Faulkner's "anxieties about his place in the world—as an artist and reporter on life, as a man subjected to the wiles of larger economic forces, as a frustrated novelist unable to focus entirely on his major vision—seem reflected in the figure of the reporter, who tellingly has no name. He is, in a sense, Faulkner's shadow." In his psychological reading of the novel, Frederick Karl detects an inner disturbance: "The entire fantasy world Faulkner had created about himself from the war divides him here."

Faulkner's anomie is akin to the flyers who are confined to stunts and have neither the equipment nor the venue to show just how good they are. Journalism is a dead end for the reporter, and the editor explains, "patiently, almost kindly," why: "The people who own this paper or who direct its policies or anyway who pay the salaries, fortunately or unfortunately I shant attempt to say, have no Lewises or Hemingways or even Tchekovs on the staff: one very good reason doubtless being that they do not want them, since what they want is not fiction, not even Nobel Prize fiction, but news." Hemingway, like the other writers the editor names, ultimately worked for himself, for the cause of literature alone, which can never be the province of newspapers. As Joseph Fruscione observes, both Faulkner and Hemingway wanted to be "*the* author of their milieu." The reporter, on the other hand, can never own his story, or root himself, as Hemingway and Faulkner did, in their work. The flyers, in other words, seek fulfillment only in flight, but are bound, nevertheless, to paymasters who determine when they can fly. Hemingway, fully established as a novelist by 1935, when *Pylon* was published, might continue to write for the newspapers but only as their special correspondent, hired precisely because of his name. He never had to work a day in Hollywood.

Nevertheless, both Faulkner and Hemingway, for all their independence, did write to suit the deadlines of employers. Well into his career, after the great successes and sales of *The Sun Also Rises* (1926) and especially *A Farewell to Arms* (1929), Hemingway became a hired hand of a press syndicate covering the Spanish Civil War. Faulkner in this same period (the mid- to late-1930s) had to take scriptwriting assignments of all kinds and also accept his removal from films like *Banjo on my Knee* (1936), which dealt with the Mississippi River denizens he knew well. For the newspapers Hemingway did not write prose like Chekhov, which is perhaps why Hemingway singled out *Pylon* for praise. He recognized himself in Faulkner's treatment of journalism, and the subordination of the writer to news.

Both writers, in effect, did not want to report the news but to create it. The reporter, for all his failings, however, wants to write literature, and thus he speaks to the ambition that Faulkner and Hemingway shared: to adapt these secondary publication milieus, journalism and scriptwriting, to their overarching imaginations. The reporter's struggle against his editor, in other words, cuts close to the psyches of these two great novelists.

In the popular imagination, as depicted in *The Front Page* and *I Cover the Waterfront*, the conflict is between the wayward reporter and his disciplinarian editor. Seldom, until *Meet John Doe* (1941) did Hollywood take on newspaper owners. But in *Pylon*, the editor could just as well be a Hollywood producer advising Faulkner to stay within the conventional boundaries of a script. And the reporter's reaction, like Faulkner's, is to drink and subside into silence rather than engage any more deeply in the corporate culture that enmeshes him. The editor is like Monroe Stahr in *The Last Tycoon* (1941) lecturing the recalcitrant writer about how to make movies. News, the editor implies, is not a narrative of lives and events per se but an account of a certain set of circumstances:

> [W]hat I am paying you to bring back here is not what you think about somebody out there nor what you heard about somebody out there nor even what you saw: I expect you to come in here tomorrow night with an accurate account of everything that occurs out there tomorrow that creates any reaction excitement or irritation on any human retina; if you have to be twins or triplets or even a regiment to do this, be so.

The newspaper reader has to get it all in one gulp, one documented day, in a "you are there drama" or movie. The reporter's thoughts, themes, or morals are inconsequential and irrelevant, unlike those of the novelist.

Of course, the repressed reporter romanticizes the flyers, who fascinate him because of their uninhibited sex lives, which the reporter as voyeur watches—but not with the journalist's practiced passivity. He yearns to be one of them, just as Faulkner coveted the role of war pilot, which his Hollywood buddy, Laurence Stallings, accorded him in a review of *Pylon*.[19] Hemingway liked this novel, probably because, as one reviewer put it, "these reckless nomads of the air are not essentially different from the graceful toreadors that court death so beautifully in the pages of Hemingway."[20] Hemingway may also have been intrigued by one of the novel's closing scenes, in which we learn that Roger Shumann is the son of a small town Ohio doctor who lived the kind of predictable, risk-averse life that Hemingway's father pursued. The reporter, emanating from that dim newspaper office and the grind of a reporter's routines, gravitates to the open spaces that the deracinated Roger, Laverne, and Jack navigate with aplomb. The air is their world elsewhere come to grief on the wasted ground of New Valois.

Like Hemingway's doomed heroes and heroines, the flyers forsake bourgeois values and live for their own sakes. They are willing to risk everything to pursue a society of their own. Faulkner, no less than Hemingway, realizes that such an uncompromising sense of self results in tragedy because of their human fallibility which is caught up in modern mechanisms over which they cannot exert complete control. Even in the air this liberated trio is fixated on those pylons that enforce the boundaries of the racers' route. Roger flying first an inferior plane, bests his competitors but crashes because the drunken Jiggs has not performed all of the necessary maintenance. Then in a dangerously experimental plane he plunges to his death. This flawed teamwork contributes to the flyers' fates as much as Feinman's machinations. *Pylon* is not a parable of economic determinism. Faulkner's characters are too implicated in their own destiny to attribute their actions to forces outside themselves. Faulkner might rail against Hollywood, but he never forgot he chose to be there to pick up the check.

In the novel's closing chapters, the journalists cluster together to chew over the crash story, just like they do in countless newspaper movies—most memorably in *Citizen Kane*, a film *Pylon* anticipates by layering together reporters, editors, and their corporate masters. Unlike the star reporters in Hollywood dramas, Faulkner's reporter is hardly a hero. What he discovers makes him ill. "I could vomit too," one of the journalists says to the reporter, "But what the hell? He aint our brother." The irony, of course, is that the reporter wants to write about his brotherly feeling for Roger. When the reporter says, "you dont understand," he might as well quote Prufrock's lament that it is impossible to say just what he means.

The reporter's final effort to tell the story ends up in fragments the copyboy picks out of a wastebasket. Like an embryonic editor or budding scholar experiencing his first joy in deciphering an unpublished manuscript, the copyboy—bright, ambitious, and with a literary sensibility—pastes together the fragments which "he believed to be not only news but the beginning of literature." After a bald summary of Roger's crash, the reporter observes that the pilot's "competitor was Death." Acknowledging Roger's honorable end—he deliberately steered his plummeting plane away from the people below—his two rivals circle the spot where he disappeared: "Two friends, yet two competitors too, whom he had met in fair contest and conquered it the lonely sky from which he fell, dropping a simple wreath to mark his Last Pylon." Less florid than the narrator of *Flags in the Dust*, the reporter nevertheless ennobles the aviators as knights of the air in a scene reminiscent of the romantic salute to war pilots in the silent film *Wings* (1927)—and also in the florid prose of Hermann Deutsch, who wrote about the dead aviator as "a gay cavalier of the skies" whose ashes are scattered from "scudding clouds," the remains of a man with "pulsing tissues" that had "once formed a living part" that had "clouded in the fine tingle of zestful living."[21] It is not hard to imagine Faulkner's scorn, and yet affection for such romantic literary effects.

Reporters in Hollywood films—like H. Joseph Miller in *I Cover the Waterfront*—are often aspiring novelists, chafing at the constraints of journalism, or playwrights like Stu Smith in *Platinum Blonde* (1931) seeking to evade the daily grind of the news. That they overcome the limitations of the trade and also, of course, win their lady loves, is precisely what Faulkner's novel contradicts as it shows how deeply mired the reporter is in events that he cannot surmount through literature. Thus the copyboy spots another draft on the editor's desk, a draft that is factual, detailed, specifying time, place, and outcome, but not the reporter's personal response:

> At midnight last night the search for the body of Roger Shumann, racing pilot who plunged into the lake Saturday p.m. was finally abandoned by a threepiece biplane of about eighty horsepower which managed to fly out over the water and return without falling to pieces and dropping a wreath of flowers into the water approximately three quarters of a mile away from where Shumann's body is generally supposed to be since they were precision pilots and so did not miss the entire lake.

Of this version, the reporter comments in a penciled note to the editor: "I guess this is what you want you bastard." The reporter's last words are directions to where he will be getting drunk, and where the editor can come with cash to pay for the drinks. This disgust with the higher-ups is typical of movie journalists who delight in charging whatever they can to their bosses, and it is also, of course, the reporter's declaration of independence. His behavior is not so different from Faulkner's conflicted relationship with Hollywood producers.

It is not surprising that Faulkner wanted to sell the novel to Howard Hawks.[22] It contains crucial elements of their earlier collaborations: a love triangle in the fraught world of flyers. Tom Dardis goes so far as to argue that *Pylon* is an homage to Hawks. It is an action story resembling the director's *Ceiling Zero* (1936) and *Only Angels Have Wings* (1939). Faulkner's characters exhibit, Dardis notes, "all of the typical Hawksian virtues of professional competence before danger, combined with stoical endurance, qualities equally esteemed by Faulkner." That the reporter can only observe these taciturn figures from the outside is of course consonant with what the camera can capture. The reporter is, so to speak, the camera eye.

Peter Lurie calls the novel's basic elements—"the courageous pilots, the love triangle, and the boldface 'headlines'" used in Faulkner's own screenplays—"Hollywood fodder." The absence of other salable features, however, argues for a more ambitious novel-cum-film. "*Pylon* evokes Wiene's classic German Expressionist film *The Cabinet of Dr. Caligari*," Susie Paul Johnson observes: "As the reporter appears for the first time, the narrator describes the way the other characters 'were now looking at something which had apparently crept from a doctor's cupboard and, in the snatched garments of an etherized patient in a charity ward, escaped into the living world.'"[23]

142   FAULKNER AND HOLLYWOOD

Faulkner's antirealism in such passages countermands the journalistic imperative to record and document. So often in *Pylon* journalists resort to their lurid imaginations when they are stymied by what they cannot see, when Roger, Laverne, and Jack are offscreen, so to speak. As Bruce Kawin concludes, the novel is "a story trying to tell a story,"[24] and such films are rare in Hollywood and evoke the kind of hostile reactions Orson Welles had to confront after the release of *Citizen Kane*. The reporter himself pivots between elite and popular culture. He is the "sensitive go-between . . . alternately the tough, alert reporter of the American newspaper tradition or his more detached, urbane, Eliotic contemporary."[25] That kind of oscillation has perplexed certain readers of a novel Hollywood would have been hard put to homogenize. Without a clear denouement, separating fact from fantasy, the novel-cum-film founders. Even the ambiguous *Citizen Kane* required an RKO resolution, a Rosebud.

And yet in 1957, Universal International released *The Tarnished Angels*, a film directed by Douglas Sirk and starring Robert Stack as Roger Shumann, Jack Carson as Jiggs, Dorothy Malone as Laverne, and Rock Hudson as the reporter. Bruce Kawin scorns the adaptation—as did most reviewers—calling it "sentimental garbage," although he observes that Hudson is "more complex and interesting than the part as written." He also praises Malone, but deplores Carson's role as an "impossible combination of Jiggs and Jack." Kawin does not argue that casting a movie star like Hudson destroys the very conception of Faulkner's frail reporter, who has no name and looks nothing like the handsome Hudson. "Sirk has no choice," it has been argued, "but to glamorize Faulkner's pathetic trio, whereas in the novel, the glamour, invisible to all under the tawdry exterior, emerged only through the newspaperman's insight into the characters' lives. These limitations, however, are only the medium's limitations. They do not prevent the film from succeeding on its own terms, or, for that matter, from being by far the best screen version of a Faulkner novel."[26] Robert Stack is so convincing as the tough—even menacing—Roger, who pushes around the hunky yet sensitive Jack Carson—that Hudson's yearning, tentative pursuit of Malone is persuasive. Hudson is grounded by doubts that never bother Shumann, and wisely the film does not allow Hudson to fly with Shumann, as he does in the novel. Carson's character is the perfect, economical solution to a film that cannot risk taking on extra scenes that would include Jack. Carson becomes, as he so often was in decades of film, the wise-cracking, worldly, but also, sometimes, the empathetic complement to the hero. Jiggs fixes airplanes and, broadly speaking, fixes things between Roger and Laverne. He is their go-between, which is to say the film develops its own emotional logic and truth, even if Roger

FAULKNER'S SHADOW: HOLLYWOOD, HEMINGWAY, AND *PYLON*   143

and Laverne talk too much about their feelings, as they never do in *Pylon*, and even if Laverne, at the reporter's urging returns to her Midwest home with not a hint that she will relinquish her child to Roger's father.

Since its release *The Tarnished Angels* has steadily risen in the estimation of critics and has even been regarded as one of Sirk's "masterworks."[27] Sirk himself called it "perhaps, after all . . . my best film."[28] He had wanted to adapt Faulkner's novel since Sirk's early years in the German film industry. Sirk, born Hans Detlef Sierck just three years after Faulkner, arrived in the United States in 1939 and experienced the Depression firsthand, making it the subject of one of Stack's terse speeches when he upbraids Carson for buying an expensive pair of boots when they do not even have a place to stay. Hudson immediately offers his apartment to these refugees, whose homelessness obviously spoke directly to the deracinated Sirk. Faulkner's fiction is full of wanderers from Quentin Compson, Joe Christmas, and Lena Grove to Lucius Priest and Ned McCaslin—all of whom experience disequilibrium and discomposure that so often dogged Faulkner away from home. They are his emigrés.

James Harvey observes that *The Tarnished Angels* is the "closest thing to an art movie he [Sirk] ever got to make at Universal," a studio better known for its horror and science fiction films. Next to Howard Hawks, no director in Hollywood had a greater reverence for Faulkner's work or a sensibility receptive to what many of Faulkner's American critics consider one of his weakest works. Sirk does not seem to have consulted Faulkner, and there is no record of contact between them, but Faulkner recognized their affinity when he called *The Tarnished Angels* "pretty good, quite honest."[29] Since he did not elaborate, a critic can only surmise what he meant. The film captures much of the novel's bleakness, especially in the way, it intercuts the gawdy—even sinister—Mardi Gras scenes, emphasizing a society besotted with masking and dumb shows that make the heroism of Roger Schumann into just another carnival appearance. His World War I exploits are revered but also made into a poster, so that he becomes a prop of fandom, so to speak.

Not surprisingly, though, Faulkner drew a line between the film and his book, saying of the former, "I'll have to admit I didn't recognize anything I put into it."[30] Sirk would not have objected, admitting that he had to "unFaulknerize" the film. Presumably the director had in mind the requirement to make the characters explain themselves, so that even the taciturn Stack tells Malone he loves her just before taking off in the plane that will crash and end his life. In *Pylon*, Roger and Laverne are unable or unwilling to express themselves because they are the antithesis of the world the reporter wants to put into words. They elude the explicit.

After so much work in Hollywood, Faulkner understood the possibilities and limitations of popular cinema, just as he had mastered the art of writing popular magazine stories, conflating, as David M. Earle puts it, "modernism and pulpism." Judging by Faulkner's response to *The Tarnished Angels*, he realized better than reviewers and academics how his work arose out of both elitist and popular sources. If he drew distinctions between his novels, screen work, and adaptations of his novels, he did not ignore their synchronicity. With *Pylon*, after all, he had Howard Hawks in mind. If the novel was not made to order for Hollywood, it had—as all critics agree—the basic elements, especially the love triangle he had worked out in earlier Hawks films. And Faulkner himself had done his share of Hollywood reductionism to suit the demands of the film medium.

If *Pylon* has not been deemed Faulkner's worst novel, it has certainly been ranked well below his greatest achievements. A far more confident man and writer than Hemingway, Faulkner does not seem to have been bothered by those who treated his work as a property to be exploited, or that he might exploit himself—for, yes, the money, but also, I think, out of a never explicitly expressed desire to impress his themes on the world at large using many different media and platforms. He might appear to be shy in public and reticent, speaking in that hushed soft patter, if he spoke at all, and yet he served in the role of writer as ambassador that Hemingway, for all his cultivation of a public image, did not. Those later diplomatic junkets to Japan and Greece, Faulkner holding court at the University of Virginia and West Point, were part of his work and became a part of his persona. Surely he did not have to go to work for Howard Hawks on *Land of the Pharaohs*. By 1955, his income was assured. He could say he was doing a favor for an old friend, but Hawks could not have been desperate for Faulkner's services. Hemingway, who never deigned to work for the Hollywood he disdained while cashing its checks, would surely have regarded working on a movie after the award of a Nobel Prize as demeaning. Howard Hawks said Hemingway told him, "he didn't know whether he could be a good writer of movies."[31] Although Hawks's testimony has been challenged, it seems reasonable to suppose that the highly competitive Hemingway would have been concerned about perceptions of him as a Hollywood hack—just one of those schmucks with typewriters that Jack Warner dismissed and humiliated as he did with Faulkner. In 1932, both writers were offered short term contracts to write for the movies. Only Faulkner accepted. He did worry about Hollywood stunting his style, but never, it seems, about how others might devalue his work because he wrote for Hollywood. Faulkner, it appears, could look on his stints in Hollywood as just that—stints that could not bring down the

FAULKNER'S SHADOW: HOLLYWOOD, HEMINGWAY, AND *PYLON* 145

house of Faulkner that even as early as 1932 had become impregnable. As Leonard Leff reminds us, Faulkner "threaded his way through the slicks," and even published in *The Woman's Home Companion* whereas Hemingway feared his appearance in such a magazine would be regarded as a sellout.

Faulkner was very much a part of the commercial world that his flyers have to navigate in *Pylon*. He cared about great writing just as they devoted themselves to great flying. He deplored his periods of indenture to Hollywood, but even hack work became a modest point of pride and even pleasure. "I had me some fun," he told an interviewer, and even admitted to enjoying the "technical aspects of production."[32] And he was not camera-shy, as is sometimes supposed when he is compared with the self-promoting Hemingway. Faulkner would say to his agent, "Don't tell the bastards anything,"[33] but such a comment reflected a writer who wanted to be in charge of when and where he became a public spectacle whereas the bragging Hemingway liked to take on all comers. Faulkner's seeming imperviousness to the corruption that Hollywood and the slicks were supposed to exert on a writer's reputation dogged Hemingway like his own shadow and perhaps even infuriated him, which is perhaps why Hemingway implied that Faulkner did not know what was good for him.

I can imagine Howard Hawks saying, "Bill, I know you don't need the money now, but I'd appreciate your helping me out on this *Land of the Pharaohs*. And we might have us some fun." Was it for old time's sake? How could Faulkner resist making Pharaohs talk like southern plantation owners? This was, after all, a world class novelist who said at MGM that he had an idea for a Mickey Mouse cartoon. That remark is sometimes brought up as a joke or to show how little Faulkner knew about who owned the rights to the rodent.[34] But ignorance or naïveté seem doubtful, since Walt Disney was already a highly celebrated Hollywood figure, and Faulkner did go to the movies and had his favorites like *Citizen Kane, The Magnificent Ambersons* (1942), and *High Noon* (1952).[35] Like the reporter, Faulkner was fascinated by those ungrounded pilots who could seem like characters in a movie, unreal and yet palpably alive, figments of the imagination who remain, nevertheless, their own selves that neither the reporter nor the novelist can quite fathom.

The Stories of Temple Drake

Temple Drake has a story to tell, but she does not tell that story in *Sanctuary*. Instead she largely appears through synecdoche. First, we see her long blonde legs, then her hair in "spent red curls," followed by a "fleet revelation of flank and thigh" as she gets into a car. She looks at Popeye: "her mouth boldly scarlet, her eyes watchful and cold beneath her brimless hat, a curled spill of red hair." Tommy says "She's a right tall gal." What we hear of her is reduced to clattering heels. She faces Popeye with a "taut toothed coquetry." She appears "no more than an elongated and leggy infant in her scant dress and uptilted hat." Ruby calls her a "doll-faced slut." When those tight red curls of hers show up again they look like "clots of resin." There is something puppetlike about her "long blonde legs slanted, lax-ankled her two motionless slippers with their glittering buckles'" that "lay on their sides as though empty." At Miss Reba's whorehouse, her face is pictured as "quite pale, the two spots of rouge like paper discs on her cheek bones, her mouth painted into a savage and perfect bow, also like something both symbolical and cryptic cut carefully from purple paper and pasted there." In short, she is a conceit, a cartoon, a paper-mâché confection.

What could Hollywood do with such a creation? On June 6, 1931, writer/producer Lamar Trotti answered the question: Nothing. In his report on *Sanctuary*, he called it unfilmable and unthinkable as a motion picture. It was a brilliant book but also, in Trotti's estimation, the "most sickening novel ever written in this country." And this was three years before the production code was strictly applied to the treatment of love and sex. Yet in the spring of 1933, *The Story of Temple Drake* appeared in movie theaters, receiving some surprising reviews. The Jackson, Mississippi *Clarion-Ledger* did not seem outraged at all, praising Miriam Hopkins for portraying with "perfect understanding the complexities of literature's most spirited character . . .

THE STORIES OF TEMPLE DRAKE

a strange composite of good and evil forces, a curious mixture of conventional attributes and uncontrollable desires." That description might also fit the Temple Drake of *Requiem for a Nun*, a character Faulkner had not yet conceived of when he wrote *Sanctuary*.[1]

Faulkner had nothing to do with the scripting of *The Story of Temple Drake*, although Jean Negulesco, showed Faulkner the sketches he made for the film, including the rape scene, sketches that the novelist admired. Miriam Hopkins, the film's star, apparently wanted to meet Faulkner, but so far as I know never did fulfill her desire, although she dated his friend Ben Wasson. The film is not as boldly expressionistic as Negulesco's sketches, which captured Temple, as Faulkner did, by synecdoche. For the film to succeed, it had to show the whole of Temple Drake, although vestiges of Faulkner's teasing vignettes remain the first time we are introduced to Temple in the film. We see nothing so suggestive as a leg or a spill of red, curled hair, but rather her hand holding on to a door. We can hear, but not see, her telling a gentleman-pursuer, "No," rejecting his advances as his hand covers hers in an attempt at appropriation that she successfully rebuffs. Only then does she enter the room and expose herself to our full view. She is desirable and knows it, but she will only go so far in satisfying the lust of her pursuers and the ogling of filmgoers.

Temple appears in the film without Virginia-educated gentleman, Gowan Stevens, who is replaced by a composite Faulkner character, Stephen Benbow, romantically interested in Temple. I guess that is why Toddy Gowan, the Gowan Stevens replacement in the film, says he goes to the state university that is clearly not Virginia, since no one attending the University of Virginia would *ever* leave out its name. We first see Stephen Benbow, the moral center of the film, in a courtroom defending the very idea of justice, which is what Gavin Stevens does in *Requiem for a Nun*, the courthouse playing a signal role in both the dramatic and narrative portions of the novel. Stephen Benbow is the unsullied ideal of the gentleman, refusing to accept Temple's statement that she is bad, which reminds me, of course, of Temple Drake's statement in *Requiem* that she liked and was attracted to evil. *The Story of Temple Drake*, in other words, is about Stephen Benbow's struggle to force Temple to express her better self, to be replaced in *Requiem for a Nun* by Gavin Stevens's more problematic efforts to get her to redemption.

I try to imagine what Faulkner thought as he watched this film, a reworking of *Sanctuary* so that it could have a happy ending, liberating Temple from confinement by salacious synecdoche in Faulkner's novel. Miriam Hopkins portrays Temple as a character very much in line with the Me Too movement. She has been raped and has to explain how it is that she winds up in a whorehouse with her rapist. As Hopkins plays it, Temple is not attracted to Trigger

(Hollywood's name for Popeye), but is dazed at what he has done to her and certain that she can never return to her family and community as a respectable woman. To survive, she has to be silent about what has been done to her.

That is why Stephen Benbow, whom she has earlier dismissed as being too good for her, has to convince her otherwise—that she is worthy of his love and her community's respect. He subpoenas her to take the stand to testify that Lee Goodwin did not murder Tommy, but to do so she has to explain not only that she witnessed Trigger shoot Tommy, but that Trigger cannot be brought to justice because she has shot him just as he is about to rape her a second time, although the word "rape" is not uttered in the film. Benbow gets as far as compelling Temple to explain she witnessed the murder, but when he has to reveal what happens afterward to Temple in the Memphis cathouse, he balks and declares he is withdrawing his witness. Why? Because he loves Temple and cannot bring himself to humiliate her, to degrade further this fallen specimen of southern womanhood. But Temple, after hesitating in a brilliant moment that is tantamount to reliving her rape and the murder of Trigger, tells the court the whole story, and the film abruptly ends with her fainting and with Stephen Benbow carrying her out of the courtroom, telling her grandfather, the judge, that he should be proud of her. "I know I am," Stephen declares.

The film is obviously not on the level of *Sanctuary*, although the expressionist lighting, the dialogue, and the performance of Florence Eldridge as Ruby, is riveting, and captures the tenor of the novel. The film may also have made Faulkner realize he was not done with Temple, or I should say, in Faulknerian terms, she was not done with him. I say this in all confidence knowing that Faulkner never believed that the pages of a novel fixed his characters forever. He was free to recreate them, and so was Hollywood. Young Bayard Sartoris in Faulkner's film script, *War Birds*, is very different from the young Bayard of *Flags in the Dust*, just as the old Bayard of *Flags* has changed from the boy/man of *The Unvanquished*, and the Sutpen of *Revolt in the Earth*, Faulkner's filmic transformation of *Absalom, Absalom!* is different from his namesake in the novel, and Judith Sutpen who dies in the novel is reborn in *Revolt in the Earth* and lives in England.

Could it be that Hollywood—not only in *The Story of Temple Drake* but in films like *Drums Along the Mohawk*, for which Faulkner did a script, made him rethink his notions of sex, romance, the gentleman's code, and so much more? It is what I argue in my biography of him as a writer who saw his characters as part of a greater intertextuality that he and Hollywood could draw on at will.

The Temple who takes the stage in *Requiem for a Nun* is "very smart, soignée, in an open fur coat, wearing a hat and gloves and carrying a handbag.

Her air is brittle and tense, yet controlled." She becomes a kind of collaborating Hollywood screenwriter debating with Gavin Stevens and later with the Governor of her state in the telling of her story.[2] This is not the Temple of *Sanctuary* or of *The Story of Temple Drake*. In *Requiem*, we see her whole, sans synecdoche. She looks and acts more like Joan Williams, with whom Faulkner wanted to write his play, and more like most of the women he became involved with from Meta Carpenter to Jean Stein—all of whom, at one time or another, met Faulkner's niece, Dean Faulkner Wells. Dean came away from those meetings thinking these women had been good for her uncle,[3] who, you know, could sometimes carry himself like Stephen Benbow and think of himself as a romantic savior. Faulkner often said he believed people could be better than they thought they were, which is what happens to Temple in *The Story of Temple Drake*, which became, certainly in darker Faulknerian terms, the Temple Drake/Mrs. Gowan Stevens of *Requiem for a Nun*.

"Tomorrow" and *Tomorrow*

Faulkner into Film

With few exceptions film adaptations of Faulkner's fiction have been disappointing failures. The density and complexity of his language is difficult, if not impossible, to convey in the primarily visual medium of film. The variety of narrative voices, the shifting points of view, and the use of several seemingly independent stories within a novel appear to have baffled or simply put off filmmakers, who have not tried to follow Faulkner's manner or method.[1]

I

Tomorrow (1971) manages to avoid some of these problems not by following the story's structure, or its use of several narrators, but by relentlessly exploring the life of its central character, Jackson Fentry, as if Fentry himself were detachable from Faulkner's fiction—a character so powerfully conceived that new images of him can be projected in a different medium. A close reading of the short story suggests that the film is not so much a reenactment—or even a version—of a literary work as it is a reaction to that work, in the sense that the film specifies and concretizes images of Fentry's life which the narrators struggle to create.[2]

In Faulkner's story, "Tomorrow," Jackson Fentry never speaks for himself; we are never simply immersed in his experience. No one in the short story is able to recreate the whole man. Gavin Stevens's initial description of him is as "thin" as the man himself: "a thin man, small, with thin gray hair and that appearance of hill farmers—at once frail and work-worn, yet curiously imperishable—who seem to become old men at fifty and then become invincible to time."

"TOMORROW" AND *TOMORROW*: FAULKNER INTO FILM   151

Fentry is made to conform to a type and is not distinguishable from numerous others of the type whom Stevens has observed. Fentry's endurance will become of major concern to Stevens, but at this early point in the story his other qualities are not even suggested. By the end of the story we certainly know more about Fentry as an individual; he is no longer just a type. Yet Fentry himself in all his particularity is not the subject of "Tomorrow." Indeed the story insists on his elusiveness, his inarticulateness, so that Stevens's putting the events of his life into coherent form for himself, for the community, and for his nephew Chick Mallison stands as the triumph of the story. What we learn about Fentry is clearly subordinated to, and understood in terms of, Stevens' view of "all human beings who at bottom want to do right, want not to harm others; human beings with all the complexity of human passions and feelings and beliefs, in the accepting or rejecting of which we had no choice, trying to do the best we can with them or despite them."

Fentry's story is important because he epitomizes what all human beings must go through in one way or another. In the same circumstances Chick would have done the same as Fentry, Stevens maintains in the face of his nephew's objections. Throughout the story Chick offers the picture of a young Gavin Stevens who "more than twenty years ago" set out bright, intent and eager, refusing to be baffled by the obstacles to his overwhelming desire "to know." As Mary Dunlap observes, Stevens "struggles to identify himself with the life around him." He is turned away by Fentry's furious father who menaces him with a shotgun and refuses to tell the attorney anything about his son. Without a sign of fear or frustration Stevens departs quickly; his grave demeanor suggests the seriousness of his investigative enterprise. He proceeds with no hesitation to ask his neighbors, the Pruitts, to tell him whatever they know about Fentry. Although he has ventured to discover why Fentry was the only juror who refused to acquit his obviously innocent client Bookwright, who in self-defense killed Buck Thorpe, a notorious "swaggering bravo," it is clear to people that what Stevens "asked was not just for his own curiosity or his own selfish using. As the Pruitts inform him of Fentry's work and family, Stevens's interest and imaginative projection into that hard life are suggested by his eyes, which "had just got brighter, as if whatever it was behind them had flared up, steady and fiercer, yet still quiet, as if it were going faster than the telling was going."

The Pruitts themselves have a special kinship with Fentry because their own lives have been almost as hard as his; and though Stevens has to ask them to "Wait," as Shreve asks Quentin to "Wait" in *Absalom, Absalom!* he absorbs the details of Fentry's life faster than he can understand them just so the Pruitts will be able to tell him all of the story as they have come to know it.

Thus Mrs. Pruitt is allowed to describe how she heard about Fentry's bringing a baby home before Stevens (and the readers of "Tomorrow") have any notion of how such an event should figure in the story. Telling of Fentry's constant devotion to the baby under the most trying circumstances, his and the boy's sudden disappearance the next summer, and Fentry's return alone five years later is as far as the Pruitts are able to take the story. They reached an impasse when they tried to question Fentry about the boy: "What boy?" Fentry asked.

Stevens stays with the Pruitts only so long as they can function as an incremental part of the story he is searching out and shaping, leaving them as soon as their steady flow of information and insight flags. Their account, which is uncluttered with irrelevant detail and as clean and neat as Mrs. Pruitt's white apron, drives Stevens to consult Isham Quick, the son of the sawmill operator for whom Fentry worked. Quick is a man with a "dreamy kind of face and near-sighted eyes, until you saw there was something shrewd behind them, even a little quizzical." He tells Stevens that he has been expecting him, since he, like the Pruitts, is part of a community which anticipates and empathizes with the attorney's desire "to know." Quick gives Stevens information about Fentry which is at first incomprehensible to Stevens and to the reader. Again the attorney eschews questions in favor of letting Quick "Just tell it."

Like Mrs. Pruitt, Quick is portrayed in a habitual pose which defines his personality and place in the community, though his manner of just telling it is the opposite of hers, which was to sit "in a low rocking chair, shelling field peas into a wooden bowl." Quick, on the other hand, "sprawled on the bench beyond Uncle Gavin, loose-jointed, like he would come all to pieces the first time he moved, talking in a lazy sardonic voice, like he had all night to tell it in and it would take all night to tell it." Unlike the Pruitts, he has not shared Fentry's kind of hard life. His sardonic tone and casual behavior reflect his distance from a man he had measured too soon. As in the case of Stevens and Chick, who judge Fentry too quickly, Quick admits he had made too easy an equation between Fentry and the rough and crude environment from which he had come: "What I seem to have underestimated was his capacity for love. I reckon I figured that, coming from where he come from, he never had none a-tall, and for that same previous reason—that even the comprehension of love had done been lost out of him back down the generations where the first one of them had had to take his final choice between the pursuit of love and the pursuit of keeping on breathing." Thus Quick shrewdly sums up his limited perceptions and the inconspicuous depth of Fentry's feelings.

Fentry was not an easy man to know. Quick has to work hard at imagining how Fentry had taken up with a woman who was about to have a baby. He doesn't know if Fentry "found her somewhere, or if she just walked into

"TOMORROW" AND *TOMORROW*: FAULKNER INTO FILM   153

the mill one day or one night," or if just that suddenly Fentry fell in love with her. Given the woman's background Quick believes that she was too proud to return to her family after having left them for a husband whom her family could not accept. Quick deems it "likely" that her husband "cut and run soon as she told him about the baby." He "reckons" that when Fentry proposed to her she knew she would never survive the baby's birth and that she said yes to him only because "it wouldn't make no difference nohow." Throughout Quick's narrative it is important to be aware of just how much he is reconstructing rather than reporting Fentry's and the woman's behavior and beliefs. It is absolutely essential to Quick's own sympathetic attitude that he invent some of the details of the situation as it unfolded and extrapolate his interpretation of Fentry's life from such details as seem reasonable and compelling to him. Like Stevens, Quick uses Fentry's story to express his own sense of life—in this instance his view that "this world ain't run like it ought to be." This last comment is Quick's response to the injustice of the scene in which the Thorpes (brothers of the woman whose child Fentry had loved and taken care of for years) brutally reclaim their sister's child. Fentry fights against the loss of his boy but fatalistically accepts it once he is physically subdued by the brothers. Quick tries to help him by suggesting that perhaps Fentry can recover the boy by using the very law which has taken the boy away from him. Fentry does not even acknowledge Quick's suggestion and walks away as lost and unrecoverable as the boy himself, who turns out to be a drunken delinquent, whom (according to Quick) Fentry sees just once more in his life. Quick concludes by remarking, "Of course [Fentry] wasn't going to vote Bookwright free."

As with the Pruitts, Fentry was not able or willing to share his feeling about the boy with Quick; and like the Pruitts, Quick did not know how to aid this incommunicative man. Both the Pruitts and Quick tried to act on the compassion they felt for Fentry; and for each of them the sad and painful failure of their efforts is as important as Fentry's failure to fulfill his love for the boy. Quick implies that Fentry's refusal to vote Bookwright free was the last act of love which Fentry could bestow on the boy who had been the heart of his life. It is Stevens, however, who actually explains to Chick Fentry's behavior on the jury and what has been learned from the narratives of the Pruitts and Quick: "It wasn't Buck Thorpe, the adult, the man. [Fentry] would have shot that man as quick as Bookwright did, if he had been in Bookwright's place. It was because somewhere in that debased and brutalized flesh which Bookwright slew there still remained, not the spirit maybe, but at least the memory, of that little boy, that Jackson and Longstreet Fentry, even though the man the boy had become didn't know it, and only Fentry did. And you wouldn't have freed [Bookwright] either. Don't ever forget that. Never." As

154 FAULKNER AND HOLLYWOOD

one of the "lowly and invincible of the earth—to endure and endure and then endure, tomorrow and tomorrow and tomorrow," Fentry enacts a paradigm of the truth which Stevens has sought to show to Chick: good faith, love, care and compassion persist as an integral part of the sum of human experience.

Each narrator in the story has welcomed Stevens's struggle to understand Fentry because each narrator supports Stevens's vision of life and has regarded him as the one who must study the experience of a community and integrate into that experience the seemingly intractable behavior of one individual who appears (at the beginning of the story) to dissent from the community's standards and values. Part of what we come to learn is that like Bookwright, who tried to save his daughter from Buck Thorpe, a daughter "incapable of her own preservation," Fentry tried to save a woman similarly situated, and "solved that problem to the best of his ability and beliefs, asking help of no one, and then abode by his decision and his act." Indeed the parallels between the plights of Fentry and Bookwright, the man he would not "vote free," ironically underscore the universality of the whole story each narrator tries to tell. Through Stevens an important aspect of Fentry's humanity has been recovered and reclaimed by the community; through him the voices of Yoknapatawpha as we hear them in the story converge and unify and are passed on to a new generation represented by Chick Mallison. Chick, in turn, gives us the story of Fentry's life as the history of a community, and as part of a community in the process of defining its own history. The community has to remember, recover, and invent its history in order to achieve a desired image of humanity and tradition of belief. In this tradition people are primarily concerned with the past that impinges on the present, and thus with how the past relates to present needs. For all of the narrators in the story the recovery of a lost chapter in the past is both an exercise in self-definition and a way of articulating the symbolic significance of Fentry's life.[3] Memory has an extraordinarily important place in "Tomorrow"—not only the memories of all of the narrators but Fentry's memory, too, are what ties together experience and establishes continuity between past and present, and harmony among several generations of a community.

II

In the film *Tomorrow* (1971) the events of Jackson Fentry's life unfold directly before our eyes in an evolving present. Absent from the film are the speculations of the narrators who remember and recreate their visions of Fentry within the contexts of their own lives. A montage of opening scenes

"TOMORROW" AND *TOMORROW*: FAULKNER INTO FILM
155

rapidly—perhaps too rapidly—recounts and dramatizes Bookwright's killing of Buck Thorpe, Gavin Stevens's (renamed Douglas) address to the jury, and Fentry's stubborn refusal to acquit Bookwright. For someone who has not read the story it is easy to be mystified by exactly what is happening. The film seeks to establish very quickly that the following dramatization of Fentry's life is actually the product of Douglas's imaginative investigation, but for the most part the film visualizes a side of Fentry that is the outcome of surmise in the short story. In other words, through the film we become the privileged observers of precisely those facets of Fentry's character which he would not share with the story's narrators, and which others had difficulty appreciating.[4]

The film focuses on Fentry at a point that is not reached until the short story is more than half over. He is seen taking up his job and trying to make himself comfortable in the crude conditions at Quick's mill—lighting the stove in his cramped living quarters, working the well pump on a cold morning, exchanging a few words with his employer. Fentry's face seems devoid of emotion; he looks toughened by a hard life and does not respond very readily to Quick's timid efforts to strike up a conversation:

ISHAM: Don't you get lonesome by yourself out here this way?
FENTRY: Nope.
ISHAM: Do you ever go hunting?
FENTRY: I hunt some.
ISHAM: Maybe when you come back we can go hunting together sometimes.
FENTRY: All right.[5]

Fentry is agreeable but taciturn and leaves the impression that he does not have much feeling to express. He does not dwell on—perhaps he cannot even conceptualize—what it means to live in such an isolated, barren, and bleak environment. Horton Foote's dialogue skillfully renders Fentry's inaccessibility and remoteness. Faulkner's Fentry would say no more than he had to, even in a social conversation.

In the short story, Faulkner makes no effort to describe the shack in which Fentry lives, though he clearly impresses us with the unpromising, meager quality of the land from which Fentry comes: "the poor soil, the little tilted and barren patches of gaunt corn and cotton ... the roads ... less than lanes, winding and narrow, rutted and dust choked." In the film, the setting is an abiding influence on the way we view Fentry. Shot on location in Mississippi, the film makes us see Fentry as the expression of an environment. As Bruce Kawin observes, the black-and-white cinematography is "closely patterned after Walker Evans's work in James Agee's *Let Us Now Praise Famous Men*: one can practically chart the grain in each plank of the sawmill's walls. Both lighting and composition are rigorous, formal, and tender—studies in the eloquence of the simple."[6] Though Fentry, superbly played by Robert Duvall, rarely changes expressions, every detail of his demeanor and dress is registered by the camera in what George Bluestone calls the "microphysiognomy of the screen image." As Fentry is forced to encounter experience for which he has had no preparation, the steady focus of the camera on his face is a perpetual disclosure of his steadiness and calmness, his incredible ability to cope with suffering and hardship.

Even though the finely detailed scenes which appear at the beginning of the film are not given with so much elaboration in the short story, they do not contradict or distort the reading of Fentry's character and his world which the story's narrators supply; in fact, some of the film's scenes dramatize the knowledge which Stevens eventually accumulates and articulates in the story.

The next set of scenes do more than complement the story, since they show how Fentry meets and deals with the woman he eventually marries and who bears the child he will raise. What the film now portrays is Fentry's experience—not the narrators' recreation of it—making of a life with this woman, and his understanding of precisely what such a life means to him. As he prepares to leave the mill to go home for Christmas, he hears a faint moaning and discovers a woman lying in the snow. She is exhausted, and he persuades her to take shelter in his shack. He says very little but offers her his strength to lean on and the warmth of his home. He learns that she has been rejected by her family and abandoned by her husband. He does not commiserate with her; he simply listens to her and urges her to sleep on his bed in order to recover her strength.

Throughout these early scenes the camera concentrates on Fentry's features, on his attempts to keep the woman warm and well fed, while the woman is kept in the background watching him, speaking to him, and waiting for his invariable one-or two-sentence replies. Gradually we get more and more closeups of her frail face, but these closeups are usually put into the context of her conversations with Fentry. As they get to know each other, the woman becomes talkative; Fentry's manner does not change, but we are always aware of his compassion because we are shown his constant attention to her.

Fentry does not go home for Christmas. He stays with the woman and begins to ask her about her kin, her husband, and her plans. His questions are not intrusive, nor does he express an idle curiosity about her. When it is absolutely clear that her family will not take care of her, he insists that she stay with him until the child is born. His treatment of her is formal and

"TOMORROW" AND *TOMORROW*: FAULKNER INTO FILM   157

courteous, without a sign of familiarity. When she breaks down and gives way to her emotions, he asks: "What are you crying for, lady?" He does not rush to comfort her, but his question expresses his growing concern. The camera registers the distance between the woman crying on the bed and Fentry standing some six or seven feet away from her. As she speaks to him, he draws nearer to her and enters into the intimacy that characterizes the remaining time they will spend together.

Sarah's speech and her character are Horton Foote's creation that is entirely in consonance with the few speculations that Quick makes about her in the short story. It is to Foote's credit that he convincingly fashions a person whose sensitivity and candor summon forth Fentry's humanity: "I don't know. I'm just tired and nervous, I guess. I've been crying a lot lately. It don't mean anything; I quit as soon as I start. (She wipes her eyes.) See. I never used to cry before. When I was a girl, people used to accuse me of being hardhearted, because nothing could get me to cry. . . . When my Papa told me I had to leave home after I married my husband, I didn't shed a tear. I said if that's how it has to be, that's how it has to be. . . . But lately that's all changed. Somebody'll walk up to me and say good morning or good evening, and I'll cry, or ask me what time is it, and I'll cry. Did you ever hear of anything like that? I didn't use to talk this way either. I used to go a whole day without saying a word. And now I can't stand it silent or quiet." Like Fentry, she has been regarded as "hardhearted," stoical, and laconic. Olga Bellin plays Sarah perfectly. Without histrionics she is plain spoken and reserved, in spite of the lengthy speech she must deliver. Bellin clearly and confidently acts the role of a proud, independent woman, who has never asked for anyone's help. In her self-reliance, her suppressed tenderness, and loneliness she again resembles Fentry. Out of her isolation she speaks to the isolation in him. This moment is a revelation for Sarah, for Fentry, and for the viewer. There is nothing like it in the short story, which depends for the most part upon retrospective summary of events, and brief but vivid description and dialogue. Neither Fentry nor Sarah has any self-pity; Sarah cries but does not sentimentalize her grief. They are a perfect match, so much so that Fentry is willing to admit to feelings that he would usually not acknowledge in the presence of others, or perhaps even to himself:

SARAH: Don't you miss having somebody to talk to?
FENTRY: Sometimes.

His terse admission of loneliness may not make it seem that he has divulged much of himself, but Fentry is a man who has spent his time in silence. It is

158 FAULKNER AND HOLLYWOOD

characteristic of Foote's masterly adaptation of Faulkner's story that he can dramatize Fentry's engagement with Sarah without ever ruining the story's careful development of his reserved character.

Subsequent scenes show Fentry and Sarah sitting at a table eating together. Numerous shots which place them together—around the stove taking in its warmth,[7] outside the shack where Fentry washes his clothes and Sarah sits in a chair watching him, walking together in the woods—emphasize Fentry's way of making a life not just for the woman but for himself. As he washes his clothes, he says to her: "Marry me," for he has realized just how close they have become. She is startled but not put off by his proposal. Again the camera records that same six or seven-foot distance between them as Sarah replies that she cannot marry him because she has a husband. Fentry does not argue; instead he shows her the site of the house that Quick has promised to build for him. It is his intention, as he later tells her, to provide for her and her child in that house.

As the time of the birth approaches, Sarah confesses to Fentry that she is afraid that she will die. She has looked worn and tired throughout the movie and has eaten very little in spite of his persistent attempts to give her nourishment. In a very determined manner he replies to her: "You're not going to die. You hear me. You are not going to die. I won't let you." He again asks her to marry him, pointing out that her husband has deserted her. Although she refuses him once more, there is no change in his attitude or actions.

Finally Sarah's labor begins and Fentry sends Quick for the midwife. The remoteness of the setting, the crude furnishings of the shack, the frail woman in the agony of childbirth, the strong yet helpless man who shapes a small crib and paces outside awaiting the outcome of her labor, and the industrious, unruffled midwife—all of these scenes are intercut in the film to expose a complex view of vulnerable human beings in an inhospitable world. Somehow they manage to get through their ordeal without any illusions about how much it has cost them. Their actions echo Sarah's words: "if that's how it has to be, that's how it has to be." The midwife tells Fentry that she very much doubts that the mother will survive. Sarah herself knows as much and so consents to marry Fentry as he paces the floor absorbed in gazing at the newborn baby.

Fentry's moment of recognition and dedication is the climax of the film. The camera captures him seated beside Sarah's bed speaking in a direct, simple, and economical language that sums up his reaction to what he and Sarah have shared and articulates his whole way of being:

I don't know why we met when we did or why I found you when you was all wore out, and I couldn't save you no matter how bad I

"TOMORROW" AND *TOMORROW*: FAULKNER INTO FILM 159

wanted to. I don't know what they done to you to make you turn so on them; but I don't care. I promised you I'd raise him, and I will. Like he was my own. (He goes to the box and looks down at the baby.) Your Mama is dead, son. But I'm gonna take care of you and see to you. I'll be your Mama and your Papa. You'll never want or do without while I have a breath of life in my bones.

The twice repeated "I don't know" followed by "I promised . . . I will. . . . I'm gonna. . . . I'll be" dramatically demonstrates Fentry's puzzlement at the vagaries of existence, his wonderment at the peculiar position in which he has been placed, and his unshakable commitment. Like Sarah, he says "I don't know," yet he quietly pledges his life to the fulfillment of his promise. Even in this speech which verges on the sentimental and seems to call for Fentry to display emotions which are carefully avoided in the story—where Quick only alludes to Fentry's capacity for love—Duvall refrains from changing the reticent voice or the subdued physical gestures of his character.

Shortly after Sarah is buried Fentry returns home to his father, and we get a montage of scenes that show Fentry working in the field, carrying the boy on his back in a sack, and plowing. Several shots of the baby toddling behind Fentry, of Fentry making clothes for the boy, and of Fentry playing with the boy in a pond strikingly portray what is obliquely presented in the story: the love and devotion and joy which the "father" and "son" experience. We get brief but very revealing glimpses of Fentry's humor and sensitivity, and the boy's happy responsiveness. The film's focus on the dim, enclosed, grim world of the mill is relieved by quick transitions from one daylight shot to another of Fentry's opening up of the world to the boy. The dynamism of human growth is everywhere apparent. The form of Faulkner's story does not allow for such richness and contrast of imagery. The very rapidity with which these scenes are projected saves them from becoming merely sentimental, and the swift shifting from one image to the next is an extension of the sudden flashes of insight into Fentry's capacity for love which the narrators of the story convey. Thus it is hard to agree with Bruce Kawin who regrets that "the relationship between Fentry and his 'son' is so hurriedly summarized."

When the Thorpes show up to take away the boy, the film modifies the scene as it is written in the short story, where Fentry immediately tells the boy to run and begins to fight the Thorpes. In the film, he stands in the road beside his home watching the men approach. The boy is several feet away from him. The suspense begins to build as Fentry recognizes Quick and begins to look over the Thorpes. They are tall, brutish men who warily scrutinize Fentry. The camera pans over the group and then in a medium closeup concentrates our attention for a prolonged moment on one robust brother who squints and looks sideways at Fentry. The brothers embody a gruff masculinity which is antithetical to Fentry's tender regard for the child. Though Fentry has seemed at the beginning of film as roughhewn as the Thorpes, he now exudes a warm sensitivity and vulnerability which is to be crushed in this confrontation. A few words of greeting are exchanged which serve to heighten the sense of foreboding. Fentry holds the boy close, tells him to say hello to the strangers, but carefully secludes the child behind his back. Then the scene bursts into violence as Fentry urges the boy to run and tries to wrestle himself free from the Thorpes. As soon as it is clear that it will do no good to resist the overwhelming force, Fentry relinquishes the fight, ignores Quick's advice on how to recover the boy, and with his back turned away from the camera which has opened up his life for us, he walks toward the fields, and back into his isolated and inaccessible life.

Douglas's [Stevens's] narration at the end of the film, as in the story, commemorates all of the lowly who will suffer but also endure for as long as there will be a tomorrow. Although the film claims to operate within the context of a story being told and passed on, in fact its images and scenes speak for themselves and do not gain much from the intervention of a narrator. The best that the voice-over narrator can do is to ratify what we have already experienced in our hearts and minds and perhaps to tell us why we have been immersed in Fentry's life in the first place. Through montage—the dynamic juxtaposition of images—crisp dialogue, the peculiar rhythm of sounds and silences which help to define the pattern of Fentry's life, and the "guitar-and-concertina score—a brilliant set of variations on the folk songs of the period,[8] the film presents an intense and authentic experience.

Certainly a film adaptation of "Tomorrow" might have attempted to introduce more narrators, to work at the sense of Fentry's life evolving out of the words and memories of many people; and so at least one critic has been disappointed that "Faulkner's involuted structure of plot-revelation is downplayed in the interest of dramatic 'clarity'"[9] Yet relatively few films, such as *Citizen Kane*, have experimented successfully with multiple narration, or, like *Last Year at Marienbad*, with following the characters' subjective impressions of what was happening.[10] Bruce Kawin has made a suggestive case for the ability of film to translate in visual terms even some of Faulkner's most complexly told stories. It does not seem fair, however, to fault "Tomorrow" for not following what might have been a more adventurous and authentic course in film adaptation. Copying the narrative structure of the story would ensure an accurate rendition of the fiction; copying might also result in a dull, confusing, and—in a sense—unfaithful dramatization of a stimulating story. A film has to succeed on its own terms; and in doing so it may still capture the essential spirit of a work of fiction. At any rate, the filmmaker has to select from and improvise upon the fiction which constitutes what might be called his "raw material."[11]

The film adaptation of "Tomorrow" began with certain advantages that other film adaptations of Faulkner's work have not enjoyed. The filmmakers did not have to compress a full-length novel into the limits of a screenplay. Thus the film could use the material of a compact short story, proceeding to develop a simple plot, a clear reading of a few characters, and one essential theme. Nor did the film have to worry over a work of literature which freely enters the consciousness of its characters. In "Tomorrow" Faulkner avoids getting into the minds of his characters, and so the filmmakers did not have to find visual equivalents for the characters' thoughts. Michael Millgate speaks of Faulkner's creating in "almost minimal terms," and of the short story's "leashed power."[12] The film reflects one convincing way to accomplish further exploration of a character who haunts our imagination by presenting a compelling enactment of the integrity of individual life.

The Reivers
On and Off the Screen

I

The Reivers (1962) is William Faulkner's final novel, published just a month before he died. He may have intended the work as his ultimate triumph. It casts a retrospective and ruminative eye on the history of Yoknapatawpha, his mythical county. Critics and biographers have called the book nostalgic, because in the mellow tones of a grandfather the narrator tells his grandchildren about the Mississippi of 1905, focusing in the main on a seemingly simpler era, when an automobile was a work of wonder, and when a trip from Jefferson (Faulkner's version of Oxford, his hometown) to Memphis could seem like an epic adventure.

In the novel, Lucius Priest (the grandfather) recounts the time he and Boon Hoggenbeck, a family retainer, became reivers (thieves) when they "borrowed" the Winton Flyer belonging to Boss Priest (Lucius's grandfather) and set off for the big city, where Boon could visit Miss Corrie in a Memphis cathouse, and introduce eleven-year-old Lucius to a world that (Boon assures him) Lucius will one day understand and avail himself of.

Lucius has been brought up to be a gentleman, so his escapade with Boon requires him to lie to his family about Boon's scheme, a lie made possible by Boss Priest having taken the train to attend the funeral of his wife's father, Lucius's other grandfather. Boon is supposed to lock up the automobile and not use it while Boss is away. The meaning of gentleman, which involves taking responsibility for one's actions and abiding by a code of honor, is developed in references to Yoknapatawpha history in the first chapters of the novel, in which descriptions of the Sutpens, the Compsons, the McCaslins, and all the county's important families impinge on Lucius's consciousness. What he does, in other words, will be measured against what his forebears

THE REIVERS: ON AND OFF THE SCREEN 163

and predecessors have done. In effect, Lucius's decision to lie, to leave home, is a declaration of independence, but it is also another act in the drama of his community's history. In effect, Lucius as "grandfather" is telling his children their history, showing how the individual has to understand it in order to come to terms with himself.

Calling *The Reivers* nostalgic and a summation of Faulkner's Yoknapatawpha saga is understandable but also misleading, since doing so suggests that the novel is not in the same class as his earlier and presumably greater novels. Indeed, in just this way many critics and biographers have discounted *The Reivers*, taking the narrator's relaxed tone as a sign of the author's more indulgent and less complex art. This assumption, however, ignores the circumstances of the telling: a grandfather addressing his grandchildren. His narration is all about the child's discovery of the adult world as told by an adult to his own kin who will, in turn, discover the world in their way. To confuse Faulkner with his narrator—no matter how many similarities between them can be assembled—is to wreck the fiction and to deny Lucius Priest his independent existence as a character.

Certainly the darker events of Faulkner's earlier novels—the suicide of Quentin Compson, the castration of Joe Christmas, and revelations about the evils of slavery—are not explored. But their consequences are— especially in the figure of Ned McCaslin, Boss Priest's coachman, whom Lucius refers to as "our family skeleton." Ned is a Black man, born in 1860, who claims that his mother "had been the natural daughter of old Lucius Quintus Carothers himself," the original progenitor of the clan. In other words, Ned claims direct descent from a founding father, whereas Lucius's line "were mere diminishing connections and hangers-on." To readers of Faulkner's other novels—especially *Go Down, Moses*, which explores the McCaslin genealogy and the white family's inextricable connections with the lives of the McCaslin slaves—Ned's pride and self-assurance are all the more appreciated. When Ned stows away in the Winton Flyer because he, too, wants a trip to Memphis, Boon cannot gainsay his presence, even though as a white man Boon ought to be able to master his so-called inferior in this highly segregated society.

Except that such segregation and racial distinctions keep breaking down and dissolving in the world of Faulkner's fiction. Ned represents the novelist's deft way of showing that dissolution even in an adventure story intended to entertain children. Compared to the wily Ned, Boon and Lucius are innocents abroad. M. Thomas Inge has rightly called Lucius a "motorized Huck Finn," and yet it is as if Faulkner takes the slave Jim off the raft and puts him in control of the story that becomes *The Reivers*.

Ned turns the seemingly simple road trip that Boon and Lucius have planned into a rococo plot that involves getting his kinsman, Bobo Beauchamp, out of trouble by trading the Winton Flyer for a racehorse, which Ned will then put up in a race against another horse, with the prize being the automobile and other winnings that will pay off Bobo's debts and return the vehicle to Boss Priest. So devious and intricate is Ned's strategy that it is not revealed until near the end of the novel, which becomes the denouement of a mystery of Ned's devising. In fact, only after the race is won does Ned divulge to Boss Priest the intricate series of events and developments that neither Lucius nor Boon has been able to explain. Without Ned as the mastermind, the novel has no engine, no way to proceed or to resolve itself.

Because Lucius is telling the story, remembering his childhood even as he invokes his status as a grandfather, *The Reivers* has a double perspective: Lucius then, Lucius now; the world then, the world now. Although a good deal has changed since 1905, the moral values Lucius seeks to impart remain the same and belong to the historical continuum that the novel itself enacts.

Ned is the conduit of that continuum. He is forty-five years old in 1905, Lucius reports. Ned will live to the age of seventy-four, "just living long enough for the fringe of hair embracing his bald skull to begin to turn gray, let alone white (it never did. I mean, his hair: turn white nor even gray)." Although Ned responds to change, represented by the automobile, he has no interest in driving it or learning about the new technology. Yet his very steadfastness in the midst of change, his knowledge of his own mind and his place in the world, renders him able to adapt to every new and unforeseeable situation on the ride to Memphis and in its aftermath. In short, he cannot be distracted by novelty or deflected from his purpose.

On the other hand, the slow-witted Boon (he failed the third grade twice) is impulsive, a man who acts in the moment without taking aim. His poor shooting is legendary. He is all id to Ned's ego, with Lucius trying to manage his own inclinations and adhere to his upbringing while coping with the behavior of the shrewd Black man born into slavery and the excitable white man saved from undoing himself by the grace of his gentlemen employers, beginning with old General Compson. Boon may be six-feet-four and weigh 240 pounds, but he has the "mentality of a child." He is a rough-hewn woodsman, with a "big ugly florid walnut-tough walnut-hard face." This physical description suggests an impermeable quality in Boon, who cannot learn from experience as Lucius does, or profit from it as Ned can. Boon can drive the action forward, just as he drives the Winton flyer, but he cannot plot his adventures or predict their pitfalls.

A case in point is Boon's confident belief that he can drive the automobile through Hell Creek bottom, a treacherous bog maintained that way by a farmer who makes his living dragging vehicles out of the mud. Even though Boon paid the man two dollars the summer before to pull out the Winton Flyer, he thinks that this time, with Ned and Lucius helping, he can use block and tackle to move the car through the sludge. After several efforts that saturate Boon and Ned with muck, Boon pays the man with the mules two dollars per passenger to rescue them from the mire. This episode is a perfect example of Boon's self-defeating actions, which tend to make his dilemmas worse than they were to begin with. In short, Lucius's up to now pristine existence, guided by the courtly examples of his father and grandfather, is enveloped in the mess Boon makes of his life.

Arriving in Memphis, the action shifts to the brothel, where Miss Reba is enchanted with Lucius's manners, such a contrast to the conniving Otis, a young nephew Miss Corrie is trying to reform. Lucius is smitten with Miss Corrie, whom he describes as a "big girl. I don't mean fat: just big, like Boon was big, but still a girl, young too, with dark hair and blue eyes and at first I thought her face was plain. But she came into the room already looking at me, and I knew it didn't matter what her face was." She may be a whore, but there is an innocence in her that Lucius connects with, and they quickly form a bond that leads to Lucius being cut by Otis's knife in a fight that starts when Lucius strikes out at Otis for denigrating Miss Corrie. She, in turn, decides to reform herself in order to be worthy of Lucius's devotion. Set against her sincerity is Mr. Binford's cynicism. He turns a critical eye on Lucius and tries to corrupt him, offering beer even though Lucius steadfastly refuses the drink, announcing that he has promised his mother that he will not imbibe until he is of age.

The novel's action shifts again when Ned shows up with a horse he has named Lightning, informing Boon that the Winton Flyer can only be recovered by winning a horse race. On the way to the race site, Ned, Boon, and Lucius encounter the sadistic deputy sheriff Butch Lovemaiden, who arrests Boon and Ned for possessing a horse that is stolen property. The price of their release, Butch informs them, is a night with Miss Corrie. Seeing no way out, she complies and is later assaulted by Boon, who thus loses Lucius's respect.

The novel's exciting denouement centers on the horse race. Ned admits to Lucius that he believes he can make their horse a winner (Lightning has lost races against his rival, Acheron), but the neck-and-neck heats in which the neophyte jockey Lucius rides make the result anything but certain. After their triumph, Ned explains that he has studied the psychology of his horse and discovered its liking for sardines, which Ned carries with him at the finish line in sight of the galloping Lightning.

166   FAULKNER AND HOLLYWOOD

In the coda of the novel, Lucius comes home for his punishment, but he is spared the beating his father is prepared to give him when Boss Priest intervenes, suggesting that it is punishment enough for Lucius to live with a sense of his transgressions: "A gentleman accepts the responsibilities of his actions and bears the burden of their consequences, even when he did not himself instigate them but only acquiesced to them, didn't say No though he knew he should." To the young Lucius, expecting corporal punishment, the psychological and moral burden his grandfather places on him seems overwhelming. But Boss tells him, "A gentleman can live through anything." And this is surely what Lucius, as narrator, is telling his grandchildren without actually saying so directly. Lucius has lived to tell the tale and is the better for it.

All along, Ned has been preparing Lucius for the moment when he will have to confront Boss. Ned has known from the start that they could not get away with their adventure, or even just accept their punishment and be done with it. Instead, as in all of Faulkner's fiction, the past is never past. It has to be borne and contended with as an inextricable part of a community's and an individual's history.

II

The Reivers (1969), a film directed by Mark Rydell, and starring Steve McQueen and Juano Hernandez, who played Lucas Beauchamp in the film adaptation of *Intruder in the Dust* (1950), was generally well received by critics as a well-made family film. As Roger Ebert puts it, it was the kind of film that "neither insulted nor challenged the intelligence of any member of the family." Ebert also notes, however, that the film does not "particularly carry a Faulkner flavor," and is closer to Mark Twain because of its simplified adventure plot.[1] Even so, most of the best lines in the screenplay are taken from Faulkner's novel. What the movie lacks is a narrative frame, even though it includes voice-over commentary by Burgess Meredith, which captures the memoirlike quality of *The Reivers* but cannot situate the significance of the story into the context of Yoknapatawpha history. Mitch Vogel deftly portrays Lucius's innocent but growing awareness of the adult world. But the production is seriously flawed in its casting of two major characters, Boon Hoggenbeck and Ned McCaslin, on which so much of the action and the morality of the novel pivots. McQueen, an actor with leading-man looks who was more successful in dramatic roles, lacks Boon's curious combination of crudity and sensitivity—more a failing of the role as written than of the performer. And Rupert Crosse is too manic to play the sly and deliberate Ned;

THE REIVERS: ON AND OFF THE SCREEN 167

the result is a caricature of one of Faulkner's most fully realized characters. But most of the remaining cast and the screenplay capture the essence of the novel's minor characters, especially Charles Tyner as Edmonds, the owner of the Hell Creek bottom mud patch; Ruth White, playing Miss Reba, the brothel madam; Michael Constantine (Mr. Binford), who presides over the Memphis brothel; Juano Hernandez (Uncle Possum), Ned's ally and Lucius's refuge; Clifton James (Butch Lovemaiden), the mean deputy sheriff who covets Miss Corrie (Sharon Farrell), Boon's beloved whore; and Will Geer as Boss Priest, Lucius's grandfather, looking every inch the southern gentleman.

The Reivers was shot in fourteen weeks almost entirely on location in Carrollton, Mississippi, "a time warp," according to McQueen's wife: "It was America still in the early 1900s.[2] Only the horse race was filmed on the Walt Disney ranch in Southern California. Steve McQueen seems to have had second thoughts almost immediately after agreeing to star in the picture. As his biographer Marc Eliot puts it, "Audiences wanted Steve," the star of *Bullitt* and *The Thomas Crown Affair*, to be "the king of cool, not a sweaty southern country boy." Moreover, McQueen was counting on William Wyler, one of the great Hollywood directors, who had filmed such classics as *The Little Foxes* (1941) and *The Best Years of Our Lives* (1946), to add depth and prestige to the film. But Wyler bowed out, and his replacement, Mark Rydell, dismayed McQueen, who knew the director from early work in television, and did not like him. Rydell was simply not in Wyler's league. And indeed, the film does, in some respects, go for the easy comedy of a made-for-television movie, even though the screenwriters, Irving Ravetch and Harriet Frank Jr., had successfully adapted parts of *The Hamlet*, "Spotted Horses," and "Barn Burning" as *The Long Hot Summer* (1958), starring Paul Newman, and wrote *Hud* (1963), another of Newman's best films. McQueen may well have thought their screenplay would do for him what it had accomplished for Newman.

McQueen's doubts about his taller, six-foot-five costar, Rupert Crosse, complicated the production further. Boon is supposed to be the big man in the story, not Ned McCaslin. Even worse, Crosse, an untested actor in his first big role, seemed to take too long to warm up to his part, going through several takes that tried McQueen's patience. Boon is in fact a role for a great character actor—say McQueen's contemporaries, Randy Quaid or Warren Oates—and there was simply no way for McQueen to lose himself in his part. Indeed, according to Eliot, after one or two takes McQueen had nothing left to contribute to a sharper interpretation of his character. Even with such problems, *The Reivers* was nominated for two Academy Awards: Rupert Crosse as best supporting actor (the first Black actor to be nominated in this category), and John Williams for the musical score. But in both categories the film lost: to Gig Young in *They Shoot Horses, Don't They?*, and to Burt Bacharach for *Butch Cassidy and the Sundance Kid*. *The Reivers* was a very modest success at the box office, and critics seemed unwilling to accept McQueen in an offbeat performance.

The film begins with shots of light glistening on a leaf and a boy in a boat fishing out on a calm lake, then introduces the dulcet voice of Burgess Meredith recalling life as a boy "a long time ago" in Jefferson, Mississippi, among a "pleasant and courteous people attending to our own business." It is unimaginable that Faulkner could write such a sentence, so ungrounded in particulars. The novel begins with grandfather describing the outlandish Boon Hoggenbeck and how he fit into the scheme of things in Jefferson.

Although filmed on location, the southern setting seems generic, except for a Black man picking cotton and a few shots of Black people tending garden plots beside small shacks. The action picks up with the arrival of the Winton Flyer by railcar, with the first shot of Boon and Ned standing next to one another full of anticipatory glee about the appearance of this new invention. In the novel, however, Ned never cares much for the vehicle and does not engage in the sort of bosom-buddy rivalry that the film sets up between him and Boon. What saves the film at this point is the closeup on McQueen's face in a shot that reveals a dreamy, lovesick expression, a yearning for this shiny yellow conveyance that seems to transport Boon out of his everyday life and into the realm of fantasy. But then the film turns into farce as Ned wrests control of the automobile from Boon and goes off across town on a tear, thus destroying the carefully delineated differences between characters Faulkner drew.

Of course, film foreshortens a novel's narrative, which provides context and background. Thus the film shifts quickly from Ned's joy ride, to Boss Priest's departure from town, to Lucius's lying to facilitate the unauthorized journey to Memphis. The highlight of the trip is their descent into Hell Creek bottom, with an amused Edmonds rocking on his porch just waiting for the moment when Boon will beg for his mule team to pull out the automobile. Several cutaway shots of Edmonds build on his smirk, which becomes full-throated laughter as Boon and Ned try to lever out the vehicle, splattered with mud from the spinning rear tires. The dialogue that ensues, as Edmonds brings up his team, is pure Faulkner and a classic of Southern humor. When Edmonds demands two dollars for each passenger, Boon tries to knock down the price by saying Ned is not white. The mules are color blind, Edmonds retorts.

The film includes some nice touches, such as Boon giving Miss Reba a hearty kiss when he enters the brothel, then turning to Lucius to tell him to make his manners—which includes executing a courtly bow. Meeting Miss Corrie,

THE REIVERS: ON AND OFF THE SCREEN   169

however, again spoils the scene, since she is not the big country girl turned whore of Faulkner's novel, but an elegantly dressed, beautiful model who would not be out of place in a Gilded Age painting. In short—except for the overdone makeup—she is not the girl who belongs to Faulkner's Boon, although she is a looker who might well attract Steve McQueen. At the same time, Mr. Binford's arrival at dinner and his quick, none-too-pleased glance at Lucius, signal a return to the atmosphere of Faulkner's novel. When Lucius stands to make his manners and puts out his hand, Mr. Binford, absorbed in his dinner, eyes the boy and puts a plate of food in his hand, ignoring the courtesies Lucius has been brought up to observe. When one of the girls arrives late to dinner, Mr. Binford rails about the "trouble with you bitches" who do not know how to act like ladies. A shocked Lucius bows his head. "Don't you like it or can't you get it," Mr. Binford taunts Lucius, who refuses the offer of beer and is immune to Mr. Binford's sophistries, as he argues that Boss and mother are not there, and that Lucius is "on a tear" with Boon anyway. The ugliness of the scene is true to Faulkner, as Miss Reba objects to Mr. Binford's blunt language, and Mr. Binford tells her to "use your mouth to eat your supper with."

Just as Lucius is learning his way around the whorehouse, Ned shows up outside and calls to Boon. Obviously drunk, Ned announces he has traded the automobile for a horse. Ned would never behave this way in Faulkner's world because Ned is not reckless. He calculates risk and does not go off on sprees. But in the film he is made to appear the buffoon, and Boon becomes merely a comic character who upsets the evening in the brothel when he comes crashing down the stairs to confront Ned. Unlike the taciturn Ned of the novel, whose plans are divulged in a piecemeal, laconic manner, the movie's boisterous Ned simply states that acquiring the horse—and ultimately winning a horse race along with the automobile—is the only way the group can exonerate themselves in Boss's eyes. The Ned of the novel, on the other hand, knows that all he can do is ameliorate, not wipe out, the punishment for stealing the automobile.

The film veers back on course when Deputy Sheriff Butch Lovemaiden interrupts the progress to the race site. Clifton James plays Butch with just the right amount of easygoing menace, giving Miss Corrie the eye, and establishing his authority by sending Lucius to Uncle Possum's melon patch to retrieve a melon and a saltshaker for Butch's delectation. He is going to enjoy that melon the same way he will enjoy Miss Corrie. But this superb way of dramatizing character is spoiled because Butch becomes brutal too quickly. He shoves Boon over—not an action that could occur in Faulkner's novel, where Butch is more cunning and offensive, pushing Boon a little too hard, but not hard enough to start a fight. Once again, the novelist's subtle development of action is sacrificed for a broader, slapstick humor. Juano Hernandez saves the scene with a single line (taken from the novel). When Butch says Uncle Possum knows him, Hernandez replies so dryly that no one can miss the point: "Everyone knows you, Mr. Butch." Uncle Possum is Ned's ally, who has seen Lightning in action.

After this point, the action speeds up, centering on the horse race in a series of scenes that adhere closely to Faulkner's novel. But there is a moment, when the horse race is presented in slow motion, which Burgess Meredith's awestruck, lilting voice announces as the film cuts between closeups of Lucius on the horse and the pounding of the horses on the track: "Carried on the back of Lightning, racing on a jet black shape, it took me completely. Blood, skin, bowels, bones, and memory. I was no longer held fast on earth but free, fluid, part of the air and the sun, running my first race, a man sized race, with people, grown people, more people than I could remember at one time before, watching me run it. And so I had my moment of glory, that brief fleeting glory, which of itself cannot last, but while it does it's the best game of all." These lines are not in the novel, and yet they evoke not only Faulknerian style, but the denouement of the film about a boy's coming of age—if not by any means quite the story the novelist conceived—nevertheless encompassing a moment that Faulkner himself might well have emphasized in his own screenplay. The rhythms and repetitions of the speech sum up not merely the style of *The Reivers*, but also of Faulkner stories about flying, leaving the earth, and attaining a brief kind of exaltation and apotheosis of what it means to be a striving, questing human being.

In the midst of the celebrations over the winning the horse race, Lucius looks up to see Boss Priest, whose authority is emphasized in a low angle shot making him seem statuesque in his uncompromising dignity. The stern moment is softened when Boss inquires of Lucius, "What happened to your hand?" But before Lucius can explain, Boss says, "Never mind. We can talk about it later. I can see you are busy now." Lucius keeps glancing back at Boss, as members of the crowd lift the boy to their shoulders. The scene prepares, of course, for the reckoning back home, which occurs in a beautifully shot interior scene, in which Lucius's father is seen to be about to whip him when a door is heard to open, and Boss comes down the steps. The dialogue is close to Faulkner's own. Again, the low angle shots—this time of Boss seated in a rocking chair scrutinizing a cowed Lucius—emphasize how much the boy has to answer for, which is more than a beating can possibly rectify, Boss has told Lucius's father, Maury. The deep focus of the scene, with an ashamed Lucius, his back turned away from his grandfather, standing some eight feet away, confessing, "I been telling lies." Boss says dryly, "I've been aware of that." But then he leans forward and opens his arms, telling Lucius to "come here," thus proffering his understanding of the gentleman's code exactly as Faulkner wrote it. Lucius may suffer his grandfather's loss of respect and trust for "a while," but not forever, Boss assures him—again with open arms, as Lucius runs to his grandfather's embrace. Burgess Meredith's voiceover, as in the speech about riding Lightning, admirably sums up the ethos of Faulkner's novel, as Lucius remembers "my face against the stiff collar of his shirt, and I could smell him, the starch and the shaving lotion, and the chewing tobacco. And finally the faint smell of whisky from the toddy which he took in bed every morning before he got up." As Will Geer, almost in tears himself, bids the crying boy to wash his face—as a gentleman always does—rocks back in his chair, it is hard not to believe that Boss, too, is remembering his youth and what it was like to break the rules and pay for breaking them.

Like the novel, the film wraps up loose ends. Boon wants to make it right with Lucius, who is still offended because Boon hit Corrie. McQueen, playing Boon at his ingratiating best, informs the boy that he is going to marry Corrie. The scene plays well in cinematic terms, because Lucius and Ned are seated in the automobile, which is, for once, not in motion, instead serving as a resting point for the story as these reivers reckon with the consequences of their actions. Boon, standing by the right front fender, says Lucius will feel better a year from now when he visits Boon and Corrie and their new baby, named Lucius Priest McCaslin Hoggenbeck. "Only name he could have," Boon tells the beaming Lucius, who sighs with satisfaction as Boon cranks up the Winton Flyer. Then the camera pulls back so that the automobile is shown to be on blocks, the wheels removed. Obviously Boss is taking no chances. The credits begin to roll as the threesome pretends to be setting off on another adventure.

The novel ends with a short scene between Miss Corrie and Lucius, after she has married Boon and had their child. Lucius looks at the child and remarks that it is just as ugly as Boon. Lucius wants to know what she is going to call "it." Not "it," she replies, "Him. Can't you guess?" Lucius asks "What?" "Lucius Priest Hoggenbeck," she announces, putting an end to the novel. Perhaps Faulkner's ending is just as cute as the film's, but it is a little more down-to-earth, emphasizing the impact Miss Corrie has had on Lucius. Her presence at the novel's conclusion emphasizes the sense of responsibility, obligation, and respect that are reaffirmed for Lucius. The film, on the other hand, returns Lucius to the scene of the crime. Given the film's emphasis on the adventure story aspect of the novel, this tack makes sense—if not exactly Faulkner's sense.

The film of *The Reivers*, while sometimes capturing the mood and ethos of Faulkner's novel, is nevertheless very much a Hollywood product, suiting plot and character elements to the star. Darwin Porter recounts, "[T]o virtually everyone on the set, it soon became obvious that the movie's plot was being too greatly altered from Faulkner's original."[3] Boon is an uncomfortable fit for Steve McQueen, although the actor has the physicality, ruggedness, and exuberance appropriate to playing Boon, and it was daring of the star to want to deviate from his glamorous tough guy persona. McQueen struggled to make the film authentic and objected when this line from Faulkner's novel was cut from the screenplay: "What's it going to look like, me, a white man, chauffeuring a [n----r] to Memphis." Rupert Crosse agreed with McQueen because, as Penina Spiegel reports, "[I]t was honest as well as historically accurate. That was the way people in real life *spoke*."[4]

For his part, Mitch Vogel seems pitch perfect—an achievement which, in part, can be credited to McQueen who, according to Vogel, treated the young actor in a tender, avuncular way, just as Boon does Lucius in the film.[5] Rupert Crosse played his role as written with superb grace and humor, but the character simply does not measure up to the subtleties of Faulkner' s Ned McCaslin, a role that Morgan Freeman could play to perfection in a remake of the movie.

The Reivers is, as Penina Spiegel notes, a "lark of a film, happy and infused with warmth, a slice of bygone Americana . . . a film of youth tinged with sadness at the all-too-certain knowledge of its passing."[6] In this respect, the film captures a vital aspect of Faulkner's novel, which is, after all, subtitled "A Reminiscence."

Part Four
Faulkner and Race

The White Man's "Negro" in Faulkner Country

In a long, handwritten and undated letter to Professor Floyd Watkins, John B. Cullen set out the basic story of what would become their work of collaboration: *Old Times in the Faulkner Country*, published by University of North Carolina Press in 1961.[1] Cullen had been one of Faulkner's hunting buddies, and the two men remained on cordial terms even after Cullen published his memoir. Faulkner seemed indifferent to the book, although if asked he probably would have advised Cullen not to publish it. While the book conveys important information about Faulkner's background that helps to illuminate his fiction, Watkins and Cullen sanitized important aspects of Cullen's racist attitudes, which were very much representative of his community, as can be seen when compared to John Dollard's classic *Caste and Class in a Southern Town* (1937), based on his five-month research study based in Indianola, Mississippi, about 110 miles from William Faulkner's home.[2] How much Faulkner knew about Cullen's racism cannot be determined, but what Cullen said could not have come as any surprise and might well have been repeated by others in Faulkner's circle. That Faulkner did not take part in discussions of race is almost certain, since Cullen expressed his surprise at Faulkner's support of integration and supposed the novelist was simply catering to his Northern audience. In short, Cullen never heard anything like what began to emerge in Faulkner's public statements in the 1950s. To Cullen, that Faulkner was unrecognizable. How could that public man have coexisted with the private one who hunted with arch segregationists, believers in Black inferiority as a matter of principle?

Cullen started out his letter by paying tribute to the "life and death of a dear old negro woman that was loved not only by the Falkner family but by many other white people. There was and are still millions of such characters living here in the south of both races." He was referring to Caroline Barr, the Faulkner family retainer who helped raise William Faulkner and his brothers and to Faulkner's tribute to her at the time of her death. Barr had looked after Estelle Oldham too and went to live with William and Estelle. Cullen called her "their old nurse . . . getting old but never was there a thought by the Falkners of displacing her for a younger woman in the Falkner home. She had her own room and garden, a "privileged character now around the Falkner home." Women like her, raised in slavery, soothed any anxiety Cullen may have felt about its aftermath. Of Barr, he said: "Born in slavery she now felt that the Falkner family belonged to her. It would have broken her old heart to have been forced to leave them." In fact, he is "sure that this thought ne'er entered her mind." Well, Carolina Barr left the service of the Falkner family several times and returned only after her other plans, usually having to do with marriage, did not work out. This is not to discount her affection for Falkners, but she seemed to have treated them more like a default solution to her predicaments rather than a first choice. That Faulkner cherished her is certain. Cullen mentioned how he would kill a hog and give her first pick of the parts. "He wanted to gladden her heart," Cullen observed. He caps off his tribute with saying her funeral was in the living room of Faulkner's home. So it was—much to the outrage of Barr's family, as Faulkner scholar Judith Sensibar later learned—only, however, with the aid of an African American researcher, since Sensibar knew that Barr's family would probably not level with a white woman.[3]

Cullen's paean to Barr was but a prelude to quite another recitation of race. "Now I am going to tell you of another type that did and probably still exists among the negro race. Education civilization and environment have done much to eliminate that type of negroes in the past fifty years to my personal knowledge." Cullen then relates what happened to him as a boy, when in 1909 he participated in the lynching of Nelse Patton. Cullen's father, a deputy sheriff, received a telephone call saying a "negro had just killed a woman out north of Oxford and for him to come at once." The father instructed his boys—John and his old brother A. B.—to stay home and "keep out of this." But they picked up a shotgun and set off on the route they believed the killer would travel, and they were right, hearing gunfire and spotting a "big negro running, across the railroad at Saddlers Crossing about two hundred yards ahead of it." The brothers caught up with him in a valley clearing heading toward a thicket where he could conceal himself. Patton spotted them and tried to run past John who yelled at him to stop. Patton ran and John brought him down with two blasts of squirrel shot from the shotgun. John ordered Patton to put up his hands. Patton refused,

THE WHITE MAN'S "NEGRO" IN FAULKNER COUNTRY   177

probably (John supposed) looking for an opportunity to seize the gun. Just as John was about to shoot Patton between the eyes, Sheriff Guy Taylor rode up. Taylor's search of Patton yielded a bloody razor "with one corner broke off in his pocket."

Patton, a powerful man, had nearly decapitated Mrs. McMillan. Dr. Young examined her body and discovered a piece of razor in her neck bone. Cullen had no doubt about what Patton had intended: "The purpose of that cruel vicious crime was perfectly clear. Nelse had gone to that home, watched it, and when he saw Mrs. McMillan in one room and her young sixteen year old daughter in another, entered and cut the mother's head off to get her out of his way so that he could satisfy his sexual lust on the daughter." This could have been a scene out of *Birth of a Nation*. Cullen implied that he knew his man— in fact, historian Joel Williamson discovered that Patton was well known in Oxford, a bootlegger who sold to white and Black alike. Cullen, sure he understood Patton's motivations, added: "After doing this had his plans worked out he would have probably killed the daughter." She had barely escaped his slashing razor and had run to neighbors, who had called Cullen's father.

A crowd soon gathered at the jail, where a local judge came out on the porch and pleaded with the crowd to "let the law take its course." Then Senator W. B. Sullivan made a "fiery speech telling the crowd that they would be weaklings and cowards to let such a vicious beast live until morning." The sheriff tried to prevent violence by leaving town with the keys to the jail. Cullen said his father remained as one of the guards. "Had he had the slightest doubt of Nelse's guilt I am convinced," Cullen insisted, "he would have talked to that mob and that if this had not proved successful that they would have entered the jail over his dead body." Perhaps so. John Dollard pointed out that half the time lynchings were prevented by the intervention of law enforcement and the clergy. But the worked-up mob, incited by Senator Sullivan's speech, "began pitching us boys through the jail windows and no guard in that jail could have dared shoot one of us. Soon we had a crowd inside and I and my brother held my father and the sons of the other guards held theirs in this way we took over the jail."

Although Faulkner claimed never to have witnessed a lynching, he went to school with Cullen and Cullen's older brother, so that it is hard to believe that this event did not register in twelve-year-old Billy Faulkner's memory in creating scenes like the one in *Light in August* with Percy Grimm, who flouts the authority of the local American Legion, and collects his own militia to lynch Joe Christmas. Grimm, like Cullen's young contemporaries, feels called on to exert a terrifying mastery over one Black man who surely represents to them more than one individual's crimes. "It took from eight o'clock that night to two a.m. for the mob to cut through the jail walls with sledge hammers and crowbars," Cullen reports, "and when they broke the lock off the murderer's cell Nelse had armed himself with a heavy iron coal shovel handle and from a corner near the door fought like a tiger seriously wounding three men of that mob." He was "shot to death thrown out of the jail a rope tied around his neck and drug down the street then hung to a walnut tree limb just outside the south entrance to the court house and left hanging there until the next day some time as a detriment to others who might have his same kind of ideas to see." In effect, the mob did not regard the crime as unique. The lynching was a show of power, such as law enforcement officers, could not demonstrate.

Cullen went on to detail the case of a "negro trusty over at Parchman who was given an easy job by one of the wardens. He repaid the warden's kindness by taking an axe, slipping into the room where the warden and his wife were sleeping and slaughtering them in bed. Then forcing their sixteen-year-old daughter to go with him into the woods and assaulted her several times." He "chewed her breast to shreds," before a crowd intercepted and lynched him. Cullen then took as truth the story of Emmett Till who had tried to assault a white woman. "The press in our country mad a great hurrah over this and pictures of him as the young innocent son of a hero father [Louis Till] who had given his life for our country when the truth was he was executed in France for the murder and rape of three women over there and there is plenty of reason to suspect that he may have committed other brutal crimes that will never be known." In fact, as John Edgar Wideman later discovered, Louis Till's conviction is suspect: "darkness, hoods, masks, shock, confusion made it impossible to identify the men who attacked" the women.

None of this mythologizing, needless to say, became part of the published collaboration of Cullen and Watkins, which focused more narrowly on Patton's crime without investigating, as Joel Williamson did, the close connections between Patton and the white woman he attacked. It is likely that liquor was involved, but what really happened quickly became enveloped in the lore about Black people that Cullen perpetuated in order to declare: "Such crimes that we know without doubt have been committed by negroes have caused the people of the south to oppose integration because we know—that if it is forced upon us at this time that it will renew racial strife." Not a word of this warning makes it way in *Old Time in the Faulkner Country*: "millions of men here in the south . . . will blast the daylights out of any man regardless of race regardless of the Supreme Court or anyone else who tries to brutalize our women folks." Dollard summarized the consensus Cullen spoke for: "The southern conception of the matter plainly is that without such segregation patterns for Negroes the amount of open violence between the races would be greatly increased. Their existence is therefore a matter of holding aggression in check." Dollard also pointed out the fallacy and the detriment to understanding that segregation promoted: "In case segregation be justified on the ground that it prevents race friction, one should also note the correlated disadvantage, that it prevents knowledge, sympathy, and cooperative attitudes from developing."

Did Cullen know, as John Dollard pointed out, that half of the lynchings in the South had nothing to do with sex crimes? Instead Cullen complained in another passage absent from his book: "Why is it that William Falkner [Cullen always used the family spelling of the last name] can write stories exaggerating on the worst and lowest type of white people who ever lived here in the south and the rest of us can't get the truth about the negroes published." Cullen then went on to the kind of self-exculpatory expressions that became all too familiar to Dollard: "I want to state that most of the negroes I have known have been and are good loyal citizens and I have many friends among them. However the greater majority of brutal crimes committed here in the south are committed by negroes." This is breathtaking blindness not only to the violence of lynching, but to a history of white terrorism in the post-Reconstruction, Jim Crow South, but just this sort of myopia remained a feature of William Faulkner's Oxford years.

Cullen, like Dollard's white informants, claimed to support the same rights for Black and white alike, so long as the association of the races was not forced on either race. Faulkner, Cullen argued, felt the same way and wanted the "right to choose the people he wishes to associate with. And I defy any one to force themselves upon William Falkner." Cullen, like all members of a privileged caste, could not see beyond the boundaries that had been set up for him: "The whole behavior of white caste members," Dollard reported, "is so routinized that it is only infrequently possible to see the aggression which invests their segregation practices against Negroes." Is it any wonder, then, that Cullen lamented: "Faulkner didn't bring out the good as he should but he has brought out the fact of the mistreatment of the [n----r]."

In a recorded interview with Watkins, Cullen expatiated on race: "There is a difference in the nature of a white man and a [n----r]. There are good [n----rs], bad [n----rs]. Good white folks, bad white folks. But God did not make them the same." Well, what was the difference? "Whites have raised [n----rs] from savagery." Cullen saw no irony in an additional comment on Patton's lynching: "I was proud. Somebody cut his balls off. Somebody scalped him."

The talk of a vestigial savagery in "[n----rs]" is what John Dollard heard again and again. In the absence of slavery and of total control, African

Americans were required to obey a rigid caste system that could only be maintained by "quick active aggression" to punish any deviation from the white supremacist norm.

That norm is often exposed in Faulkner fiction, but nowhere do we find a character like John Cullen in the novels and stories, although Cullen comes to mind in Gavin Stevens's account of a white storekeeper in *Intruder in the Dust*: "He has nothing against what he calls [n----rs]. If you ask him, he will probably tell you he likes them even better than some white folks he knows and he will believe it. . . . All he requires is that they act like [n----rs]." Cullen hunted by William Faulkner's side but never understood the other side withheld from him. And perhaps to get along himself, William Faulkner never felt equipped outside his fiction to reckon with the John Cullens he had to live with most days of his life. And that is why Cullen, with a good conscience, could say when affirming the separation of the races, that the Faulkner he knew was the Faulkner who "believes like I do."

The Twilight of Man in "Delta Autumn"

On December 16, 1940, Faulkner's story, "Delta Autumn" arrived in his agent Harold Ober's office. At Christmas, his stepson received a gift of Earnest Albert Hooton's *Twilight of Man* (1939), inscribed to "Malcolm A. Franklin / from Mama and Billy."[1] Malcolm, a herpetologist, the family scientist, began reading in biology and anthropology "under the spur of his stepfather's interest," Joseph Blotner writes in his one-volume Faulkner biography.

By the time of *The Twilight of Man*, Hooton was a nationally known figure, a prominent advocate of eugenic practices that would improve the human breed, although the word eugenics never appears in the book the Faulkners gave to Malcolm. But the question of race, and the fate of humanity—such a great concern for Hooton—suffuses "Delta Autumn" and *Go Down, Moses* (1942), the novel that absorbed the story. Even if Faulkner had not read Hooton, the ideas in *The Twilight of Man*, were very much a part of the ether, which Malcolm may well have discussed with his stepfather, his mentor. In fact, in a memoir, *Bitterweeds*, Malcolm claimed to have spent more time in William Faulkner's company than anyone else. Faulkner had shaped his sensibility over the previous decade, and later in his diaries and letters to his mother, Malcolm would attest to his pride in his kinship with a great man and writer.[2]

I include all this biographical background to suggest that not only through his books but through his nurturing of Malcolm, Faulkner was pursuing certain deeply founded principles that he had absorbed in his experience and that became explicit in "Delta Autumn." It may well have been that Hooton confirmed what Faulkner had already derived from his acute observations of human beings and of nature.

Although Faulkner often said that life is motion and change is inevitable, that did not mean he believed in human progress—or at the least, human advancement was not a given. To prevail was not the same as to improve. As

181

he said to Malcolm Cowley, life was the same "frantic steeple-chase toward nothing everywhere and man stinks the same stink no matter where in time."[3]

This is where Hooton is close to Faulkner's thinking. "As an anthropologist, I am perturbed by the fact that human invention has outstripped man's organic development, and his control of nature his control of himself." Such statements nod toward *Go Down, Moses*, which demonstrates that by so efficiently eliminating the wilderness in which Ike McCaslin hunts, human beings have lost touch with the very environment out of which they have emerged. You have to understand the "organic basis of mechanical achievement and the cause of man's physical and social lag in relation to his material progress," Hooton proclaimed in *The Twilight of Man*. Without the proper scientific study of man's biological development, all the other disciplines of knowledge will not benefit humankind, the anthropologist, like the novelist, asserts. "Machines get better and better, while man gets worse and worse."

Hooton wrote in the aftermath of World War I and the imminent breakout of World War II. Like Faulkner, he doubted the efficacy of politics and never overlooked an opportunity to scorn politicians, totalitarian and democratic alike, for their dishonesty in government, because "man has always identified himself with his own creator, who, according to Genesis, 'saw everything that he had made, and, behold, it was very good.'" Morons had put into public office "persons of similar endowment, or men who successfully substitute for real intelligence a kind of low cunning." Much of the American myth of the settling of the frontier, the "Winning of the West," Hooton dispatched in a pithy phrase: the "alternation of massacre and fraud." The future, he argued, "depends not upon New Deals and the promulgation of political and moral platitudes, but upon the maintenance of high qualities in human organisms. Progressive evolution of an animal organism is a biological phenomenon; it is not a producer of politics, industry, labor, economics, nor even of medical science." Hooton quoted Bernard Shaw on man as "only an ape with acquirements."

Sounding like Faulkner, Hooton contended those acquirements can be retained only if an organism progresses." In short, man is "an animal which has forgotten itself." Progress for the human species, Hooton warned, is impossible without understanding the animal nature of man,[4] and how that nature has been circumvented by geniuses who have "made it possible for millions to live comfortably and luxuriously without even understanding the machines which produce for them." He called this ignorance the "wages of biological sin," a crime, really, against humankind itself.

To Hooton, humanity was in a bad way. Faulkner, attracted to twilight as an evocation of time, decay, sex, and death, may have found in *The Twilight of Man* a harbinger of his darkest thoughts about the degeneracy—one of

Hooton's favorite words—of mankind, even as Faulkner shared with Hooton a hope that it was not too late to excite a positive response to the coming calamity, or doom—another word Faulkner liked, and which strikes at the heart of Ike McCaslin's attachment to the wilderness in "Delta Autumn":

> Because it was his land, although he had never owned a foot of it. He had never wanted to, not even after he saw plain its ultimate doom, watching it retreat year by year before the onslaught of axe and saw and log-lines and then dynamite and tractor plows, because it belonged to no man. It belonged to all; they had only to use it well, humbly and with pride. Then suddenly he knew why he had never wanted to own any of it, arrest at least that much of what people called progress, measure his longevity at least against that much of its ultimate fate. It was because there was just exactly enough of it. He seemed to see the two of them—himself and the wilderness—as coevals, his own span as a hunter, a woodsman, not contemporary with his first breath but transmitted to him, assumed by him gladly, humbly, with joy and pride, from that old Major de Spain and that old Sam Fathers who had taught him to hunt, the two spans running out together, not toward oblivion, nothingness, but into a dimension free of both time and space where once more the untreed land warped and wrung to mathematical squares of rank cotton for the frantic old-world people to turn into shells to shoot at one another, would find ample room for both—the names, the faces of the old men he had known and loved and for a little while outlived, moving again among the shades of tall unaxed trees and sightless brakes where the wild strong immortal game ran forever before the tireless belling immortal hounds, falling and rising phoenixlike to the soundless guns.

"Delta Autumn," let alone the whole of *Go Down, Moses*, does not endorse Ike's decision to have nothing to do with land ownership and his patrimony, but at the same time the awareness of what it means to plunder the land must be paramount as we go forward and shoot one another in war and sever the ties to nature that has made us what we are.

By losing ties to the land, humankind loses a kinship with itself—a fate that overtakes Ike in "Delta Autumn," notwithstanding his reverence for nature. Alone in his tent during a hunting trip, he is awakened by Roth Edmonds, who has accepted ownership of the land, the birthright Ike has renounced. "There will be a message here some time this morning, looking for me. Maybe it wont come. If it does, give the messenger this and tell

184   FAULKNER AND RACE

h—say I said No." Edmonds hands Ike an envelope containing a "thick sheaf of banknotes." Then Edmonds is more explicit: "Tell her No . . . Tell her." Ike compares Roth's behavior to "coon-hunting," Faulkner's ironic wording for what Ike is about to learn about kinship and race. He berates Roth with a question: "What did you promise her that you haven't the courage to face her and retract?" Roth replies "Nothing!" This is all of it. Tell her I said no." All of what? Roth leaves without saying more.

Ike hears an approaching boat which seems virtually simultaneous with Roth's departure, as if there have been "no interval" as the tent flap lifts again and a young woman with an infant swaddled in a blanket enters. Ike cries out: "Is that his? . . . Don't lie to me!" She says yes and tells him Roth has gone. "Yes, he's gone," Ike replies, "You wont jump him here. Not this time. I don't reckon even you expected that." He acts as though the woman has been hunting Roth, as if he is her prey, as he hands her the envelope. Instead of taking the money, she says: "You're Uncle Isaac." He takes her address to him as simply a recognition of what Faulkner calls Ike at the beginning of "Was," the first story in *Go Down, Moses*: "uncle to half a county and father to no one." She tears open the envelope and as the notes spill out on Ike's blanket, she says "That's just money." Ike questions her and confirms that Roth has not offered marriage, and she has not expected a proposal from a man she has been involved with for less than two months. So what does she want? Ike asks. She begins to recite the McCaslin family history and says in regard to Roth: "He's not a man yet. You spoiled him. You, and Uncle Lucas and Aunt Mollie. But mostly you." She tells a dumbfounded Ike that he spoiled Roth when "you gave to his grandfather that land which didn't belong to him, not even half of it by will or even law." He treats her like an educated, but loose Northern woman going off with Roth and getting pregnant. He reveals how obtuse he has become when he asks, "Haven't you got any folks at all?" She does, mentioning an aunt in Vicksburg who took in washing, and that detail suddenly triggers recognition:

> He sprang, still seated even, flinging himself backward onto one arm, awry-haired, glaring. Now he understood what it was she had brought into the tent with her, what old Isham had already told him by sending the youth to bring her in to him—the pale lips, the skin pallid and dead-looking yet not ill, the dark and tragic and foreknowing eyes. Maybe in a thousand or two thousand years in America, he thought. But not now! Not now! He cried, not loud, in a voice of amazement, pity, and outrage: "You're a [n----r]!"

THE TWILIGHT OF MAN IN "DELTA AUTUMN"   185

"Yes," she said. "James Beauchamp—you called him Tennie's Jim though he had a name—was my grandfather. I said you were Uncle Isaac." Tennie's Jim is a part of many memorable scenes in *The Bear*, the centerpiece of *Go Down, Moses*. He holds Lion, "the passive and still trembling bitch," who, in the words of Ike's mixed-race mentor, Sam Fathers, "would have to be brave once so she could keep on calling herself a dog." Tennie's Jim pours the whiskey which is like a sacrament to the hunters. He holds the hounds on leash, saddles the mules, wakes Ike up on the morning when he and Boon go into town for whiskey. Tennie's Jim is the Black man who pulls the towsack off of the horse that Boon and Ike purchased, and he is the one who is sent to the doctor for Boon, Lion, and Sam after they bring down the bear "Old Ben," Faulkner's Moby-Dick. He stays with Sam after the white men leave.

This family history is what the woman has brought into the tent with her, confounding Ike who cannot imagine a world where miscegenation and marriage are conceivable in the same sentence. He banishes her, saying "I can do nothing for you! Cant nobody do nothing for you!" But then asks her to wait and offers the money again, which she rejects saying she does not need it. She and Roth have an understanding: "Besides the money he sent to Vicksburg. Provided. Honor and code too. That was all arranged." However, at his insistence, she takes up the money, and then he asks her to wait again, the "dry old man's fingers touching for a second the smooth young flesh where the strong old blood ran after its long lost journey back to home." As a young man Ike had gone in search of Tennie's Jim, and now he murmurs: "Tennie's Jim." He asks her to wait a third time as he rises from his bed to give her a hunting horn, "the one which General Compson had left him in his will." She thanks him. He advises her to go North and marry a man of her race:

> "You are young, handsome, almost white; you could find a black man who would see in you what it was you saw in him, who would ask nothing of you and expect less and get even still less than that, if it's revenge you want. Then you will forget all this, forget it ever happened, that he ever existed—" until he could stop it at last and did, sitting there in his huddle of blankets during the instant when, without moving at all, she blazed silently down at him. Then that was gone too. She stood in the gleaming and still dripping slicker, looking quietly down at him from under the sodden hat. "Old man," she said, "have you lived so long and forgotten so much that you dont remember anything you ever knew or felt or even heard about love?"

After half-acknowledging and half-repudiating his own kin, Ike rejects the contemporary scene in a tirade worthy of Hooton's own revulsion at the "horrible state of affairs in which 'civilization' has involved itself." Man's tools, in Hooton's harangue, are "no longer accessories, the tail now wags the dog and even thinks for him." Are there, Hooton wonders, "uncorrupted minds which yet arrest the course of man's degeneration"? Ike thinks not:

> This land which man has deswamped and denuded and deriverer in two generations so that white men can own plantations and commute every night to Memphis and black men own plantations and ride in jim crow cars to Chicago to live in millionaires' mansions on Lakeshore Drive, where white men rent farms and live like [n----rs] and [n----rs] crop on shares and live like animals, where cotton is planted and grows man-tall in the very cracks of the sidewalks, and usury and mortgage and bankruptcy and measureless wealth, Chinese and African and Aryan and Jew, all breed and spawn together until no man has time to say which one is which nor cares. . . . No wonder the ruined woods I used to know dont cry for retribution! he thought: The people who have destroyed it will accomplish its revenge.

In spite of Ike's racism, he seems similar to Hooton in excoriating the whole of humanity, which results in a kind of perverse belief in equality. "I stand firmly upon the platform of racial equality," Hooton declared, rejecting the idea of inferior or malign races: "the range and mean of individual capacity within the several human races has never been proved to differ significantly. Each has, in all probability, its own array of points of strength, offset by weaknesses; and these points do not always coincide in all of the different races. Add them all together in any single race, and I am afraid that it amounts to zero—or, in other words, it comes out even." But Ike cannot conceive of Hooton's next step: race mixing, selecting for "survival those individuals in whom fortuitously or by genetic law the strong qualities of the parent races are combined, and eliminate the rest." Sounds like eugenics, which Faulkner, so far as I know, never endorsed. And though he made comments about how the Black and white races did not wish to congregate or copulate, he also suggests that in three hundred years Black and white would be so assimilated that race itself would not be an issue. This seems to be where Shreve is headed at the end of *Absalom, Absalom!* when he declares "in a few thousand years I who regard you will also have sprung from the loins of African kings."

The question, though, of degeneracy that provoked Hooton plagues "Delta Autumn," and is mixed in with earlier talk, before Ike's tent scene diatribe,

THE TWILIGHT OF MAN IN "DELTA AUTUMN" 187

about politics and hunting animals—not coons but deers, especially the doe Ike is certain has been killed at the end of the story. Like Hooton, Faulkner returns, again and again, to the biological nature of human experience, casting doubt on history as the way to explain human actions. "Times are different now," one of the hunters says, acknowledging the diminution of the wilderness: "There was game then" Ike agrees. Another puts in a dig at Roth and his mistress: "Besides, they shot does then. . . . As it is now, we aint got but one doe-hunter in—." He is cut off by Roth who directs his ire at Ike: "And better men hunted it." Ike counters: "There are good men everywhere, at all times. Most men are. Some are just unlucky, because most men are a little better than their circumstances give them a chance to be. And I've known some that even the circumstances couldn't stop." This is a view of human nature quite at odds with his tent scene broadside. Roth's choice of words in his attack on Ike is especially Hootian: "So you've lived almost eighty years. . . . And that's what you finally learned about the other animals you lived among. I suppose the question to ask you is, where have you been all the time you were dead?" This put down silences everyone until Ike says "Maybe so. . . . But if being what you call alive would have learned me any different, I reckon I'm satisfied wherever it was I've been."

The argument is over human nature, with Roth contending that man is an animal who behaves only when a man in blue with a badge is watching him. Ike denies that, and so do the other hunters. "I still believe," Ike affirms as the tension mounts, and what he believes is the love of men and women, which he holds sacred, and which Roth scoffs at. He has already told his companions that this will be his last hunt, a declaration that provokes the question "Why?" Because Roth has lost the belief Ike clings to. "After Hitler gets through with it?" Roth asks. "Or Smith or Jones or Roosevelt or Willkie or whatever he will call himself in this country?" Sounding like Hooton in his dismissal of New Deals, Roth rejects the argument that "We'll stop him in this country. . . . Even if he calls himself George Washington." Roth is skeptical of gestural patriotism, the "singing God bless American in bars at midnight and wearing dime-store flags in our lapels." Ike resists this defeatism, even though he acknowledges its force: "This country is a little mite stronger than any one man or group of men, outside of it or even inside of it either. I reckon, when the time comes and some of you have done got tired of hollering we are whipped if we dont go to war and some more are hollering we are whipped if we do, it will cope with one Austrian paper-hanger, no matter what he will be calling himself." Referring to the Civil War Ike notes that "better men than any of them you named tried to tear it in two with a war, and they failed." Roth won't have it:

Half the people without jobs and half the factories closed by strikes. Half the people on public dole that wont work and half that couldn't work even if they would. Too much cotton and corn and hogs, and not enough for people to eat and wear. The country full of people to tell a man how he cant raise his own cotton whether he will or wont, and Sally Rand with a sergeant's stripes and not even the fan couldn't fill the army rolls. Too much not-butter and not even the guns—

The debate between Ike and Roth reflects the tensions in Faulkner's own psyche and his role as farmer and hunter decrying the desecration of the land he loved in the name of progress and the New Deal and honoring, all the same, a national purpose he served in his patriotic Hollywood scripts and his later service for the State Department. He dreaded his own sense of doom, that he was witness to the twilight of man, even as he volunteered for military duty in World War II knowing he was too old to last a week in combat. No single character could ever speak for him because he was suspended between polar opposites. Ike's own final riposte to Roth relies on his faith in families as what men in war ultimately are fighting for. So it is all the more terrible that Ike should let down his own principles when he meets Roth's mixed race lover. That hunting horn is, perhaps, a feeble gesture of consanguinity but it counts. Ike has defeated himself, but in his tragic awareness of his own defeat, the family carries on, no matter how rent it has been by the racism of his patrimony. That tragic sense that is both a loss and gain for humanity is more than Hooton could imagine in the fading light of his own pessimism, which has a purchase on Faulkner's imagination that his art nevertheless transcends.

"Shooting Negroes"

William Faulkner supported the Montgomery Bus Boycott, begun on December 5, 1955, and ended December 20, 1956, when segregated public transportation was declared unconstitutional. In the midst of the national uproar about integration, journalist Russell Warren Howe interviewed Faulkner, who said:

> I don't like enforced integration any more than I like enforced segregation. If I had to choose between the United States government and Mississippi, then I'll choose Mississippi. . . . As long as there's a middle road, all right, I'll be on it. But if it came to fighting I'd fight for Mississippi against the United States even if it meant going out in the streets and shooting Negroes. After all, I'm not going out to shoot Mississippians.

In *The Free World: Art and Thought in the Cold War*, Louis Menand notes that "Faulkner was speaking in the context of a bus boycott, which does not even count as civil disobedience, since it breaks no laws." So why was he so riled up?" That seems to be the implication of Menand's comment.

For Faulkner, the context was not merely a bus boycott, but that is all Menand chooses to see: "The remarks about shooting Negroes (who were apparently not Mississippians) got attention," including reports in *The New York Times* and *Time*. "Faulkner tried to retract them, hinting that he had been drunk (certainly a possibility). But the damage was done." Why Menand says a possibility is mystifying. Joseph Blotner's edition of *Selected Letters* includes Faulkner's admission to Joan Williams that he had been drinking for days. He was wrought up, but what troubled him was not a bus boycott, and he did not retract what he said to Howe.

It may be that Faulkner did not remember exactly what he said. Howe insisted he was relying on his own verbatim shorthand notes. Faulkner never disputed what Howe wrote but simply repudiated his remarks as nothing a sane man would say. Faulkner in the 1950s began to experience blackouts and even had himself medically examined because he said he was not himself. The medical results were inconclusive or seem so now since all we have to go on was Faulkner's report that a doctor said there was something about his brain that made his responses to drinking abnormal.[1] In short, Faulkner might well have thought he had been out of his mind during that talk with Howe.

But let's return to the Montgomery Bus Boycott, which Menand takes as the "context" for Faulkner's remarks. It wasn't. Or rather, the Boycott was just part of the accumulating pressures on Faulkner, who had responded positively to the *Brown v. Board of Education*, and thus brought down on him the wrath not only of the South, and of Oxford where he lived, but of his own family that had disowned his support for integration and for a single school system for Blacks and whites alike. This wasn't merely a difference of opinion in the Faulkner family. It went much deeper than that.

Faulkner's brother John had said he would take up arms to oppose integration. His opinion was not singular. In her memoir, Dean Faulkner Wells describes a scene in which her grandmother (Maud, Faulkner's mother) denied that the Declaration of Independence applied to Black people. No one in the Faulkner family of his generation ever spoke in favor of equal rights or integration. Phil Stone, Faulkner's mentor, and his hunting buddy, John Cullen, supposed that Faulkner's support for integration reflected his desire to appease his Northern audience. Other than a radical like historian, Jim Silver, who taught at the University of Mississippi, and had Faulkner's stepdaughter in his class, no one in Faulkner's community publicly supported his position that Mississippi should abolish segregated schools.

That Faulkner had a reputation for going it alone, that he seemed aloof from his community's denigration of his opinions and even his livelihood as a writer, is a commonplace in Faulkner biography. But when it came to family, when it came to confronting his mother about the race issue, it seems that he could not bring himself to argue with her. We do not even know if he ever had a conversation about the subject with her, and they saw one another virtually every day while he resided in Oxford. She was the only one in his family privy to this most private man's comments about his fiction. In his community, he does not seem ever to have spoken out about the treatment of Black people. So when his comments in the national press began to appear after he won the Nobel Prize, his family and neighbors were shocked that he seemed to take the side of northerners who agitated for civil rights.

He seems to have had some contentious words with his brother John. That much we know because he worked on three drafts of a letter to the Memphis *Commercial Appeal* criticizing his brother's racist attack on the Supreme

Court and the drive toward integration. We do not know exactly what John said to his brother, but it seems certain that John expressed a willingness to engage in violence, if necessary, to protect the segregationist status quo. In short, this was the context in which Faulkner had declared he would take up arms if integration was forced upon Mississippians. In his muddled mind, at the moment he said those fatal words, Mississippians would not have included Black people, because, in that drunken state he equated defense of his native land with his family, white forebears, and African Americans who served his family—not those "Negroes" in the streets, who were not Mississippians because they took the side of the federal government.

To say Faulkner was not in his right mind when he said he would "shoot Negroes"—if pushed to the extremes of resisting federal power—is not to absolve him of blame. He knew better and had to be condemned for his reactionary statements. In other comments he made in Virginia, while teaching at the university, and in Japan, it is clear that he never was able to quite relinquish the idea of a war of northern aggression.[2] To the Japanese, he said he understood them because his own land had suffered from a ruthless occupation.[3] He was alluding then to what was still a governing view of Reconstruction, abetted by southern and northern historians alike, that Reconstruction was a time of turmoil when Black people, gaining their rights, had succumbed to corruption and worse—epitomized in that scene in *Birth of a Nation*, in which Blacks shove whites shoved off the street. Faulkner had seen a stage version of *The Clansman*, the novel *Birth of a Nation* adapted, and a copy of the novel, given to him by a teacher, was in his library at the time of his death. Everything in Faulkner's culture taught him that Black people were not ready for equality and freedom as practiced by their former masters.

Coupled with this notion of backward former slaves is the myth of African primitivism. Faulkner thought he was complimenting Black people when he said in a talk to Virginians that the Black race had come so far in a few generations and had produced, for example, a Ralph Bunche, winner of the 1950 Nobel Peace Prize, who, by the way, could not stay in a Charlottesville Hotel but had to be accommodated on the grounds of the University of Virginia. Behind Faulkner's "compliment" to the progress of Black people was a southern white boy's schooling in the idea of slaves who had been brought to the American continent and civilized. Without this white intervention in African history, in other words, the natives (savages) would have remained in a retrograde state. Faulkner was hardly alone in his views. Menand cites William F. Buckley's defense of unequal rights, saying white southerners should prevail, "politically and culturally," in areas in which it does not predominate numerically . . . because, for the time being, it is the advanced race."

This deluded sort of support for white supremacy shows up to comical effect in *Flags in the Dust* (1929) when Caspey, returned from the war, is clobbered by old Bayard for being uppity. Home from abroad, Caspey has new ideas about his status, and those have to be quashed. He appears like one of those Blacks in early Hollywood films who try to act like "the quality." From the white point of view he is putting on airs. He does not know his place. *Flags in the Dust*, by and large, accepts the segregationist status quo, just as William Faulkner returned from RAF training in Toronto, accepted it. His letters then are not only full of racial slurs, but in one instance he even brags about intimidating a Black customs official so that his trunk is not inspected. Even a decade later, he strikes the White supremacist chord when he announces to his mother that he will no longer be published by Horace Liveright (a Jew) but by white people (Harcourt, Brace).[4]

And yet every novel after *Flags in the Dust* tells a different story—one that refutes white supremacy, in characters like Joe Christmas in *Light in August*, Charles Bon in *Absalom, Absalom!* and Lucas Beauchamp in *Go Down, Moses* and *Intruder in the Dust*. The very category of race, of putting a premium on one's blood, is questioned, which is to say the very idea of southern whiteness, as a concept, is subverted.

The Faulkner of those novels never quite makes it into his public statements. Why is, of course, a matter of debate. One simple answer is that Faulkner, the man, lost his nerve. He simply could not continue to live in Mississippi according to the implications of his own novels. Actually, he could not live anywhere and at the same time abrogate his upbringing. When he took his family to California, his African American driver, Jack Oliver, treated their arrival as though they were now in a foreign country, telling Mr. Faulkner that he had the "weak trembles." Yet as soon as Oliver acclimated to California, he no longer answered the phone by announcing that this was the Faulkner residence. Picking up a phone one day, he answered by identifying himself and asking the caller to whom did he wish to speak. An angry Faulkner chastised Oliver for not answering in the proper manner, saying this was the Faulkner residence. Jack Oliver did not return with the Faulkners to Mississippi. We know this because Estelle Faulkner told the story to journalist Robert Cantwell, staying in the Faulkner home. Cantwell kept that story in his notes, and it did not appear in the Faulkner profile he published in *Time*.[5]

John Cullen said that no Black character like the independent Lucas Beauchamp could have survived in Mississippi. William Faulkner would have agreed. But by creating Lucas Beauchamp, in effect Faulkner, on the page at least, was conceiving of a character who could exist in Mississippi, and by creating such a character he was exploring the rigidified caste structure that he himself could not abridge by shortening the distance between Black and white behavior. Lucas is a natural born aristocrat, refusing an inferior station, and claiming a right of pedigree that has its origins, ironically, in slavery. He is a direct descendant of white slave masters whereas Chick Mallison belongs to a white branch of less importance—as does Lucius Priest in *The Reivers*. It is almost as if, in such instances, Faulkner thought he could surmount the divisions of race by shifting attention to the claims of caste.

Only stories of the kind Faulkner created can assimilate the contradictions that he lived out in Mississippi and took with him when he traveled. On the one hand, he advanced the notion in public talks that the races could never comfortably mix, marry, and so on, and that both races felt that way, even if he realized that, legally, the barriers to racial equality had to be demolished. On the other hand, he has Shreve at the end of *Absalom, Absalom!* talking about the future in which he will have descended from the loins of African kings, which is to say the very question of race will have become moribund. White and Black will have blended. Well, how will that happen if the races don't mix? That question, so far as I know, Faulkner never addressed. His stories are far more powerful than anything he could say about the stories or about the issues the stories churned up. To Jean Stein, Faulkner claimed that unlike many of his Southern male contemporaries, he never had sex with a Black woman.[6]

Contemporary comment on Faulkner, exemplified by Louis Menand, is both ahistorical and ill attuned to the exigencies of biography, with no curiosity, and perhaps no time, to think about the man and his work in a book that is busily surveying the Cold War landscape. Menand is hardly alone, when reviews of a book like Michael Gorra's about Faulkner and the Civil War are headlined: "What to Do About William Faulkner?"[7] Our greatest writer is now viewed in the public prints as an embarrassment. It is a more complicated story, of course, as examination of contemporary scholarship on Faulkner shows. But even in the academy professors worry about how to introduce Faulkner into the classroom in front of students who want to draw their own color lines.[8]

Just now interest in James Baldwin has revived, so it is not surprising that Menand quotes Baldwin's statement that Faulkner is "so plaintive concerning this 'middle of the road' from which 'extremist' elements of both races are driving him that it does not seem unfair to ask just what he has been doing there until now. . . . Why—and how—does one move from the middle of the road where one was aiding Negroes into the streets—to shoot them?" Ralph Ellison and Albert Murray (great admirers of Faulkner's fiction) felt betrayed: "he forgets the people he's talking about are Negroes and they're everywhere in the States and without sectional allegiance when it comes to the problem," Murray said. To Faulkner's go-slow advice, Ellison observed that Black people had been waiting a while for three hundred years. . . . Faulkner thinks he can end this great historical action just as he ends a dramatic action in one of his novels." Murray noted Faulkner's travels abroad "selling humanity for the State Dept and then going back home pulling that kind of crap at the first sign of real progress."[9]

Faulkner's comments about shooting Black people will never be less than shocking and reprehensible, but how those comments are contextualized, and how we get to Menand's summary judgment, reveals how, over time, views of Faulkner and of race have evolved. The first book by an African American scholar, *Faulkner and the Negro* (1965) by Charles H. Nilon does not address the Howe interview, since Nilon is exclusively concerned with Faulkner's treatment of Black characters in his novels and short stories. Nilon nonetheless offers a context for considering Faulkner's offensive remarks, by describing what Nilon calls a "social theory" which is derived from Faulkner's analysis of "a misuse of power. Federal intervention to correct social evils in the South would, from Faulkner's point of view, also involve the use of power, a use which he thinks would continue the evils that should be destroyed."

It is a pity that Nilon does not apply his statement of Faulkner's social theory to the Howe interview, preferring to stay safely within the precincts of Faulkner's fiction. But we can extrapolate from Nilon's description of that social theory to say that sometimes, going into the streets to oppose the centralized state, as in *A Fable*, is the individual's only recourse.[10] Faulkner's distrust of governmental power cannot be exaggerated.[11] It appears everywhere—in his novels as well as in his movie scripts. In his adaptation of *Drums Along the Mohawk*, for example, he transforms Kenneth Roberts's historical novel about the American Revolution into a three-way conflict—not only between the British and the Americans, but between local colonists and the Continental Congress.

In "Faulkner and the Howe Interview" (*CLA Journal*, December 1967), Charles D. Peavy summarized the reaction of many who treated Faulkner as unreconstructed racist. Peavy made a distinction between Faulkner's moral and ethical support of racial equality and his insistence he had to side with his native land, even if it meant, as it did for his great-grandfather, fighting against the federal government. He also noted Faulkner's later comment that he would never have permitted the statement about shooting Black people to appear in print. He takes Faulkner's comment that no sane or sober man would make such statements as a "repudiation" of them. Faulkner's comments leave open some ambiguity, given what he suggested about his disordered state to Joan Williams.

The diligent Peavy contacted Russell Warren Howe, who stood by his report and noted Faulkner "gave no impression of inebriation; he was slow-spoken as usual, but didn't slur, misconstrue sentences or do anything else associated with people who are drunk. He chose the time and place of the appointment himself. . . . And confirmed it a few hours before, so presumably felt himself in a fit state to be interviewed. I sat about three or four feet from him the whole time, and caught no odor of bourbon." In a second letter, Howe conceded the perhaps he was "too unfamiliar with Faulkner" to recognize his drunken state.[12] Another journalist, Horace Judson, told Peavy he had two sources in the "academic and publishing worlds" that had confirmed Faulkner's drinking.[13]

In 1968, James B. Meriwether and Michael Millgate reprinted the Howe interview in *Lion in the Garden: Interviews with William Faulkner, 1926–1962* and observed that the statement about shooting Black people had been "quoted out of context." They also say Faulkner took "pains" to repudiate the statement, which was at odds with what he said in the rest of the interview. They note that because the interview appeared in a short version in the London *Sunday Times* and a longer one in *The Reporter*, the "interview must be treated with considerable caution, not only because Faulkner repudiated parts of it, but also because the two published versions differ from one another." Differ, yes, but the two versions do not contradict each other.

In 1974, Joseph Blotner's monumental biography provided more context, noting that African American Autherine Lucy's attempt to enroll at the University of Alabama had made Faulkner frantic, fearing that she would be killed. Blotner reports that Faulkner's support of integration had provoked phone calls threatening his life. Southerners were wrong, he told Howe and anybody else who would listen, but they would fight to maintain the status quo. Blotner comments very little on why Faulkner made his remark about shooting Black people, except to say that his brother John's way of saying he would shoot Black people had "slipped perversely" into Faulkner's own speech.

Would a journalist, as well established as Howe, make up such an inflammatory statement? To quash Howe, Faulkner, who carried no gun, could have simply issued a one-sentence statement: "I didn't say that." Instead his "repudiation" came with a good deal of leeway. In his 1984 revised and updated Faulkner biography, Blotner added this important sentence, after explaining the interview had taken place in the office of Faulkner's editor: "Saxe Commins did not dispute Russell Howe's convincing rejoinder and assertion of accuracy."

At a 1977 Faulkner and Yoknapatawpha Conference, in a talk on "Faulkner and Race," Margaret Walker Alexander went much further even than Baldwin, Ellison, and Murray in her critique:

Black students and even some whites who read "The Bear" may be bothered by some things in it that they see as racist. Faulkner was, in fact, a racist—but two or three things are important to note. First of all, he knew that and knew it thirty-five or forty years before anyone much talked in such terms. Secondly . . . he knew that the whole of American society in these United States—North and South—was racist. Thirdly, he moved beyond where many people are today to discover that in an important way, to say one is racist is to say one is human and the product of his culture. And, fourthly, and finally, and more importantly, he did not conclude that this realization (that is to be a racist is to be human) removed any of the guilt and responsibility from the perceiver. For Faulkner devoted a good share of his work, his ability, to the problem of coming to terms with his racism (in a social context). Learning this, and attempting to do something about it, is what "The Bear" is all about, particularly part five.[14]

For those who so admire Faulkner's brilliant fiction, the label "racist" is hard to accept in such a bald way, and biographers continued to ignore or palliate the possibility that he would shoot Black people.

Biographies by Judith Wittenberg and David Minter in 1979 and 1980 do not mention the Howe interview. Walter Taylor, in *Faulkner's Search for a South* (1983) did better, pointing out that Faulkner's comments on the Howe interview were "agonized and ambiguous, strained to the point of inanity to avoid outright denial of what they were written to deny."

Should one statement about shooting Black people stand, as it does in Menand's book, to characterize Faulkner's feelings and convictions? Certainly not, but how can a biographer ignore it? Yet in a 484-page biography, Richard Gray does just that. Also odd is Jay Parini's using the statement about shooting Black people as an epigraph to a chapter in *One Matchless Time: A Life of William Faulkner* (2004) and then virtually ignoring the controversy over its significance.

In a Yoknapatawpha Conference collection devoted to *Faulkner and Race* (1986), there is only one statement in a footnote referring to Faulkner's "intemperate outburst" as "anomalous." In *William Faulkner: The Man and Artist* (1987), Stephen B. Oates seems to think Faulkner complained that he had been misquoted. But that's not what Faulkner said. He said that if he had seen the interview beforehand, he would have taken out the quotation about shooting Black people. If you have done interviews, or understand how most interviews work, the interviewees sometimes give interviews with the stipulation that the interviewee will see the interview before it is printed so as to correct or change any imputations. Before the publication of his *Paris Review* interview, Faulkner went over it carefully with Jean Stein, but he did not request that Howe show him the interview before it was published. Faulkner did say he had never held the opinion Howe had reported, but, again, that's not the same thing as saying he did not say it. Oates treats Faulkner's words as unfortunate: He had "blurted out things that would haunt him for the rest of his life. No wonder he thought that man's greatest curse was the ability to speak."

Frederick Karl, in *William Faulkner: American Writer* (1989) is prone to thinking that Faulkner was "out of his mind with anguish and alcohol." Karl is the first biographer to suggest that Howe goaded Faulkner: "This note of hostility drove Faulkner crazy and created the context for his reply—to say something off the wall which Howe could then use to support what he thought all along: that every white Southerner, including Faulkner, was a racist at heart." Karl's assumptions are presumptuous biography. He knows what Howe really thinks. He knows why Faulkner reacted with a reprehensible reply. Then Karl veers toward another Faulkner comment, sent to W. C. Neill who had been taunting Faulkner, calling him "Weeping Willie," to which Faulkner replied on January 12, five weeks before the Howe interview: "I doubt if we can afford to waste even on Congress, let alone on one another, that wit which we will sorely need when again, for the second time in a hundred years, we Southerners will have destroyed our native land just because of [n----rs]." Karl wonders if Faulkner was telling Neill, a resident of North Carrollton, Mississippi, that they spoke the "same language," or was making a "sarcastic play on Neill's racism; or, the worse scenario, was it Faulkner's way of speaking without regard for the degrading nature of '[n----r].'" Are we supposed to take our pick? It is part of a biographer's responsibility to canvass all the possibilities, so perhaps Karl should not be faulted for laying them out. On the last point, it has to be admitted that Faulkner frequently used the term "[n----r]" in his letters and in conversation with no noticeable use of irony. He talked as if the word was normal; he sometimes talked as if he owned his help. He told Howe that he believed 90% of Black people were on his side—that is, that they did not want enforced integration. That's making a lot of assumptions.

Karl spends more time on the Howe interview than most biographers but what he ends up with is a contradictory muddle. After suggesting Howe goaded Faulkner, the biographer then says that the "major part of the interview does not lead up to shooting Negroes in the streets. Quite the contrary." Faulkner was in an agitated state before he met Howe, and it is difficult to see how the reporter is, in any way, to blame for what Faulkner said. In *William Faulkner: Life Glimpses* (1990), Louis Daniel Brodsky, following Karl, thinks

198   FAULKNER AND RACE

that access to Howe's questions might well provide more context and perhaps reveal the reporter's "baiting remarks."

A blunter, unapologetic assessment is rendered by Joel Williamson in *William Faulkner and Southern History* (1993). However measured and even progressive some of Faulkner's statements on integration, he "lost all credibility" in his statement about shooting Black people.

André Bleikasten, one of Faulkner's finest critics, published his biography in French in 2007,[15] and treated the Howe interview without apologies for Faulkner, saying that in the interview—all of it—he "asserted his ultimate priorities." As Bleikasten observes, Faulkner's so-called retraction was nothing of the kind but was instead "a barely disguised confession." If Howe had, in Bleikasten's words, "probably trapped him," the biographer had no doubt that the reporter had faithfully rendered Faulkner's words. In effect, Bleikasten concludes, following James Baldwin, that Faulkner had affirmed his "tribal allegiance."

To say that Faulkner, in his right mind, would not speak the terrible words that appeared in the Howe interview is not enough for Philip Weinstein in *Becoming Faulkner* (2009). Here is a context far broader and deeper than any biographer or critic heretofore had put in just the right words. Weinstein writes of

> Faulkner's abiding twinship with blacks and his no less abiding difference from them, by way of his whiteness. The dark face he sees—as a Southerner—in the mirror proposed by race cannot be his own, yet he fleetingly glimpses himself there as well. More broadly, for several centuries in the South, the two races have been intertwined and cordoned off—at once inseparable and unreconcilable, scandalously connected by blood though segregated by law. Most of his fellow white Southerners denied the twinship, insisting instead on the unbridgeable difference between whiteness and darkness. But Faulkner—caught in a weave of racial realities he could neither master nor escape—moved through this uncertain territory like a man careening between the poles of blindness and insight. Deeply fissured within, he found himself making incompatible utterances, each true to incompatible experiences. Recurrently he appeared—and heard himself as—not-Faulkner. He knew at once too much and not enough. His lifelong immersion in the sea of race enacts this paradox in a range of ways.

Weinstein's insight strikes at Faulkner's core, relieving generations of biographers of their earnest efforts to somehow wish away what Faulkner said

"SHOOTING NEGROES"   199

about shooting Black people. "The default pole in Faulkner's paradoxical racial stance is disidentification," Weinstein concludes. In other words, he could think and say he was not in his right mind, that he never held such an opinion about the conceivable need to "shoot Negroes," and he would want to believe that was the truth. What was inconceivable he had conceived.

Weinstein won't let Faulkner go: "It is hard to imagine his saying 'shooting whites,' no matter how much he had been drinking. Somewhere inside his psyche, inculcated there and confirmed by his region's truisms, he could envisage shooting Negroes." It is difficult to stop quoting Weinstein:

> His words to Howe further reveal his incapacity to enter black lives. "I have known Negroes all my life," he proclaimed, "and Negroes work my land for me. I know how they feel." Warming to his theme, he added that, if it came to violence, "My Negro boys down on the plantation would fight against the North with me. If I say to them, 'Go get your shotguns, boys,' they'll come" The master/slave model is patent. He is the master of the plantation, they its obedient workers; he is the man, they the boys; he owns the guns and gives the orders, they follow suit. He is the active subject, they the docile object. This widely shared fantasy failed the South in the Civil War, when black slaves—given the chance—fled in huge numbers from their astonished Southern masters. The fantasy is all the more outrageous when sounded in 1956. Even intoxicated, he had to have known that neither his home (Rowan Oak) nor his farm (Greenfield Farm) was a plantation. Or is it that in foundational matters, the passage of time itself seems illusory? That beneath and behind the twentieth-century Southerner's home and farm there lurks the destroyed yet indestructible antebellum plantation?

Then Weinstein delivers the final blow: "the Howe interview reveals that in the matter of race, Faulkner thought in terms of place."

In *The Saddest Words: William Faulkner's Civil War*, Michael Gorra wastes no time: "Faulkner knew what he had said. He knew how shameful his words had been. He spoke in fear and he spoke in fever, the fever of whiskey and in fear not only of the white South but of himself too; of how much he still had in common with the world from which he'd come." In my own treatment of the Howe interview in the second volume of *The Life of William Faulkner*, I fastened on his reference to his family heritage: "My [great]-grandfather had slaves and he must have known that it was wrong, but he fought in one of the first regiments raised by the Confederate Army, not in the defense of his ethical position but to protect his native land from being invaded." This is what generations of southerners had told themselves: Their fight was for states' rights, and Faulkner was declaring his support

But consider the implications of Faulkner's use of "must have." If he did not know what his great-grandfather thought about owning slaves, he might have obtained an answer from his Aunt Bama (1874–1968), as the family called her. She was the old Colonel's youngest daughter who told William Faulkner many things about his great-grandfather, especially that after the Civil War he had been a public benefactor supporting the education of African Americans. But she did not tell him what he needed to know when he spoke with Russell Warren Howe. In effect, William Faulkner arrived at Saxe Commins's office for the interview unprepared. Evidently no one in the Faulkner family had reckoned with its slave owning past, even though that past was so much the subject of *Go Down, Moses* (1942), not to mention other stories and novels. Only through fiction, it seems, could Faulkner get anywhere near what his own family had done that led to his statement about "shooting Negroes" in the streets.

Phil Stone, Faulkner's mentor, said that the family acted like a law unto themselves.[16] They were not in the habit of questioning their motives, or in seeing the social and political consequences of their actions. They were not alone, of course, in this attitude, but not every family was quite that impregnable to self-criticism. Stark Young, another Faulkner mentor, confessed in a memoir, *The Pavillion*, that his Mississippi family remained troubled about the legacy of slavery. Nowhere in Faulkner's surviving letters to his family does the issue of slavery or of civil rights appear.

Until winning the Nobel Prize, Faulkner had not been questioned closely about race. Nothing he said before the Nobel was likely to attract newspaper headlines. On the page, in his fiction—all through the 1930s and 1940s—Faulkner family matters really did not intrude. Faulkner hardly had a public voice. The stories he wrote could be ignored if that is what family members wanted to do. Faulkner was not close to his brothers, and judging by their memoirs they never discussed his writing with him, and he did not invite their commentary. The one extant letter from his brother Jack about his brother Bill's writing concerns *The Reivers*, which Jack liked for its portrait of their father and for evoking fond memories of their childhood.

It seems that in order to feel on the right side of his family, after he began to express opinions about race that branded him as a "[n----r] lover," Faulkner had to cross a line, the one that his brother John drew when he said he would shoot Black people rather than accept integration. The trouble with Faulkner—it had always been the trouble with him—is that he could not stay put on the family side. He had the rest of the world to think about.

Caste from a Faulknerian Perspective

Intruder in the Dust

John Dollard (1900–1980), trained in sociology at the University of Chicago and in psychoanalysis at the Berlin Institute, brought the sensibility of a novelist to a five-month study in Indianola, Mississippi, which he wrote up as *Caste and Class in a Southern Town* (1937). Dollard went South, but what he found applied in the other direction: The "caste line is drawn in the North as effectively, if not as formally, as in the South," which meant "We are still deliberately or unwittingly profiting by, defending, concealing or ignoring the caste system." Caste, he argued, had far reaching implications: "Our social system has come under world inspection and is literally being looked at by several billion people or their competent agents." Faulkner would say or imply as much not only in essays and speeches in the 1950s, but in his wartime Hollywood screenplays, like the unproduced *Battle Cry*, in which he named an African American character America, a wounded warrior carried to safety by a white southern good-old-boy soldier.

It is unlikely that Dollard had anything new to convey to a reader like William Faulkner, if, in fact, Faulkner ever read the book in Oxford, which is about 110 miles from Indianola. But *Intruder in the Dust* (1948), nonetheless, reads like a remarkable reification of the caste system, not only as Dollard discovered it, but as Isabel Wilkerson, acknowledging Dollard's influence, has tracked on a global canvas: "Throughout human history, three caste systems have stood out. The tragically accelerated, chilling, and officially vanquished caste system of Nazi Germany. The lingering, millennia-long caste system of India. And the shape-shifting, unspoken, race-based caste pyramid in the United States."

Wilkerson's phrasing—"shape-shifting, unspoken, race-based caste pyramid"—leads right into the opening pages of *Intruder in the Dust*. Jefferson,

Mississippi "had known since the night before that Lucas [Beauchamp] had killed a white man." Of course, Jefferson knows no such thing. Lucas, Black and notoriously independent, flouts his place at the bottom of the race pyramid, and a lynching will be the white retribution for a crime and will also serve to put down all others of his subordinate race. As Dollard observed of lynchings, what mattered was not punishing the right man but punishing the "Negro caste . . . through one of its representatives."

Across from the jail is a sixteen-year-old white boy, Chick Mallison, "trying to look occupied or at least innocent." He is part of what is "unspoken." He is not supposed to acknowledge what is about to happen anymore than the novelist was ever to admit what he knew concerning Nelse Patton's lynching in 1909, just a few blocks from twelve-year-old Billy Faulkner's home. Only in fiction, did Faulkner dare to reveal what he knew about the code of caste.[1]

Chick knows Lucas Beauchamp "as well that is as any white person knew him." Behind that statement is a regime of dominion over African Americans that Dollard found paradoxical. His white informants often touted how well they knew "their Negroes" while nearly at the same time complaining that Black people were mysterious and hard to read. In this respect, Lucas Beauchamp, who keeps his own counsel, is the instigator of a white uneasiness, Dollard surmised, that hid a fear of revolt—if the enforcement of caste was not unremitting. With any let up at all the individuality that Lucas personifies might well overwhelm caste boundaries.

Four years earlier, Chick, then twelve, fell through the ice in a creek during a hunting expedition on the property of white landowner Roth Edmonds, which is near Lucas's home. Lucas had ordered the white Edmonds boy and Chick's Black companion, Aleck Sander, to get Chick out of his ice hole. Climbing an embankment Chick looks up at a man with a hat like Chick's grandfather would have worn. The shape of caste has shifted. Lucas crowns himself, making no effort to get Chick out of the creek. It is one of those intervening moments, Wilkerson writes about, when a member of the upper caste suddenly realizes what it means to be brought low.[2] Lucas looks out of his skin as if he "had no pigment at all not even the white man's lack of it, not arrogant, not even scornful: just intractable and composed."

The white Edmonds boy addresses Beauchamp as "Mister Lucas," a title no white is supposed to use for his inferior. When Dollard called his African American informants by Mr. or Mrs. he outraged the white community who called him a "[n----r] lover." When two boys told Faulkner he was called a "[n----r] lover," the novelist replied that it was better than being a fascist.[3] "To be a '[n----r] lover,'" Dollard observed, "suggests the person is a traitor to his caste, and that his fondness for Negroes is headlong and impractical." The

CASTE FROM A FAULKNERIAN PERSPECTIVE: *INTRUDER IN THE DUST*   203

epithet also reflected, as Faulkner's novel and Dollard's study make apparent, the "constant and potent pressures to compel every white person to act his caste role correctly."

Lucas Beauchamp is descended from the old Carothers McCaslin's slave who was also old Carothers's son, and that lineage matters, as Dollard learned when African American informants mentioned their pride in their white blood, although Lucas deviates from the Dollard pattern by not expressing, as the sociologist's informants did, any sense of being "scorned and rejected" by their own white relations.

Lucas shows no deference to Chick, no fear, no sense of dependence on his white caste masters. He turns his back on Chick and issues a command: "Come to my house." In effect, Lucas takes on the paternal power of the upper caste. When Chick says he will return to the Edmonds house, Lucas ignores him and says to the Black boy: "Tote his [Chick's] gun, Joe." Dollard would have recognized Lucas's dominance as not merely an affront to the caste principle but as a blow to this white boy's pride of place. Or to state the obverse: "a member of the white caste has an automatic right to demand forms of behavior from Negroes which serve to increase his own self-esteem." When that subservient behavior was not forthcoming, Dollard saw that white image of self, of "being something special and valuable," deflated.

John Cullen, author of *Old Times in the Faulkner Country*, told his collaborator, Professor Floyd Watkins: "Lucas Beauchamp was more independent than he could actually get away with as a real person in Oxford."[4] Indeed, John Dollard found no African American like Lucas Beauchamp, unafraid of white retaliation. Dollard concluded: "Every Negro in the South knows that he is under a kind of sentence of death; he does not know when his turn will come; it may never come, but it may also be at any time." Faulkner creates a character who could not have existed but who is absolutely necessary so that the novelist can expose what did exist and why it could not continue.

Lucas strides ahead "incapable of conceiving himself by a child contradicted and defied." Chick is on Lucas's sovereign ground, deeded to him by his white first cousin, ten acres of land "set forever in the middle of the two-thousand-acre plantation like a postage stamp in the center of an envelope." Black land owners, Dollard reported, were at special risk of being driven off their property and often retained it only with the support of what was called an "angel," a white man who served as a protector, which is exactly what Mr. Edmonds is. "It seems that every white family has some Negro or Negroes whom it protects," Dollard learned.

Lucas orders the sodden Chick to "strip off" and dry himself. As Robert Hamblin puts it, Chick is "stripped of his whiteness," in a "near-drowning" that is a "very appropriate symbol."[5] Chick tries again to recover his caste authority, announcing that he will take his dinner at the Edmonds home. Lucas now is devoid of his racial designation: "The man neither protested nor acquiesced. He didn't stir; he was not even looking at him [Chick]. He just said [referring to his wife], inflexible and calm: 'She done already dished it up now.'" After the meal, Chick attempts to give Lucas four coins. "What's that for?" Lucas asks, refusing to acknowledge he has done a service for the white boy. Chick drops the coins on the floor and orders Lucas; "Pick it up!" Lucas ignores Chick and tells the Edmonds boy and Aleck Sander to pick up the money and return it to Chick, who is then dismissed: "Now go on and shoot your rabbit. . . . And stay out of that creek."

Wilkerson's *Caste* dramatizes many such moments in her life and in the lives of others when the demeaning aspects of caste are exposed in an intervention of a kind that virtually no white person in Faulkner's time could imagine. As Wilkerson notes, "without intervention or reprogramming, we act out the script we were handed. Caste is installed in the "subconscious of every one of us," as well as the "fear of losing caste." Lucas triumphs because he will not allow caste to work against him in the large and small ways that, as Wilkerson puts it, "elevate or demean, embrace or exclude." After his encounter with Lucas, Chick has to choose, in Wilkerson's words: "We can be born to the dominant caste but choose not to dominate. We can be born to a subordinated caste but resist the box others force upon us." A "world without caste, she proclaims, would set everyone free."

A chagrined Chick thinks: "Lucas had beat him." Chick is so desperate to assert his white privilege that he thinks: "*If he would just be a [n----r] first, just for one second, one little infinitesimal second.*" This is not merely Chick's dilemma. He expresses his community's anxiety, since submission cannot be extorted from Lucas Beauchamp. Dollard discovered a few cases where African Americans tried to assert themselves as Lucas does and they were "driven out of the community or otherwise disposed of."

When Chick tries to send a Christmas gift of a dress for Molly, Lucas's wife, a white boy on a mule shows up with Lucas's gift of a gallon bucket of sorghum molasses. In short, "what would or could set him [Chick] free was beyond not merely his reach but even his ken." How ironic that it is the white teenager who cannot be "set free."

When Lucas arrives at the jail in the sheriff's custody, he looks at sixteen-year-old Chick and issues a command: "You, young man. Tell your uncle I wants to see him," and then calmly walks into the jail. Beauchamp is not without resources. Half the time, Dollard reported, lynchings were prevented by "conscientious white citizens and law officers."

CASTE FROM A FAULKNERIAN PERSPECTIVE: *INTRUDER IN THE DUST* 205

Faulkner casts doubt on Lucas's guilt. The crime occurs in Beat Four, a violent stronghold of the Gowries, white supremacists. But Lucas has been apprehended with the purported murder weapon in his hand. Chick's uncle, county attorney Gavin Stevens, supposes Lucas is performing his part in the caste pyramid: "blew his top and murdered a white man," which is what white people expect, Stevens observes. "Whites have raised [n----rs] from savagery," John Cullen told Floyd Watkins, reflecting what many Southerners of Faulkner's generation believed and what they told John Dollard—that in certain circumstances Black people would return to their primitive state. A lynching seemed to Cullen a vindication of white supremacy. Present at the lynching of Nelse Patton, Cullen said without a trace of irony about who was savage: "I was proud. Somebody cut his balls off. Somebody scalped him. I don't know who done that. I was just a bystander."

When Stevens and Chick enter the jail to visit Lucas, he is asleep, confirming Chick's conception of caste: "He's just a [n----r] after all for all his high nose and his stiff neck and his gold watch-chain and refusing to mean mister to anybody even when he says it. Only a [n----r] could kill a man, let alone shoot him in the back, and then sleep like a baby as soon as he found something flat enough to lie down on." This is the preposterous thinking Dollard encountered everywhere, a mindset that typed African Americans as children or primitives unaware of the consequences of their actions. It never occurs to Chick that Lucas is asleep because he has not killed a man. Stevens tells Lucas: "I don't defend murderers who shoot people in the back." Stevens is upset because Lucas won't call him mister. He yells at Lucas about how the Gowries are going to lynch him. Finally, Stevens calms down enough to absorb Lucas's story about how he has observed two white timber mill partners, one cheating the other, hauling timber late at night, selling it, and pocketing the profits. Stevens doesn't wait to hear the rest and simply concocts what he thinks the arrogant Lucas did: tell a white man another white man is cheating him and getting knocked down by the white man cursing him and calling him a liar, which, in turn, results in Lucas shooting him in the back. Stevens advises Lucas to plead guilty and let his lawyer argue that his old age and lack of a criminal record deserves a merciful verdict—being sent to the penitentiary. Realizing the garrulous Stevens is hopeless, Lucas bids Stevens goodbye, saying: "If you stay here you'll talk till morning."

Lucas needs to find another way to save himself, to stage another intervention, so he turns to Chick. Stevens departs, but Chick returns the same night to Lucas's cell, because of the unspoken understanding between them. As he enters, he says "All right. What do you want me to do?" But Chick already knows. He has to dig up Vinson Gowrie's body to prove, as Lucas tells him, that Gowrie was not shot with Lucas's gun. It has to be Chick, because neither the sheriff nor Stevens would countenance such a request. As another old Black man once said to Chick: "Young folks and women's, they ain't cluttered. They can listen." When Chick doubts he can get to the grave and return all in one night, the laconic Lucas replies: "I'll try to wait."

Faulkner was fond of detective stories and read them in cheap paperbacks right off the rack in Oxford's drugstore. Mysteries made a mockery of convention and caste, with the detective often being the outsider in terms of class or iconoclastic even if in the upper caste. With *Intruder in the Dust* he had first set out to tell a detective story, but he discovered that the very notion of pursuing clues depended on the ability to see them in a society cluttered with all that cant about Black people and their willing participation in the rightness of whiteness. Characters like Lucas and Chick stand out, as an affront to the casuistry of caste.

How is Chick going to dig up a body in a cemetery several miles from town? In desperation, he calls on his Uncle Gavin, who dismisses Lucas's defense, saying any man, Black or white, would say it was not his gun. Besides, how could the attorney ever convince the Gowries to dig up their dead kin to exonerate a "[n----r]." Chick rules out his father, realizing he would get the same answer, but then hears the same thing from his Black companion, Aleck Sander, who adds: "It's the ones like Lucas makes trouble for everybody." Everybody, in short, is implicated in a caste paradigm that no one is willing to challenge. But out of friendship, Aleck Sander helps Chick saddle up a horse and tote the pick and shovel needed for the exhumation.

In yet another intervention, Miss Habersham, who happens to be in Stevens's office when Chick barges in, follows the boys as they saddle up to save Lucas. She asks Chick about what Lucas told him. She is the oldest surviving member of the town's founding families and is interested because of Molly, Lucas's wife, who is the same age as Miss Habersham and a descendent of one of Doctor Habersham's slaves. Molly and Miss Habersham have grown up "like sisters, like twins," taken care of by Molly's mother. "Miss Habersham had stood up in the Negro church as godmother to Molly's first child." As soon as Chick tells her that Lucas said it was not his pistol, Miss Habersham replies immediately: "So he didn't do it." She is in a position to understand that killing a low-caste white man like Vinson Gowrie is beneath Lucas's dignity, his caste pride.

Miss Habersham exercises the privileges of her upper-caste position, bound to make its own rules and execute its own plans when necessary, as she muses about Lucas. "Naturally he wouldn't tell your uncle. He's a Negro and your uncle's a white man." She takes over, using her truck as well as

CASTE FROM A FAULKNERIAN PERSPECTIVE: *INTRUDER IN THE DUST* 207

Chick's horse to tote the body from the grave to the truck. When they open the grave, Vinson Gowrie is not there. Instead they find Jack Montgomery, a "jackleg timber buyer." Now Chick, Aleck Sander, and Miss Habersham have to apply to Stevens and Sheriff Hampton to make yet another intervention before the Gowries get to town to lynch Lucas.

Stevens looks at Miss Habersham and ventures: "But if a woman, a lady, a white lady." The nature of caste is so ingrained that Miss Habersham understands her mission: She is to sit on the steps in front of the jail barring the lynchers who would not dare to run over her. As a mob gathers in front of the jail, Chick realizes that all of the county has made the lynching possible:

> It seemed to him now that he was responsible for having brought into the light and glare of day something shocking and shameful out of the whole white foundations of the county which he himself must partake of too since he too was bred of it, which otherwise might have flared and blazed merely out of Beat Four and then vanished back into its darkness or at least invisibility with the fading embers of Lucas' crucifixion."

Faulkner prolongs the suspense halfway through the novel when Stevens starts to talk too much in what Chick earlier calls the "significantless speciosity of his uncle's voice," or what Dollard terms the "defensive ideology" of southerners who attack a federal government that is interfering with the high caste privilege of setting African Americans free since the North has not been able to do it. This is the same Gavin Stevens that in *Light in August* spouts nonsense about white and Black blood.

The case against Lucas collapses as soon as the grave is opened. After some convoluted plot twists it is discovered that Crawford Gowrie, an army deserter and criminal, involved in a timber deal gone wrong, has murdered two men, his brother Vinson and Jake Montgomery who has been blackmailing Crawford. Faulkner, never good as the sheer mechanics of detective story plotting, is more interested in Chick Mallison's reaction to the lynch mob that rushes away from the town square when they realize Lucas Beauchamp is not their prey. Stevens tries to palliate Chick's disgust with the mob, suggesting they ran to save their consciences: it was run or stand there and admit they were wrong. They are running, Stevens adds, from Crawford Gowrie, although Stevens does not explain what he means. Presumably, what troubles the mob is that the murderer is white and a fratricide, and they are ashamed.

The caste consensus collapses and then is reconstituted when Chick muses that the instant the "bullet struck Vinson Gowrie . . . Lucas was

208   FAULKNER AND RACE

already dead . . . in the same instant," and theirs [the mob's] was merely to preside at his suttee." This is Faulkner's notion of time: "It's all *now* you see. Yesterday wont be over until tomorrow and tomorrow began ten thousand years ago." That could be said as well for the Indian conception of caste, of a widow who performs suttee, flinging herself on her husband's funeral pyre in her devotion—sometimes coerced—to caste. Lucas is no widow, but Stevens had earlier supposed that any white man would now take Lucas "out and burn him all regular and in order and themselves acting as he is convinced Lucas would wish them to act: like white folks; both of them observing implicitly the rule: the [n----r] acting like a [n----r] and the white folks acting like white folks and no real hard feelings on either side." In short, this is the ritualistic southern version of suttee.

At the beginning of Caste, Wilkerson describes a 1936 photograph of Hamburg shipyard workers all facing the same direction and "heiling in unison," except for one man, August Landmesser, who folds his arms and refuses to give the Nazi salute. An Aryan and a Nazi, he fell in love with a Jew. Forbidden to marry her, he began to understand the perverted nature of Nazi ideology. Wilkerson concludes that "unless people are willing to transcend their fears, endure discomfort and derision, suffer the scorn of loved ones and neighbors and co-workers and friends, fall into disfavor of perhaps everyone they know, face exclusion and even banishment, it would be numerically impossible, humanly impossible, for everyone to be that man." Faulkner wrote to a European friend, "I am doing what I can. I can see the possible time when I shall have to leave my native state, something as the Jew had to flee from Germany during Hitler."[6] Faulkner's fiction is his version of the 1936 photograph. Intruder in the Dust stands apart from both the lynchers and southern whites like Stevens, implying that history changes slowly, but sometimes dramatically, one individual at a time.

What Faulkner Could Not Imagine

The Life of James Meredith

On September 29, 1962, a riot broke out on the University of Mississippi campus. James Meredith was on his way to becoming the first African American to enroll at Ole Miss. Segregated schools were still the norm, and violence, as William Faulkner had forecast, would come if the federal government enforced integration.

The plan was to murder James Meredith, as Kathleen Wickham recounts in *We Believed We Were Immortal.* Jimmy Faulkner, William Faulkner nephew, son of arch-segregationist John Faulkner, and an Air Force veteran, drove a bulldozer onto campus toward the Lyceum, where wounded Union soldiers had once been housed, where James Meredith remained, protected by US Marshals since Mississippi law enforcement had withdrawn.

Jimmy Faulkner had not counted on his brother Murry, a member of the federalized Mississippi National Guard, standing in his way. At the last moment, Jimmy veered away from his brother and drove the bulldozer into a tree, hoping to use that as cover for riflemen who would shoot and storm the Lyceum, but the FBI swarmed over the bulldozer as Jimmy fled, never to be apprehended.

When William Faulkner predicted violence over forced integration, he never imagined it would be brother against brother in his own family, even though that is what happened in his Civil War novel, *Absalom, Absalom!* But Murry had taken an oath to the United States, and he was determined to abide by it.

But it wasn't just William Faulkner who was wrong about what would happen when Ole Miss and other schools were integrated. In the fall of 1962, two months after Faulkner had died, even Thurgood Marshall thought Meredith was crazy to confront segregation in the most reactionary Southern state, as you will learn in *James Meredith: Breaking the Barrier*, edited by Kathleen Wickham. In her important collection of articles by and about Meredith and the desegregation of Ole Miss, you will discover a composite biography that not even this country's greatest novelist could have imagined.

Meredith, in his own words and those of others who watched him, was not a movement man. He was always his own man, determined to force an entire state to capitulate to his desire to be recognized, as he put it, as an American citizen. An Air Force veteran, Meredith had served in Japan in the 1950s at the time William Faulkner visited. Did Faulkner notice, as Meredith did, that African Americans serving there were treated as equals? Meredith decided, right then, he would return home and liberate an entire state: liberate not only his fellow African Americans but his fellow white citizens, prisoners of discrimination and hate.

Like Faulkner's Lucas Beauchamp, that larger than life figure in *Go Down, Moses* and *Intruder in the Dust*, Meredith was fearless. Beauchamp grows up on a piece of land his white masters have carved out of a plantation as his own domain. Meredith hailed from Kosciusko, Mississippi, the ancestral home of Estelle Faulkner, on a piece of property that his father had established to protect his son from precisely those people who would later try to murder him.

Faulkner could not imagine an African American as courageous as Meredith, and yet Meredith confirmed the great novelist's conviction that only individuals, not movements, would change history. Only when Meredith refused to pull out of what looked like a suicidal quest did Thurgood Marshall, Robert Kennedy, and the weight of the federal government come down on his side.

But the story, as with that confrontation between brothers, is far more complex, with the white editor of Ole Miss's student newspaper supporting Meredith's right to enroll and later, much later, being awarded for her stance, rescinding the earlier censure of her for doing so, and achieving, as a result, more than even Chick Mallison could have imagined possible.

The stories of a Black journalist and others showing how dangerous it was to report the story of Meredith's heroic quest make *James Meredith: Breaking the Barrier* essential reading, along with Edwin Meek's photographs in *Riot* that documents what happened when a university campus became a "war zone."

Acknowledgments

The following articles appeared in somewhat different form in these publications:

"Building a Better Biography," *Fear of Theory: Towards a New Theoretical Justification of Biography*, edited by Hans Renders and David Veltman, Brill, 2022.

"The Historians of Yoknapatawpha": *New York Sun* and *University Bookman* Interview with Michael Gorra: https://podcasters.spotify.com/pod/show/carl-rollyson/episodes/Episode-45-William-Faulkners-Civil-War--a-talk-with-Michael-Gorra-about-his-new-book-eq1au7.

Interview with Taylor Brown: https://podcasters.spotify.com/pod/show/carl-rollyson/episodes/A-Faulknerian-novel-in-which-Faulkner-appears-e1isord.

"Counterpull: Estelle and William Faulkner," *South Atlantic Quarterly* 85, no. 3 (Summer 1986): 215–27.

"Faulkner's Conservatism," *The Imaginative Conservative*, September 24, 2021, https://theimaginativeconservative.org/2021/09/old-rowan-oak-conservatism-william-faulkner.html.

"Faulkner the Antifascist": *Moment*, http://momentummag.com/summer-issue-2020.

"Faulkner the Futurist": *The Hedgehog Review*, Fall 2022, https://hedgehogreview.com/issues/america-on-the-brink/articles/faulkner-as-futurist.

"Faulkner's Shadow: Hollywood, Hemingway, and Pylon." *Faulkner and Hemingway*, edited by Christopher Reiger and Andrew B. Leiter. Southeast Missouri State University Press, 2018.

"'Tomorrow' and *Tomorrow*: Faulkner into Film": *Mississippi Quarterly* 32, no. 3 (Summer 1979): 437–52.

"Caste from a Faulknerian Perspective": *Spectator World*, https://thespectator .com/book-and-art/cast-american-class-system-faulkner/.

"A Revisionist Review of 'The Reivers': Novel into Film April 29, 2020, http://classicmovieman.blogspot.com/2020/04/a-revisionist-view-of -reivers-novel.html.

I'm grateful to Heather Ostman for her careful copyediting of this book, and to Valerie Jones for additional editorial assistance.

Notes

Building a Better Biography

1. Joseph Blotner, *Faulkner: A Biography* (1974), *Faulkner: A Biography* (1984); Judith Wittenberg, *Faulkner: The Transfiguration of Biography* (1979); David Minter, *William Faulkner: His Life and Work* (1980); Stephen B. Oates, *William Faulkner: The Man and the Artist* (1987); Frederick Karl,: *William Faulkner: American Writer: A Biography* (1989); Joel Williamson, *William Faulkner and Southern History* (1993); Jay Parini, *One Matchless Time: A Life of William Faulkner* (2004); Philip Weinstein, *Becoming Faulkner: The Art and Life of William Faulkner* (2009); André Bleikasten, *William Faulkner: A Life Through the Novels* (2017).

2. M. Thomas Inge, *William Faulkner* (2006); Carolyn Porter, *William Faulkner: Lives and Legacies* (2007); David Rampton, *William Faulkner: A Literary Life* (2008); Robert W. Hamblin, *Myself and the World: A Biography of William Faulkner* (2016); Philip Weinstein, *Simply Faulkner* (2016); Kirk Curnutt, *William Faulkner* (2018).

3. For biographical chapters, see Michael Millgate, *The Achievement of William Faulkner* (1965); Michael Grimwood, *Heart in Conflict: Faulkner's Struggles with Vocation* (1987); Joseph Urgo, *Faulkner's Apocrypha* (1989); Doreen Fowler, *Faulkner: The Return of the Repressed* (1997); Kevin Railey, *Natural Aristocracy: History, Ideology, and the Production of William Faulkner* (1999). These are by no means the only biographical chapters but simply those that came to my attention and that seemed especially relevant to this essay.

4. Bruce Kawin, *Faulkner and Film*; *Faulkner's MGM Screenplays* (1982). The work of Hamblin, Lurie, and Solomon is represented in Peter Lurie and Ann J. Abadie, eds., *Faulkner and Film*; see also Sarah Gleeson-White, ed., *William Faulkner at Twentieth Century-Fox: The Annotated Screenplays*; Ben Robbins, "The Pragmatic Modernist: William Faulkner's Craft and Hollywood's Networks of Production." *Journal of Screenwriting* 5, no. 2 (June 2014): 239–57.

5. "Hollywood 1943 by Meta Carpenter Wilde and Orin Borsten," in *Faulkner: A Comprehensive Guide to the Brodsky Collection Volume IV: Battle Cry, A Screenplay by William Faulkner*, Robert W. Hamblin and Louis Daniel Brodsky, eds.; Carl Rollyson, *The Life of William Faulkner: This Alarming Paradox, 1935–1962, Volume 2* (University of Virginia Press, 2020).

NOTES

6. Sotheby's, http://www.sothebys.com/en/auctions/ecatalogue/2013/books-manuscripts-n09066/lot.259.html.

7. James G. Watson, *Thinking of Home: William Faulkner's Letters to His Mother and Father, 1918–1925* (W. W. Norton, 1992).

8. George Sidney's dissertation, "Faulkner in Hollywood: A Study of His Career as a Scenarist," University of New Mexico, 1959, remains a useful study of the tensions inherent in Faulkner's effort to conform to studio standards: "Thus twice during his screen writing career Faulkner repudiated Hollywood's "manual of style," his obligations to his employers, his assumed role—and wrote for himself." Sidney is referring to *Banjo on my Knee* and *Country Lawyer*, underestimating how many times Faulkner went against Hollywood orthodoxy in *Sutter's Gold*, *Drums Along the Mohawk*, and *The Left Hand of God*, although I am not certain Sidney saw Faulkner's adaptation of Barrett's novel.

9. M. Thomas Inge, ed., *Conversations with William Faulkner* (University Press of Mississippi, 1999).

10. Frederick Karl mistakenly assumes that Faulkner was "reunited" with Bogart, but the released film is based on another writer's script, with a different director, long after Faulkner had departed from Hollywood.

11. See Stefan Solomon, *William Faulkner in Hollywood: Screenwriting for the Studios* (University of Georgia Press, 2017).

12. Maud Falkner to Sallie Burns, January 16, 1951, Carvel Collins Papers, Harry Ransom Humanities Research Center, University of Texas at Austin.

13. Lowrey to Phil Stone, February 28, 1951, Louis Daniel Brodsky and Robert Hamblin, eds. *Faulkner: A Comprehensive Guide to the Brodsky Collection. Volume II: The Letters* (University Press of Mississippi, 1984).

14. The film was not released until July 1952, but I think the reason Faulkner liked it is because it accorded with his redemptive vision in *The Left Hand of God*.

15. For a chapter-length study of the "Monument of the Famous Writer," focusing on Blotner, see Dennis W. Petrie, *Ultimately Fiction: Design in Modern American Literary Biography* (Purdue University Press, 1981), 59–110.

16. See "Biographical Criticism," in Charles A. Peek and Robert W. Hamblin, eds. *A Companion to Faulkner Studies* (Greenwood Press, 2004). Railey's is the single best essay-length discussion of Faulkner biography. Also of great value is Mary Phyfer's Gillis's PhD dissertation: "Faulkner's Biographies: Life, Art, and the Poetics of Biography," University of Alabama, 2002.

The Foreigner in Faulkner

1. All quotations are from James G. Watson, ed., *Thinking of Home: William Faulkner's Letters to His Mother and Father 1918–1925* (W. W. Norton, 1992).

2. For the details of Faulkner's time in Toronto, New York City, and New Orleans, see Carl Rollyson, *The Life of William Faulkner: The Past Is Never Dead, 1897–1934, Volume 1* (University of Virginia Press, 2020).

NOTES 215

3. For more on Faulkner's *Big Sleep* and *Dreadful Hollow* screenplays, see Carl Rollyson, *The Life of William Faulkner: This Alarming Paradox, Volume 2* (University of Virginia Press, 2020), and Stefan Solomon, *William Faulkner in Hollywood: Screenwriting for the Studios* (University of Georgia Press, 2017).

4. Joseph Blotner, *Selected Letters of William Faulkner* (Random House, 1977).

5. Blotner, *Selected Letters*.

6. The State Department letters lauding Faulkner's work abroad are collected in Brodsky and Hamblin, volume II.

7. Dean Faulkner Wells, *Every Day by the Sun: A Memoir of the Faulkners of Mississippi* (Crown, 2011).

Counterpull: Estelle and William Faulkner

1. See Judith Sensibar's groundbreaking, *Faulkner and Love: The Women Who Shaped His Art* (Yale University Press, 2009).

2. See the second volume of *Faulkner: A Comprehensive Guide to the Brodsky Collection*, edited by Louis Daniel Brodsky and Robert W. Hamblin (University Press of Mississippi, 1984).

3. See the second volume of Rollyson, *The Life of William Faulkner*.

4. See the description of Estelle's dance with the Prince of Wales in the first volume of Rollyson, *The Life of William Faulkner*.

5. See the second volume of Rollyson, *The Life of William Faulkner* for the description of Bezzerides's love letter to Estelle, and for her delight in the company of Felix Frankfurther.

6. Panthea Reid Broughton, "An Interview with Meta Carpenter Wilde," *Southern Review*, Autumn 1982, https://www.proquest.com/openview/74656bc31e1473f888b773c97 43bdod5/1?pq-origsite=gscholar&cbl=1819563.

7. Brodsky and Hamblin, *Faulkner*, volume 2.

8. Brodsky and Hamblin, *Faulkner*, volume 2.

9. See the next chapter of this book, "Sole Owner and Proprietor."

10. That Faulkner realized just how perceptive his wife could be is explored in the next chapter on his affair with Jean Stein.

11. Brodsky and Hamblin, *Faulkner*, volume 2.

12. Brodsky and Hamblin, *Faulkner*, volume 2.

13. Judith Sensibar, *Faulkner and Love: The Women Who Shaped His Art: A Biography* (Yale University Press, 2010).

14. Sensibar, *Faulkner and Love*.

15. Brodsky and Hamblin, *Faulkner*, Volume 2.

16. See the next chapter of this book, "Sole Owner and Proprieter."

17. The evidence of her pride in William Faulkner is everywhere apparent in the Brodsky and Hamblin collection of her letters.

18. Lisa C. Hickman, *William Faulkner and Joan Williams: The Romance of Two Writers* (McFarland, 2006).

19. Joan Williams, "Twenty Will Not Come Again," *Atlantic Monthly*, May 1980.

"Sole Owner and Proprietor": William Faulkner and Jean Stein

1. A file in Stein's papers includes typewritten excerpts from Faulkner's letters, a kind of carve-out of his correspondence that Stein permitted Blotner to use in *Selected Letters of William Faulkner*. Blotner sent her excerpts of drafts for his Faulkner biography and she crossed out passages that she thought were too personal, marking one with a big X and writing "no."

2. What looks like a draft of Stein's letters is in her papers.

3. Stein's letters are full of strikeouts, changes of wording, and I have quoted what she left unmarked in what may be only drafts of the actual letters she sent to Faulkner.

4. Faulkner misspelled the word Bunbury, as he described looking in his closet at his Burberry.

5. The misspelling is Faulkner's.

6. A T. S. Eliot poem, "McCavity: The Mystery Cat," https://poets.org/poem/macavity -mystery-cat: "There never was a Cat of such deceitfulness and suavity."

7. See the previous chapter of this book.

8. From Stein's notes recording Faulkner's comments.

9. See the description of Faulkner's pornographic drawings of lovemaking with Meta Carpenter in the second volume of Rollyson, *The Life of William Faulkner*.

10. See the first volume of Rollyson, *The Life of William Faulkner*.

11. See the account in the second volume of Rollyson, *The Life of William Faulkner*.

12. Who is speaking is not clear.

Faulkner's Conservatism

1. Carl Rollyson, "Old Rowan Oak: Faulkner's Conservatism," *The Imaginative Conservative*, September 24, 2021. https://theimaginativeconservative.org/2021/09/old -rowan-oak-conservatism-william-faulkner.html.

2. See William Faulkner, *Essays, Speeches, and Public Letters* (Random House, 1965), for the Nobel prize address and his other nonfiction essays and statements.

3. Brodsky and Hamblin, *Faulkner*, volume iv. For my discussion of *Battle Cry*, see the second volume of *The Life of William Faulkner*.

4. Sally Trotter, *Rowan Oak: A History of the William Faulkner Home* (Nautilus, 2017).

5. Starr is a valuable observer of the young, unreconstructed William Faulkner. Earlier biographies ignored Starr, but you can learn more about Starr in both volumes of Rollyson, *The Life of William Faulkner*.

6. Faulkner's scripts of *Drums Along the Mohawk* are available in Gleeson-White and discussed in the second volume of Rollyson, *The Life of William Faulkner*.

NOTES

Faulkner the Antifascist

1. For a detailed account of the Nelse Patton lynching and what Faulkner knew about it, see the first volume of Rollyson, *The Life of William Faulkner*.

2. Joseph Blotner, *Selected Letters of William Faulkner* (Random House, 1977).

3. James B. Meriwether and Michael Millgate, eds., *Lion in the Garden: Interviews with William Faulkner, 1926–1926* (Random House, 1968).

4. See volume 2 of Rollyson, *The Life of William Faulkner*.

5. Blotner, *Selected Letters*.

6. Wilde and Borsten and the second volume of Rollyson, *The Life of William Faulkner*, provide details about Faulkner's friends and social and political views while working in Hollywood.

7. Blotner, *Selected Letters*.

Faulkner as Futurist

1. Reprinted in David Minter's Norton Critical edition of *The Sound and the Fury*.

2. James B. Meriwether and Michael Millgate, eds., *Lion in the Garden: Interviews with William Faulkner, 1926–1926* (Random House, 1968).

War No More: The Revolt of the Masses in *A Fable*

1. Joseph Blotner, *Selected Letters of William Faulkner* (Random House, 1977).

2. Blotner, *Selected Letters*.

3. Blotner, *Selected Letters*.

4. Joseph L. Fant and Robert Ashley, eds., *Faulkner at West Point* (University Press of Mississippi, 2002).

5. For this period in Faulkner's life, see the second volume of Rollyson, *The Life of William Faulkner*.

6. See Robert Hamblin's comments in *Critical Essays on William Faulkner* (University Press of Mississippi, 2016) about how Faulkner inverts the story of Christ in *A Fable*.

7. Noel Polk and Ann J. Abadie, eds., *Faulkner and War* (University Press of Mississippi, 2004).

8. Blotner, *Selected Letters*.

9. Blotner, *Selected Letters*.

10. William Faulkner, *Essays, Speeches, and Public Letters* (Random House, 1965),

11. Dean Faulkner Wells, *Every Day by the Sun: A Memoir of the Faulkners of Mississippi* (Oxford University Press, 2011).

12. Polk and Abadie, *Faulkner and War*.

13. Blotner mentions the Faulkner march in volume 2 of *Faulkner* (1974).

14. Faulkner's great-grandfather was a Mason, but the extent to which Faulkner knew about Masonic practices has not been determined.

15. Blotner, *Selected Letters*.

16. Blotner, *Selected Letters*.

218 NOTES

Recreating *Absalom, Absalom!: Revolt in the Earth*

1. For an overview of Faulkner's history in Hollywood, see https://brightlightsfilm.com/the-cinematic-faulkner-framing-hollywood/#.XqCVgGhKjIU.

2. Brodsky and Hamblin, volume 2, includes many letters and memos from film producers concerning their high regard for Faulkner and his work.

3. See Sarah Gleeeson-White, ed., *William Faulkner at Twentieth Century-Fox: The Annotated Screenplays* (Oxford University Press, 2017).

4. See Stefan Solomon, *William Faulkner in Hollywood: Screenwriting for Studios* (University of Georgia Press, 2017).

5. The copy of the screenplay held at the Albert and Shirley Small Special Collections, University of Virginia, lists both Faulkner and Murphy on the title page.

6. The review is included in Carvel Collins, ed., *Early Prose and Poetry* (Jonathan Cape, 1963).

7. The script is published in Gleeson-White, *William Faulkner*.

8. Slavery was abolished in Jamaica in 1838, so perhaps Lovett is employing free labor: https://www.britannica.com/place/Jamaica/British-rule.

9. Carvel Collins, ed., *New Orleans Sketches* (Random House, 1958).

10. See the first volume of Rollyson, *The Life of William Faulkner*.

11. Faulkner employs a faux newspaper account in *Pylon* (1935).

12. See *William Faulkner Day by Day* for three instances in which Faulkner sang the song and the second volume of Rollyson, *The Life of William Faulkner*.

13. Quoted in Susan B. Delson, *Dudley Murphy: Hollywood Wildcard* (University of Minnesota, 2006).

14. Buckner's memo and the screenplay are in the Shirley and Albert Small Special Collections, University of Virginia.

15. Stefan Solomon details Murphy's significant contribution to the film, exploring, for example, the director's soundscape, which makes the sounds of Africa central to *Revolt in the Earth*. Solomon also shows how *Revolt in the Earth* draws on earlier stories, like "Evangeline."

Faulkner's Shadow: Hollywood, Hemingway, and *Pylon*

1. For the most detailed account of the short stories that culminate in *Pylon*, see Duane MacMillan, "Pylon: From Short Stories to Major Work," *Mosaic* 7 (Fall 1973): 186–212.

2. See Patricia L. Bradley, "Angelic Acrobats and Fallen Southern Women: William Faulkner and Robert Penn Warren Go to the Circus," *Faulkner and Warren*, edited by Christopher Rieger and Robert W. Hamblin (Southeast Missouri State University Press, 2015).

3. Laverne eschews the sentimentality of the wife in "Honor," who feels bound to tell her flyer-husband that she has fallen in love with his wing-walker partner.

4. Lisa Paddock, *Contrapuntal in Integration: William Faulkner's Short Story Collections* (International Scholars Publications, 2000).

NOTES

219

5. See Joseph Blotner, *Selected Letters of William Faulkner* (Random House, 1977).

6. See the second volume of Rollyson, *The Life of William Faulkner* for details about Faulkner's attendance at the air show.

7. For details about the Shushan air show, see Michael Millgate, *The Achievement of William Faulkner* (Constable, 1965).

8. Blotner, *Selected Letters of William Faulkner.*

9. Faulkner explained the genesis of Pylon in Frederick L. Gwynn and Joseph L. Blotner, eds., *Faulkner in the University: Class Conferences at the University of Virginia 1957–1958* (University Press of Mississippi, 2022).

10. Robert Hamblin, "Faulkner and Hollywood: A Call for Reassessment," *Critical Essays on William Faulkner* (University Press of Mississippi, 2002).

11. Hawks explained his reaction in Joseph McBride, ed., *Hawks on Hawks* (University of California Press, 1982).

12. Tom Dardis, *Some Time in the Sun: The Hollywood Years of F. Scott Fitzgerald, William Faulkner, Nathanael West, Aldous Huxley, and James Agee* (Scribner's, 1976).

13. Joseph Blotner interview with Hermann Deutsch, February 1965, Joseph Blotner Papers in the Louis Daniel Brodsky Collection, Center for Faulkner Studies (CFS), Southeast Missouri State University.

14. Cleanth Brooks, *Toward Yoknapatawpha and Beyond* (Yale University Press, 1978).

15. Carvel Collins interview with Murray Spain, early June 1960, in Carvel Collins Papers, Harry R. Ransom Humanities Research Center (HRC), University of Texas.

16. Interview with Richard Bradford, August 9, 1969, Joseph Blotner Papers, CFS.

17. Interview with Mrs. Roark Bradford, spring 1963, Carvel Collins Papers, HRC. See the chapter on Taylor Brown's *Wingwalkers*, which draws on this episode in his Faulknerian novel.

18. Interview with Mrs. Vernon Omlie, November 24, 1963, Carvel Collins Papers, HRC.

19. John Bassett, ed., *William Faulkner: The Critical Heritage* (Routledge & Kegan Paul, 1975).

20. Bassett, *William Faulkner.*

21. Quoted in Brooks, *Toward Yoknapatawpha.*

22. Faulkner's December 1934 letter to his agent mentions he had sent a copy of the novel to Hawks. See Blotner, *Selected Letters.*

23. Quoted in Peter Lurie, *Vision's Immanence: Faulkner, Film, and the Popular Imagination* (The Johns Hopkins University Press, 2004).

24. Bruce Kawin, *Faulkner and Film* (Ungar, 1977).

25. Donald T. Torchiana, "Faulkner's Pylon and the Structure of Modernity," *Faulkner and His Critics*, ed. John N. Duvall (The Johns Hopkins University Press, 2010).

26. Jean-Pierre Coursodon with Pierre Sauvage, *American Directors, Volume 1* (McGraw-Hill, 1983).

27. See the entry on Sirk in Richard Roud, *Cinema: A Critical Dictionary* (Seeker and Warburg, 1980).

28. Philip French, "The Tarnished Angels," *The Guardian*, September 13, 2013. http://www.theguardian.com/film/2013/sep/15/tarnished-angels-douglas-sirk-dvd.

29. M. Thomas Inge, *Conversations with William Faulkner* (Overlook Duckworth, 2006).

220   NOTES

30. Inge, *Conversations with William Faulkner*.

31. Quoted in Frank M. Laurence, *Hemingway and the Movies* (Da Capo, 1981).

32. Inge, *Conversations with William Faulkner*.

33. Quoted in Leonard Leff, *Hemingway and His Conspirators: Hollywood, Scribner's, and the Making of American Celebrity Culture* (Rowman & Littlefield, 1997).

34. Dardis believes that Faulkner was adopting a country bumpkin persona when he made the remark about Mickey Mouse.

35. Inge, *Conversations with William Faulkner*.

The Stories of Temple Drake

1. For these and other details about the novel and film, see the first volume of Rollyson, *The Life of William Faulkner* and the blu-ray release on dvd of *The Story of Temple Drake*.

2. I'm indebted for this insight to Ben Robbins, *Faulkner's Hollywood Novels: Women Between Page and Screen* (University of Virginia Press, 2024).

3. Unpublished interview with Dean's husband, Larry Wells.

"Tomorrow" and *Tomorrow*: Faulkner into Film

1. This was written in the late 1970s, long before James Franco, produced his adaptations of *The Sound and the Fury* and *As I Lay Dying*, the latter a bold attempt to render different points of view using split screen and other experimental camera techniques and placements.

2. It strikes me now that *Revolt in the Earth* is like the adaptation of the story of "Tomorrow," a work that is not beholden to the written text but is free to explore its characters in a new dimension.

3. In articulating the view of history that seems to inform "Tomorrow," I have drawn on Bernard Lewis, *History: Remembered, Recovered, Invented* (Princeton University Press, 1975).

4. Horton Foote's film adaptation of "Tomorrow" is based on his script for the Playhouse 90 television production (May 7, 1960), published by Dramatist's Play Service in 1963. In the television production (which I have not seen) Foote included scenes with the Pruitts, Charles Mallison, and Gavin Stevens in order to maintain Faulkner's emphasis on a story which emerges out of the speculations of the narrators. Mr. Foote informed me that these same scenes were also shot for the film but were eliminated in the final cutting. The elimination seems to have been justified, for the scenes might slow the action of the drama. Foote also considered having all of the narrators tell the story but rejected this possibility because he believed the film would be rendered static and diffuse by the clash of conflicting narrative styles. The film reproduces the dialogue of the 1960 screenplay for television, except for small cuts in that dialogue and the omission of the narrators' scenes mentioned above. I have quoted from the 1960 screenplay in my interpretation of the 1971 film only for the purposes of accurately recording and analyzing the same dialogue which is used in the film The shooting script for the film has not been published.

NOTES

5. Horton Foote, *Three Plays: Old Man, Tomorrow, and Roots in a Parchment Ground* (Harcourt, Brace & World, 1962).

6. Bruce Kawin, *Faulkner and Film* (Ungar, 1977).

7. The scenes centered around the stove are reminiscent of scenes in Faulkner's other fiction, especially *Go Down, Moses*, where the stove, the fire and the hearth, symbolize the solidarity of home and the continuity of family life. Thus Horton Foote cleverly manages to dramatize one of Faulkner's essential themes and makes it profoundly resonant in the film.

8. Kawin, *Faulkner and Film.*

9. Kawin, *Faulkner and Film.*

10. Kawin, Faulkner and Film.

11. For a similar view of film adaptations, see Gene Bluestone, *Novels into Film: The Metamorphosis of Fiction into Cinema* (University of California Press, 1973).

12. Michael Millgate, *The Achievement of William Faulkner* (Constable, 1966).

The Reivers: On and Off the Screen

1. Roger Ebert, Rev. of *The Reivers*, 1969, https://www.rogerebert.com/reviews/the-reivers-1969.

2. Neile McQueen Toffel, *Steve McQueen, My Husband, My Friend* (Atheneum, 1986).

3. Darwin Porter, *Steve McQueen, King of Cool: Tales of a Lurid Life: Another Hot, Startling, and Unauthorized Celebrity Biography* (Blood Productions, 2009).

4. Penina Spiegel, *McQueen: The Story of a Bad Boy in Hollywood* (Doubleday, 1986).

5. Marshall Terril, *Steve McQueen: Portrait of an American Rebel* (D. I. Fine, 1994).

6. Spiegel, *McQueen.*

The White Man's "Negro" in Faulkner Country

1. Quotations from Cullen are from the Floyd Watkins Papers, Stuart A. Rose Manuscript, Archives, and Rare Book Library, Emory University.

2. Dollard's work is discussed in the chapter, "Caste from a Faulknerian Perspective."

3. Judith Sensibar, *Faulkner and Love: The Women Who Shaped His Art: A Biography* (Yale University Press, 2010).

The Twilight of Man in "Delta Autumn"

1. The gift is recorded in Louis Daniel Brodsky and Robert Hamblin, eds., *Faulkner: A Comprehensive Guide to the Brodsky Collection. The Bibliography Volume I* (University Press of Mississippi, 1983).

2. Malcolm's letters are in special collections University of South Carolina library.

3. See Malcolm Cowley, *The Faulkner-Cowley File: Letters and Memories, 1944–1962* (Viking, 1966).

4. This is also the import of *Revolt in the Earth.*

"Shooting Negroes"

1. Faulkner's drinking and his medical history are dealt with in the second volume of Rollyson, *The Life of William Faulkner*.

2. Faulkner's statements on race and civil rights are collected in William Faulkner, *Essays, Speeches, and Public Letters* (Random House, 1965).

3. Faulkner comments on Reconstruction and race while in Japan are collected in James B. Meriwether and Michael Millgate, eds., *Lion in the Garden: Interviews with William Faulkner, 1926–1962* (Random House, 1968).

4. Joseph Blotner, *Selected Letters of William Faulkner* (Random House, 1977).

5. The full story of Cantwell's visit to the Faulkner home is told in the second volume of Rollyson, *The Life of William Faulkner*.

6. See the next chapter of this book, "Sole Owner and Proprietor."

7. Drew Gilpin Faust, "What to Do About William Faulkner?" (September 15, 2020). See my rebuttal, "The Indispensable Faulkner," *National Review*, January 2024.

8. For a brilliant explanation about how to handle Faulkner and race in the classroom, see Robert Hamblin's "Teaching Intruder in the Dust through Its Political and Historical Context" in Robert Hamblin, *Critical Essays on William Faulkner* (University Press of Mississippi, 2022).

9. Quoted in Catherine Gunther Kodat, "Unsteady State: Faulkner and the Cold War." *William Faulkner in Context*, ed. John T. Matthews (Cambridge University Press, 2015).

10. See the chapter in this book entitled "War No More."

11. Towner observes that "Faulkner's own distrust of group action and behavior sabotaged his lifelong attempts to describe group behavior: he was often a clumsy commentator on cultural phenomena because he believed, at base, only in individual reality."

12. Howe's letters are reprinted in Charles D. Peavy, *Go Slow Now: Faulkner and the Race Question* (University of Oregon, 1971).

13. Peavy says Howe offered to supply him with his verbatim notes, but Peavy does not say if he did, in fact, look at those notes. Archivists at the University of Wyoming could not locate Howe's notes in his papers.

14. Evans Harrington and Ann J. Abadie, eds., *The Maker and the Myth: Faulkner and Yoknapatawpha* (University Press of Mississippi, 1978).

15. The American edition, titled *William Faulkner: A Life through Novels*, appeared in 2017.

16. Stone's critical comments on the family appear frequently in letters that are included in Louis Daniel Brodsky and Robert Hamblin, eds., *Faulkner: A Comprehensive Guide to the Brodsky Collection, Volume II: The Letters* (University Press of Mississippi, 1983).

Caste from a Faulknerian Perspective: *Intruder in the Dust*

1. See the first volume of *The Life of William Faulkner* for a discussion of the Nelse Patton lynching and what Faulkner knew about it.

2. Robert Hamblin, "Teaching Intruder in the Dust through Its Political and Historical Context," *Critical Essays on William Faulkner* (University Press of Mississippi, 2022), notices that before Lucas has ordered Chick's rescue from the creek, "Chick and his two Black

NOTES

companions assume for that time and place the expected roles of their respective races. Chick leads the way and carries a gun, while the Blacks follow, armed with tapsticks."

3. See the description of this episode in the second volume of Rollyson, *The Life of William Faulkner*.

4. Floyd Watkins Papers, Stuart A. Rose Manuscript, Archives, and Rare Book Library, Emory University.

5. Hamblin, *Critical Essays on William Faulkner*.

6. Joseph Blotner, *Selected Letters of William Faulkner* (Random House, 1977).

Bibliography

Note: All quotations from Faulkner's fiction are from the Library of America and Random electronic editions.

Bassett, John, ed. *William Faulkner: The Critical Heritage*. Routledge & Kegan Paul, 1975.

Bleikasten, Andre. *William Faulkner: A Life through the Novels*. Indiana University Press, 2017.

Blotner, Joseph. *Faulkner: A Biography*. Random House, 1974.

Blotner, Joseph. *Selected Letters of William Faulkner*. Random House, 1977.

Blotner, Joseph. *Faulkner: A Biography*. Random House, 1984.

Bluestone, Gene. *Novels into Film: The Metamorphosis of Fiction into Cinema*. University of California Press, 1973.

Bradley, Patricia L. "Angelic Acrobats and Fallen Southern Women: William Faulkner and Robert Penn Warren Go to the Circus." In *Faulkner and Warren*, edited by Christopher Rieger and Robert W. Hamblin. Southeast Missouri State University Press, 2015.

Brodsky, Louis Daniel. *William Faulkner: Life Glimpses*. University of Texas Press, 1990.

Brodsky, Louis Daniel, and Robert Hamblin, eds. *Faulkner: A Comprehensive Guide to the Brodsky Collection. Volume I. The Biobibliography*. University Press of Mississippi, 1983.

Brodsky, Louis Daniel, and Robert Hamblin, eds. *Faulkner: A Comprehensive Guide to the Brodsky Collection. Volume II: The Letters*. University Press of Mississippi, 1984.

Brodsky, Louis Daniel, and Robert Hamblin, eds. *Faulkner: A Comprehensive Guide to the Brodsky Collection. Volume III: The De Gaulle Story*. University Press of Mississippi, 1984.

Brodsky, Louis Daniel, and Robert Hamblin, eds. *Faulkner: A Comprehensive Guide to the Brodsky Collection, Volume IV: Battle Cry: A Screenplay by William Faulkner*. University Press of Mississippi, 1985.

Brodsky, Louis Daniel, and Robert Hamblin, eds. *Faulkner: A Comprehensive Guide to the Brodsky Collection. Volume V: Manuscripts and Documents*. University Press of Mississippi, 1988.

Brooks, Cleanth. *Toward Yoknapatawpha and Beyond*. Yale University Press, 1978.

Broughton, Panthea Reid. "An Interview with Meta Carpenter Wilde," *Southern Review*, Autumn 1982, 776–802.

Coursodon, Jean-Pierre, with Pierre Sauvage. *American Directors, Volume 1*. McGraw-Hill, 1983.

Cowley, Malcolm. *The Faulkner-Cowley File: Letters and Memories, 1944–1962*. Viking, 1966.

BIBLIOGRAPHY

Cullen, John B., and Floyd C. Watkins. *Old Times in the Faulkner Country*. University of North Carolina Press, 1961.

Curnutt, Kirk. *William Faulkner*. Reaction Books, 2018.

Dardis, Tom. *Some Time in the Sun: The Hollywood Years of F. Scott Fitzgerald, William Faulkner, Nathanael West, Aldous Huxley, and James Agee*. Scribner's, 1976.

Delson, Susan. *Dudley Murphy: Hollywood Wildcard*. University of Minnesota Press, 2006.

Dollard, John. *Caste and Class in a Southern Town*. University of Wisconsin Press, 1989.

Dunlap, Mary. "The Achievement of Gavin Stevens." PhD diss., University of South Carolina, 1970.

Earle, David M. *Re-Covering Modernism: Pulps, Paperbacks, and the Prejudice of Form*. Ashgate, 2009.

Eliot, Marc. *Steve McQueen: A Biography*. Crown Archetype, 2011.

Fant, Joseph L., and Robert Ashley, eds. *Faulkner at West Point*. University Press of Mississippi, 2002.

Faulkner, William. *Early Prose and Poetry*. Little Brown, 1962.

Faulkner, William. *Essays, Speeches, and Public Letters*. Random House, 1965.

Faulkner, William. *New Orleans Sketches*. Rutgers University Press, 1958.

Foner, Eric. *Reconstruction: Updated Edition: America's Unfinished Revolution, 1863–1977*. Harper Perennial Classics, 2014.

Foote, Horton. *Three Plays: Old Man, Tomorrow, and Roots in a Parched Ground*. Harcourt, Brace & World, 1962.

Fowler, Doreen. *Faulkner: The Return of the Repressed*. University of Virginia Press, 1997.

Fruscione, Joseph. *Faulkner and Hemingway: Biography of a Literary Rivalry*. The Ohio State University Press, 2012.

Gillis, Mary Phyfer. "Faulkner's Biographies: Life, Art, and the Poetics of Biography." PhD diss., University of Alabama, 2002.

Gleeson-White, Sarah, ed. *William Faulkner at Twentieth Century-Fox: The Annotated Screenplays*. Oxford University Press, 2017.

Gorra, Michael. *The Saddest Words: William Faulkner's Civil War*. Liveright, 2020.

Grimwood, Michael. *Heart in Conflict: Faulkner's Struggles with Vocation*. The University of Georgia Press, 1987.

Gwynn, Frederick L., and Joseph L. Blotner, eds. *Faulkner in the University: Class Conferences at the University of Virginia 1957–1958*. University of Virginia Press, 1959.

Hamblin, Robert W. *Critical Essays on William Faulkner*. University Press of Mississippi, 2022.

Hamblin, Robert W. *Myself and the World: A Biography of William Faulkner*. University Press of Mississippi, 2016.

Harrington, Evans, and Ann J. Abadie, eds. *The Maker and the Myth: Faulkner and Yoknapatawpha 1977*. University Press of Mississippi, 1978.

Harvey, James. *Movie Love in the Fifties*. Da Capo Press.

Hickman, Lisa C. *William Faulkner and Joan Williams: The Romance of Two Writers*. McFarland, 2006.

Hooton, Earnest Albert. *The Twilight of Man*. Putnam's, 1939.

Inge, M. Thomas, ed. *Conversations with William Faulkner*. University Press of Mississippi, 1999.

BIBLIOGRAPHY

Inge, M. Thomas, ed. *William Faulkner: The Contemporary Reviews.* Cambridge University Press, 1995.

Inge, M. Thomas. *William Faulkner.* Overlook Duckworth, 2006.

Kawin, Bruce. *Faulkner and Film.* Ungar, 1977.

Kawin, Bruce. *Faulkner's MGM Screenplays.* University of Tennessee Press, 1982.

Karl, Frederick. *William Faulkner: American Writer.* Grove Press, 1989.

Kodat, Catherine Gunther. "Unsteady State: Faulkner and the Cold War." In *William Faulkner in Context,* edited by John T. Matthews. Cambridge University Press, 2015.

Ladd, Barbara. *Resisting History: Gender, Modernity, and Authorship in William Faulkner, Zora Neale Hurston, and Eudora Welty.* Louisiana State University Press, 2007.

Laurence, Frank M. *Hemingway and the Movies.* Da Capo, 1981.

Leff, Leonard. *Hemingway and His Conspirators: Hollywood, Scribner's, and the Making of American Celebrity Culture.* Rowman & Littlefield, 1997.

Lewis, Bernard. *History: Remembered, Recovered, Invented.* Princeton University Press, 1975.

Lurie, Peter. *Vision's Immanence: Faulkner, Film, and the Popular Imagination.* The Johns Hopkins University Press, 2004.

Lurie, Peter, and Ann J. Abadie, ed. *Faulkner and Film.* University Press of Mississippi, 2014.

MacMillan, Duane. "*Pylon*: From Short Stories to Major Work." *Mosaic* 7 (Fall 1973): 186–212.

Matthews, John T. *William Faulkner: Seeing through the South.* Wiley Blackwell, 2012.

McBride, Joseph, ed. *Hawks on Hawks.* University of California Press, 1982.

McCarthy, Todd. *Howard Hawks: The Grey Fox of Hollywood.* Grove Press, 2000.

Meek, Edwin E. *Riot: Witness to Anger and Change.* Edited by Lawrence Wells. Yoknapatawpha Press, 2015.

Meriwether, James B. *A Faulkner Miscellany.* University Press of Mississippi, 1974.

Meriwether, James B., and Michael Millgate, eds. *Lion in the Garden: Interviews with William Faulkner, 1926–1962.* Random House, 1968.

Millgate, Michael. *The Achievement of William Faulkner.* Constable, 1965.

Minter, David, ed. Norton critical edition of *The Sound and the Fury.* W. W. Norton, 1987.

Minter, David. *William Faulkner: His Life and Work.* Johns Hopkins University Press, 1980.

Oates, Stephen B. *William Faulkner: The Man and the Artist.* HarperCollins, 1987.

Paddock, Lisa. *Contrapuntal in Integration: William Faulkner's Short Story Collections* International Scholars Publications, 2000.

Parini, Jay. *One Matchless Time: A Life of William Faulkner.* Harper, 2004.

Peavy, Charles D. *Go Slow Now: Faulkner and the Race Question.* University of Oregon, 1971.

Peek, Charles A., and Robert W. Hamblin, eds. *A Companion to Faulkner Studies.* Greenwood Press, 2004.

Petrie, Dennis W. *Ultimately Fiction: Design in Modern American Literary Biography.* Purdue University Press, 1981.

Polk, Noel. *Children of the Dark House: Text and Context in Faulkner.* University Press of Mississippi, 1996.

Polk, Noel, and Ann J. Abadie, eds. *Faulkner and War.* University Press of Mississippi, 2004.

Porter, Carolyn. *William Faulkner: Lives and Legacies.* Oxford University Press, 2007.

Porter, Darwin. *Steve McQueen, King of Cool: Tales of a Lurid Life: Another Hot, Startling, and Unauthorized Celebrity Biography.* Blood Productions, 2009.

Railey, Kevin. *Natural Aristocracy: History, Ideology and the Production of William Faulkner.* University of Alabama Press, 1999.

Rampton, David. *William Faulkner: A Literary Life.* Palgrave Macmillan, 2008.

Robins, Ben. "The Pragmatic Modernist: William Faulkner's Craft and Hollywood's Networks of Production." *Journal of Screenwriting* 5, no. 2 (2014): 239–57.

Rollyson, Carl. *The Life of William Faulkner: The Past Is Never Dead, 1897–1934, Volume 1.* University of Virginia Press, 2020.

Rollyson, Carl. *The Life of William Faulkner: This Alarming Paradox, 1935–1962, Volume 2.* University of Virginia Press, 2020.

Rollyson, Carl. *William Faulkner Day by Day.* University Press of Mississippi, 2022.

Roud, Richard. *Cinema: A Critical Dictionary.* Secker and Warburg, 1980.

Sensibar, Judith. *Faulkner and Love: The Women Who Shaped His Art: A Biography.* Yale University Press, 2010.

Sensibar, Judith, ed. *Vision in Spring.* University of Texas Press, 1984.

Sidney, George. "Faulkner in Hollywood: A Study of His Career as a Scenarist." PhD diss., University of New Mexico, 1959.

Solomon, Stefan. *William Faulkner in Hollywood: Screenwriting for the Studios.* University of Georgia Press, 2017.

Spiegel, Penina. *McQueen: The Story of a Bad Boy in Hollywood.* Doubleday, 1986.

Terrill, Marshall. *Steve McQueen: Portrait of an American Rebel.* D. I. Fine, 1994.

Toffel, Neile McQueen. *Steve McQueen, My Husband, My Friend.* Atheneum, 1986.

Torchiana, Donald T. "Faulkner's *Pylon* and the Structure of Modernity." In *Faulkner and His Critics*, edited by John N. Duvall. The Johns Hopkins University Press, 2010.

Towner, Theresa. *Faulkner on the Color Line: The Later Novels.* University Press of Mississippi, 2000.

Trotter, Sally. *Rowan Oak: A History of the William Faulkner Home.* Nautilus, 2017.

Urgo, Joseph. *Faulkner's Apocrypha.* University Press of Mississippi, 1989.

Van Vechten, Carl. *Nigger Heaven.* University of Illinois Press, 2000.

Wasson, Ben. *Count No 'Count: Flashbacks to Faulkner.* University Press of Mississippi, 1983.

Watson, James G. *William Faulkner: Self-Presentation and Performance.* University of Texas Press, 2013.

Watson, James G., ed. *Thinking of Home: William Faulkner's Letters to His Mother and Father, 1918–1925.* W. W. Norton, 1992.

Webb, James W., and A. Wigfall Green, eds. *William Faulkner of Oxford.* Louisiana State University Press, 1965.

Wells, Dean Faulkner. *Every Day by the Sun: A Memoir of the Faulkners of Mississippi.* Crown, 2011.

Weinstein, Philip. *Becoming Faulkner: The Art and Life of William Faulkner.* Oxford University Press, 2009.

Weinstein, Philip. *Simply Faulkner.* Simply Charly, 2016.

Wickham, Kathleen, ed. *James Meredith: Breaking the Barrier.* Yoknapatawpha Press, 2022.

Wickham, Kathleen. *We Believed We Were Immortal: Twelve Reporters Who Covered the 1962 Integration Crisis at Ole Miss.* Yoknapatawpha Press, 2017.

Wilde, Meta Carpenter, and Orin Borsten. *A Loving Gentleman: The Love Story of William Faulkner and Meta Carpenter.* Simon and Schuster, 1976.

Wilkerson, Isabel. *Caste: The Origins of Our Discontent.* Random House, 2020.

Williams, Joan. "Twenty Will Not Come Again." *Atlantic Monthly*, May 1980, 58–66.

Williams, Joan. *The Wintering.* Harcourt Brace Jovanovich, 1971.

Williamson, Joel. *William Faulkner and Southern History.* Oxford University Press, 1993.

Wittenberg, Judith. *Faulkner: The Transfiguration of Biography.* University of Nebraska Press, 1979.

Young, Stark. *The Pavilion: Of People and Times Remembered, of Stories and Places.* Scribner's, 1951.

Index

Africa, 28–29, 87, 107, 109, 119, 124, 126, 129, 186, 191, 193, 218n15

African Americans, 9, 10, 18, 24, 29, 74–79, 85, 104, 116–18, 123, 127, 129, 176, 179, 191–92, 194, 195, 200–205, 207, 209–10. *See also* Black people

Agee, James, 156

Aircraft, 100, 136

Alabama, University of, 195

Aldridge, Leslie, 62

Alexander, Margaret Walker, 195–96

Algonquin Hotel, 57

Algonquin Round Table, 116

All God's Chillun Got Wings, 116

All the King's Men, 133

America, 9, 20, 29, 37, 39, 54, 61, 78, 83, 88, 90, 103, 119, 130, 167, 184, 191, 196, 201; army, 39; bars, 187; critics, 143; crowds, 106; frontier, 182; literature, 88; moving pictures, 99; women, 103; writers, 62

American Boy, The, 32

American Legion, 83, 85, 177

American Revolution, 194

American South, 81, 104

Americana, 172

Americans, 11, 13, 14, 15, 23, 37, 38, 40, 54, 81, 83, 107, 179, 194, 210

Anderson, Sherwood, 4, 22, 129

Anti-Communism, 15

Associated Artists, 115

Athens, 64

Baby Doll, 60

Bacher, William, 103

Baird, Helen, 42

Baldwin, James, 193, 195, 198

Baptists, 82, 120, 121, 127

Barbizon Hotel, 55

Barnstorming, 98, 133

Barr, Caroline (Callie), 10, 176

Barrett, William E., 11, 13

Barrymore, Lionel, 99

Basso, Hamilton, 132

Beck, Warren, 86

Becoming Faulkner, 10, 198–99

Bell Jar, The, 55

Bellin, Olga, 157

Bergson, Henri, 89

Berlin Institute, 201

Best Years of Our Lives, The, 167

Bezzerides, A. I. (Buzz), 44, 55, 215n5

Birth of a Nation, 77, 177

Bitterweeds, 181

Black Faulkners, 28, 79, 122

Black people, 21, 24, 25, 27, 76, 77, 118, 120, 121–26, 129–30, 168, 178, 186, 190–200, 202, 203, 205, 206. *See also* African Americans

Bleikasten, André, 9, 20–23, 198

Blotner, Joseph, 7–8, 9, 10, 16, 20, 21, 31, 32, 33, 44, 46, 51, 53, 54, 102, 132, 181, 189, 195, 216n1

Bluestone, George, 156

Bogart, Humphrey, 12, 13, 84, 214n10

Bradford, Roark, 135

Brazil, 40, 55

Brennan, Walter, 13

Brodsky, Louis Daniel, 197–98

INDEX

Brooks, Cleanth, 135
Brothels, 165, 167, 168, 169
Broughton, Panthea, 45, 47, 52
Brown, Ellen, 53
Brown, Taylor, 3, 31–36
Brown v. Board of Education, 77, 190
Bryant, Will, 75
Buckley, William F., 191
Buckner, Robert, 114–15, 130, 218n14
Bullitt, 167
Bunche, Ralph, 191
Burcham, Milo, 133
Bureaucrats, 41, 100
Butch Cassidy and the Sundance Kid, 168
Butterworth, Keen, 103

Cabinet of Dr. Caligari, The, 141
Caesar, Julius, 100, 106
Cairo, Egypt, 54
California, 32, 58, 113, 167, 192
Camus, Albert, 19
Canada, 37
Canadians, 31, 38, 80, 87
Canetti, Elias, 93, 101
Cantwell, Robert, 21, 192, 222n5
Carlyle, Thomas, 95
Carpenter, Meta, 10, 11, 38, 42, 45–48, 50, 52,
    62, 63, 67, 85, 94, 149, 216n9
Carrollton, Mississippi, 167
Carson, Jack, 142, 143
Caste and Class in a Southern Town, 175, 201
Ceiling Zero, 141
Cerf, Bennett, 66
Cerf, Phyllis, 66
Chandler, Raymond, 39
Chekhov, Anton, 138
Christ, Jesus, 93, 95, 99, 100, 217n6
Christianity, 95
Christians, 101
Citizen Kane, 137, 140, 142, 145, 160
Civil War, 23, 25–29, 184, 90, 98, 116, 193, 199,
    200; in *Absalom, Absalom!*, 74, 87, 88,
    209; in *Flags in the Dust*, 24, 98; in *Go
    Down, Moses*, 187; in *Revolt in the Earth*,
    121, 123, 125; in *The Unvanquished*, 27, 75

Clansman, The, 192
Clarion-Ledger (Jackson, Mississippi),
    118, 146
Cobb, Lee J., 13
Coindreau, Maurice, 115
Cold War, 11, 62, 189, 193
Cole, Nat King, 28
Collins, Carvel, 10, 135
Commins, Dorothy, 46, 50
Commins, Saxe, 40, 44–47, 49–51, 55, 66,
    195, 200
Communism/Communists, 13, 15, 37, 62,
    79, 82, 85
Confederacy, 27; army, 199; flag, 27;
    soldiers, 23
Conrad, Joseph, 18, 44
Conservative Mind, The, 73
Constantine, Michael, 167
Cooper, Gary, 13, 16
Cowley, Malcolm, 4, 19–20, 23, 182
Crawford, Joan, 114, 131, 134
Crosse, Rupert, 166, 167, 172
Crowds and Power, 93
Cullen, John, 28–29, 175–80, 190, 192,
    203, 205
Curnutt, Kirk, 11

Dardis, Tom, 115, 134, 141, 220n34
Delson, Susan, 115
Depression, the, 133, 143
Deutsch, Hermann, 134–35, 140
Dickens, Charles, 95
Disney, Walt, 145, 167
Dollard, John, 175, 177, 178, 179, 201–5, 207
Dos Passos, John, 69
Double Dealer, 82
Du Bois, W. E. B., 24
Dunlap, Mary, 151
Dunning, William Archibald, 77
Duvall, Robert, 156, 159

Earle, David M., 144
Ebert, Roger, 166
Ebony, 78
Egypt, 54

INDEX

Eisenhower, Dwight, 62
Eisenstein, Sergei, 116
Eldridge, Florence, 148
Eliot, Mark, 167
Eliot, T. S., 19, 136, 142, 167
Ellison, Ralph, 193–94, 195
Emperor Jones, The, 116, 117–21, 124, 127
England, 58, 90, 102, 110, 130, 148
Europe, 38, 39, 40, 54, 58, 63, 81, 82, 85, 100, 104, 108, 109, 129, 208
Evans, Walker, 156

Fascism, 38, 81–85, 86, 88, 92, 100, 107, 202
Falkner, Alabama Leroy (Aunt Bama), 43, 200
Falkner, Maud, 10, 12, 14, 17, 28, 33, 37, 41, 42, 43, 54, 68, 77, 82, 101, 190
Falkner, Murry (father), 8, 76, 104, 107, 200
Falkner, Murry (brother, aka Jack), 133
Falkner, Murry (nephew), 209
Falkner, William C. (the old Colonel), 98, 200
Falkner family, 9, 77, 78, 175–76
Far East, 44
Farrell, Sharon, 167
Faulkner, Estelle, 7, 9, 10, 21, 30, 38, 40, 42–52, 59–60, 64, 69, 176, 192, 210, 215nn4–5
Faulkner, Jill, 12, 43, 48, 49–50, 56, 60, 61, 62, 66, 69
Faulkner, Jimmy, 92, 209
Faulkner, John (brother), 79, 133, 190–91, 195, 200, 209
Faulkner, William: and alcohol consumption, 25, 30, 45, 55, 63, 64, 65, 79, 114, 115, 135, 189, 190, 195, 199, 222n1; and the American dream, 40; and aviation, 17, 33–34; childhood of, 15, 25, 33, 43, 48; and the Civil War, 23–27, 29, 74, 75, 84, 87, 88, 90, 98, 116, 121, 123, 125, 187, 193, 199, 200, 209; criticism, 9, 17–18; drawings of, 56, 216n9; and divorce, 47; education of, 25, 28; and farming, 54, 199; and Faulkner family, 7, 8, 9, 11, 25, 27, 28, 45, 46, 47, 50, 73, 74, 76, 77, 78,

79, 104–5, 109, 114–15, 122, 132, 175–76, 181, 190–91, 192, 199–200, 209, 222n26; and foreigners, 37–41, 82, 100, 109; and history, 9, 12, 16, 25, 26, 74, 75, 76, 77, 85, 95, 96, 99, 100, 103, 104, 106, 109, 116, 127, 130, 133, 154, 162, 163, 166, 179, 187, 191, 201, 208, 210, 222n3; and horses, 54, 58, 61, 68, 69, 104, 106, 132; and hunting, 59, 97, 106, 175, 180; interviews of, 4, 64, 65, 67, 79, 82, 83, 89, 145, 189, 194, 195, 196, 197, 198, 199, 200; and miscegenation, 78, 87, 185; as pilot, 98, 139; and pipes, 33, 59, 68; poetry of, 43; and politics, 82, 84, 97, 133, 182, 187; and race, 21, 23–25, 28, 76, 82, 83, 87, 88, 117–18, 121, 123, 125, 175–210, 222n8, 222n2; and religion, 14, 81, 99, 126; and uniforms, 17, 22, 33, 68, 83, 92, 97, 100, 101, 102, 107, 109, 120; and women, 10, 21, 40, 42, 45, 46, 47, 48, 49–50, 52, 62, 64, 83, 96, 124–26, 131, 134, 135, 136, 149, 176, 187, 206
Faulkner, William, characters of: Barron, Homer, 39; battalion runner, 99–100, 103–5, 107, 110; Beauchamp, Bobo, 164; Beauchamp, James, 185; Beauchamp, Lucas, 74, 108, 166, 192, 202–7, 210; Beauchamp, Philip Manigault, 108; Binford, Mr., 165, 167, 169; Bon, Charles, 26, 38, 39, 78, 80, 87, 88–90, 122–24, 130, 132, 192; Bookwright, 151, 153, 154, 155; Boss Priest, 162, 163, 166; Buchwald, 108; Burden, Joanna, 38; Cadet Lowe, 98; Captain Bridesman, 102; Captain Gualdres, 39; Coldfield, Rosa, 122–23; the corporal, 84, 95, 96, 100, 102, 107–10; Christmas, Joe, 38, 82–83, 88, 143, 156, 163, 177, 192; Compson, Benjamin (Benjy), 20; Compson, General, 121, 164, 185; Compson, Jason (father), 23, 122; Compson, Jason (son), 81, 82, 85; Compson, Quentin, 37, 77, 86, 87, 102, 143, 163; Corrie, Miss, 162, 165, 167, 168, 169, 171; Drake, Temple, 146–49; Eddie (*To Have and Have Not*),

84, 85; Edmonds, Roth, 183–84, 202–4; Eric, 126–29; Fentry, Jackson, 150–61; French architect, 39, 73; General Compson, 121, 164, 185; General Sternwood, 39; Generalissimo (old General), 94–96, 107–10, 114; Goodwin, Lee, 148; Gowrie, Crawford, 207; Gowrie, Vinson, 206, 207; Gragnon, Charles, 96–99, 102, 108, 109; Grierson, Emily, 39; Grimm, Percy, 38, 82–83, 177; Grove, Lena, 86, 143; Habersham, Miss, 206–7; Hampton, Sheriff, 207; Hogganbeck, Boon, 162, 166, 168, 171; horse groom, 103–5; Iowan, 108; Jack, 134, 136, 139, 142; Jiggs, 132, 136, 139, 142; Jones, Milly, 123; Jones, Wash, 123–24, 126, 128–29; Jones, Wash, III (grandson), 127–28; Kohl, Barton, 85; Levine, 100–102; Lovemaiden, Butch, 165, 167, 169; Mahon, Donald, 98; Major de Spain, 62–63, 183; Mallison, Chick, 77, 85, 151, 154, 193, 202, 208, 210, 220n4; the marshal, 84, 101, 107; Maury, 170; McCannon/Mackenzie, Shreve, 28, 38, 80, 87–90, 122, 151, 186, 193; McCaslin, Carothers, 74, 203; McCaslin, Ike, 74, 76, 86, 182–83; McCaslin, Ned, 105, 143, 163, 166, 167, 172; Montgomery, Jack, 107; Nancy (*Requiem for a Nun*), 279; Miriam (*Revolt in the Earth*), 126–30; old man Falls, 24; Otis, 165; Polchek, 108; Popeye, 146, 148; Pruitts, 151, 152, 153, 220n4; Quick, Isham, 152, 153, 155, 157, 158, 159, 160; Ratliff, V. K., 85; Reba, Miss, 146, 165, 167, 168, 169; reporter, 34, 132, 134–43, 145; Ruby, 146, 148; Sander, Aleck, 202, 204, 206, 207; Sartoris, Bayard (*The Unvanquished*), 27, 86; Sartoris, old Bayard, 8, 293n9; Sartoris, Young Bayard, 24, 89, 132; Sartoris, Colonel John, 77–78; Sartoris, John, 89; Sartoris twins, 113; Shumann, Dr., 131; Shumann, Laverne, 131–32, 134, 136, 139, 142–43, 218n3; Shumann, Roger, 131, 134, 136, 139, 140–41, 142–43; Shushan,

Colonel A. L., 136; Snopes, Clarence, 81; Snopes, Eula Varner, 60, 61, 62; Snopes, Flem, 85, 86; Snopes, Ike, 87; Snopes, Linda, 55, 57, 61, 84, 85, 86, 90, 100; Snopes, Mink, 85; Stevens, Gavin, 14, 22, 58, 60–62, 85, 86, 88, 106, 147, 149, 150–56, 180, 205–8, 220n4; Stevens, Gowan, 62, 147; Sutpen, Clytie, 89, 122–30; Sutpen, Henry, 26, 78, 79, 124, 125; Sutpen, Judith, 38, 89–90, 124–28, 130 131, 132, 148; Sutpen, Thomas, 19, 39, 73, 74, 78, 87–89, 107, 117, 119–31; the Sutpens, 80, 87, 162; Sutterfield, Reverend Tobe (Tooleyman), 103–6; Thorpe, Buck, 151, 154, 155; the Thorpes, 153, 159–60; Toinette, 125; Tommy, 146, 148; Varner, Eula, 60, 61, 62; Wilbourne, Harry, 32, 46

Faulkner, William, works of: *Absalom, Absalom!*, 3, 19, 21, 23, 26, 27–29, 34, 37, 38, 73–74, 78, 86–87, 89, 107, 113, 116–18, 120–24, 126–27, 129, 131, 134, 148, 151, 186, 192, 193, 209; *As I Lay Dying*, 19, 23, 35, 104, 134, 220n1; *Banjo on my Knee*, 13, 138, 214n8; "Barn Burning," 167; *Battle Cry*, 12, 73, 84, 92, 103, 115, 116, 201, 216n3; "The Bear," 69, 185, 196; *The Big Sleep*, 12, 39, 215n3; *Compson Appendix*, 3; "Country Lawyer," 16, 214n8; *The De Gaulle Story*, 92, 115; "Death Drag," 132, 133; "Delta Autumn," 181–88; *Dreadful Hollow*, 39, 215n3; *Drums Along the Mohawk*, 11, 13, 79, 114, 115, 148, 194, 214n8; "Dry September," 25; *Elmer*, 35, 44; "Evangeline," 218n15; *A Fable*, 22, 57, 61, 84, 91–110, 194, 217n6; "Fire and the Hearth," 9, 18, 221n7; *Flags in the Dust*, 23, 24, 29, 82, 89, 98, 140, 148, 192; *Go Down, Moses*, 19, 74, 76, 86, 163, 181, 182, 183, 184, 185, 192, 200, 210, 221n7; *The Hamlet*, 19, 167; "Honor," 132; *Intruder in the Dust*, 20, 77, 108, 166, 180, 192, 201–8, 210, 222n8; "Knight's Gambit," 39; *Land of*

INDEX

the Pharaohs, 13, 54, 144, 145; *The Last Slaver (Slave Ship)*, 117; *The Left Hand of God*, 11–14, 16, 214n8, 214n14; *Light in August*, 19, 23, 24, 29, 38, 82, 86, 88, 177, 192, 207; *The Mansion*, 55, 77, 84, 86, 90, 100; "Mississippi," 25; "Mistral," 81; *Mosquitoes*, 38; "An Odor of Verbena," 27; "Old Man," 47; "Pantaloon in Black," 29; *The Portable Faulkner*, 19–20, 23; *Pylon*, 3, 20, 31 34, 131–45, 218n11, 219n9; "Raid," 27; *The Reivers*, 77, 105, 162–66, 200; *Requiem for a Nun*, 12, 13, 14, 39, 61, 73–74, 75, 86, 147–49; *Revolt in the Earth*, 3, 89, 113–30, 148, 218n15, 220n2; *The Road to Glory*, 99; "A Rose for Emily," 39; *Sanctuary*, 20, 81, 146–49; *Sartoris*, 23, 31; "Shall Not Perish," 15; "Smoke," 80, 86, 88, 90, 91; Snopes trilogy, 3, 84, 86, 89; *Soldiers' Pay*, 98; *The Sound and the Fury*, 3, 19, 20, 23, 29, 35, 38, 44, 81, 82, 86, 102, 104, 114, 220n1; "Spotted Horses," 167; "Sunset," 118–19; *Sutter's Gold*, 116, 214n8; "That Evening Sun," 28; "This Kind of Courage," 134; *To Have and Have Not*, 12, 13, 84, 92, 114; *Today We Live*, 114, 131, 134; "Tomorrow," 150–61; *The Town*, 60–61, 77; "Turnabout," 93, 114, 131; *Vision in Spring*, 43; "The Waifs," 258; *War Birds*, 16, 89, 148; *The Wild Palms*, 11, 19, 20, 31, 32, 35, 36, 46, 58; "The Wild Palms," 47

Faulkner and Love, 10

Faulkner and Race, 196

"Faulkner and the Howe Interview," 194

Faulkner and the Negro, 194

Faulkner and War, 100

Faulkner's Apocrypha, 98

FBI (Federal Bureau of Investigation), 100, 209

Federal army, 78

Federal government, 191, 194, 207, 209, 210

Feinman, Colonel H. I., 131, 136, 137, 140

Feldman, Charles, 54

Feldman, Jean, 54

Fitzgerald, F. Scott, 19, 66, 82, 114

Flashbacks to Faulkner, 44, 47, 48, 49

Flaubert, Gustave, 44

Foote, Horton, 3, 157–58, 220n4

Foote, Shelby, 15, 155, 157–58, 220n4, 221n7

Ford, Ford Maddox, 116

For Whom the Bell Tolls, 84; Robert Jordan, 84

France, 22, 103, 110, 178

Franco, Francisco, 83

Frank, Harriet, Jr., 167

Frankfurter, Felix, 44

Franklin, Cornell, 43, 44, 51

Franklin, Gloria, 46

Franklin, Malcolm, 22, 91, 98, 181

Free World, The, 189

Freeman, Morgan, 172

French Foreign Legion, 102

French Revolution, The (Carlyle), 95

Front Page, The, 136, 138, 140

Fruscione, Joseph, 138

Gates Flying Circus, 132

Geer, Will, 167, 171

Genoa, Italy, 38

Gleeson-White, Sarah, 11

Gold Medal for Fiction, 97

Goldman, Morton, 134

Gone with the Wind, 24, 77, 118

Gorra, Michael, 23–30, 193, 199

Gray, Richard, 9

Great Gatsby, The, 82

Greece, 144

Greenfield Farm, 199

Greenville, Mississippi, 59, 60

Gumbel, Margery, 82

Gwynn, Frederick L., 102

Haas, Robert, 91, 98

Hamblin, Robert, 11, 46, 49, 134, 203

Hammett, Dashiell, 115

Harcourt, Brace, 192

Harlem, 116, 125, 127

Harlem Renaissance, 116

Harvard University, 77

236 INDEX

Harvey, James, 143
Hathaway, Henry, 93, 103
Hawks, Howard, 11–13, 16, 54, 103, 113, 114,
    134, 135, 141, 143, 144, 145, 219n11, 219n22
Hellman, Lillian, 82
Hemingway, Ernest, 19, 82, 84, 104, 114, 116,
    131, 132–33, 138, 139, 144, 145
Hernandez, Juano, 166–67, 170
Heyward, Dubose, 117
High Noon, 16, 145
His Girl Friday, 134; Hildy Johnson, 134, 136
Hitchcock, Alfred, 102
Hitler, Adolf, 81, 82, 85, 100, 187, 208
Holly Springs, Mississippi, 8
Hollywood, 4, 10–13, 15, 16, 34, 38–39, 47–49,
    52, 55, 73, 75, 76, 83, 85, 89, 92–94, 99,
    103, 113–15, 116, 119, 121, 123, 125, 130,
    133–36, 138–45, 148–49, 167, 171, 188, 192,
    201, 214n8
Hooton, Earnest Albert, 181–88
Hopkins, Miriam, 146–48
Hotel Beaujolais, 54, 59
Housman, A. E., 19
Howe, Russell Warren, 189–90, 194–200
Howland, Harold, 40
Hud, 167
Hudson, Rock, 142–43

I Cover the Waterfront, 136, 138, 140
Importance of Being Earnest, The, 57
Indianola, Mississippi, 175, 201
Italy, 58, 81

James, Clifton, 167, 169
James Meredith: Breaking the Barrier, 210
Japan/Japanese, 40, 62, 77, 144, 191, 210,
    222n3
Jefferson, Mississippi, 19, 26, 39, 74, 88, 162,
    168, 201–2
Jefferson, Thomas, 28
Jefferson Society, 69
Jews, 41, 81–82, 85, 108, 186, 192, 208
Jim Crow, 116, 120, 179, 186
Johnson, Susie Paul, 141

Jonsson, Else, 10, 15, 55
Joyce, James, 18, 116
Judson, Horace, 195

Karl, Frederick, 8, 21, 137, 197, 214n10
Karlova, Irina, 39
Kawin, Bruce, 11, 114, 142, 155, 159, 160
Kazan, Elia, 59, 60
Keats, John, 19, 132
Kelly, Grace, 55
Kennedy, John F., 97
Kennedy, Robert, 210
Keswick Hunt Club, 68
Kirk, Russell, 73–74, 76–80
Kosciusko, Mississippi, 210

Ladd, Barbara, 96, 103, 104, 109
Lady Go-Lightly (horse), 54
Lafayette County, Mississippi, 26
Landmesser, August, 208
Last Tycoon, The, 139; Monroe Stahr, 139
Last Year at Marienbad, 160
"Lay of the Last Minstrel, The," 38
Lee, Muna, 40
Leff, Leonard, 145
Legacy of the Civil War, The, 26
Let Us Now Praise Famous Men, 156
Levy, Harold, 82
Lewis, Sinclair, 138
Liberals, 78
Life of William Faulkner, The, 200–201
Lincoln, Abraham, 78
Linscott, Robert, 59, 66
Lion in the Garden, 195
Little Foxes, The, 167
Little League games (Charlottesville,
    Virginia), 68
Liveright, Horace, 82, 192
London, 126
Long, Huey, 133
Long Hot Summer, The, 167
Lost Cause, 24, 26
Louisiana, 119, 133
Loving Gentleman, A, 11, 39, 45, 47, 49, 50

INDEX

Lowrey, Perrin H., Jr., 15
Lucy, Autherine, 195
Lurie, Peter, 11, 141
Lynching, 25, 29, 38, 8–83, 118, 120, 176–79, 202, 204, 205, 207, 208, 217n1, 222n1
Lyon, Ben, 136

Magnificent Ambersons, The, 145
Mailer, Norman, 92, 96
Malone, Dorothy, 142, 143
Marne, First Battle of the, 92
Marshall, Thurgood, 209, 210
Masons, 103, 104, 217n14
McCarthy, Todd, 11, 12
McCarthyism, 84
McCavity the Cat, 58
McQueen, Steve, 166, 167, 168, 169, 171, 172
Meet John Doe, 138
Memphis, Tennessee, 49, 60, 115, 148, 162, 163, 164, 165, 167, 168, 172, 186, 190
Menand, Louis, 189–90, 191, 193, 194, 196
Meredith, Burgess, 166, 168, 170, 171
Meredith, James, 209–10
Meriwether, James B., 195
MGM (Metro-Goldwyn-Mayer), 114, 145
Millgate, Michael, 161, 195
Minter, David, 8, 196
Mississippi, University of, 39, 190, 209
Mississippi/Mississippians, 8, 37, 39, 48, 57, 76, 77, 78, 79, 106, 108, 115, 155, 162, 189, 191, 192, 193, 200; Indians, 75; National Guard, 209; planters, 120
Mississippi River, 80, 132, 138; Great Flood of 1927, 20, 32
Mitchell, Margaret, 24
Mobs, 91, 93
Moby-Dick, 185
Modern Library, 104
Monroe, Marilyn, 67
Montgomery Bus Boycott, 189, 190
Murphy, Dudley, 114–19, 121, 127, 130, 218n15
Murray, Albert, 193, 195
Musso & Frank, 38
Mussolini, Benito, 38, 81, 100

NAACP, 78
Naked and the Dead, The, 92, 96
Napoleon, 92, 100, 106, 120
National Book Award, 84
Negulesco, Jean, 147
Neill, W. C., 197
New Albany, Mississippi, 9
New Deal, 79, 100, 182, 187, 188
New Haven, Connecticut, 37, 76
New Orleans, 10, 31–33, 38–39, 59, 82, 88, 118, 124–25, 127, 129–30, 132, 134, 135, 137
New York City, 10, 15, 28, 37, 40, 48, 55, 57, 61, 63, 76, 82, 98, 116, 117, 126
Newman, Paul, 167
Nigger Heaven, 116–17, 123, 124, 127; Byron Kasson, 127
Nilon, Charles H., 194
Nobel Prize, 7, 11, 12, 14, 15, 19, 20, 26, 33, 73, 78, 92, 97, 138, 144, 190, 200
North, 24, 26, 76, 78, 116, 199, 201, 207
North Carrollton, Mississippi, 197

Oates, Stephen B., 8, 196–97
Oates, Warren, 168
Ober, Harold, 181
O'Brien, Pat, 136
Old Times in the Faulkner Country, 29, 175, 203
Oliver, Jack, 192
Omlie, Phoebe, 135
Omlie, Vernon, 135
O'Neill, Eugene, 116–17, 119, 130
One Matchless Time, 196
Only Angels Have Wings, 141
Oregon, University of, 21, 63
Oxford, Mississippi, 10, 26, 33, 44, 47, 48, 52, 54, 55, 56, 59, 64, 74, 75, 78, 81, 82, 92, 115, 135, 162, 176, 177, 179, 190, 201, 203, 206; Oxford Square, 75

Parini, Jay, 9, 17–18, 21, 137, 196
Paris, 58, 64, 103, 116
Paris Review interview, 64, 67, 197
Parker, Dorothy, 82

238 INDEX

Patton, Nelse, 29, 81, 176, 202, 205, 217n1
Paul, Saint, 108
Pavillion, The, 200
Pearl Harbor, 39
Peavy, Charles D., 194–95, 222n13
Peru, 40
Pfeiffer, Kathleen, 116–17
Phillips, Ulrich Bonnell, 24
Picasso, Pablo, 123
Pine Manor Junior College, 66
Plath, Sylvia, 55
Platinum Blonde, 140
Polk, Noel, 96, 100
Porter, Darwin, 172
Postcolonialism, 92, 102, 109–10
Pound, Ezra, 115
Princeton, New Jersey, 55, 62
Production code, 16, 130, 146
Prufrock, J. Alfred, 136, 140
Pulitzer Prize, 84

Quaid, Randy, 167

Railey, Kevin, 16
Rand, Sally, 188
Random House, 26, 40, 56, 59, 66, 104
Ravetch, Irving, 167
Reconstruction, 24, 28, 77, 79, 179, 191, 222n3
Ringdove (sloop), 58
Red River, 13
Reivers, The (film), 166–72; Edmonds, 167, 168
Resisting History, 103
Rio Bravo, 13
Riot, 210
Ripley, Mississippi, 121–22
RKO, 142
Robbins, Ben, 11
Roberts, Kenneth, 194
Robeson, Paul, 116, 119, 120, 124
Rome, 58, 66, 108
Roosevelt, Franklin, 79, 187
Rowan Oak, 52, 59, 60, 74–75, 77, 97, 199
Royal Air Force, 37

Royal Flying Corps, 101
Rugby Road, 68
Russians, 37
Rydell, Mark, 166, 167

Saddest Words, The, 199
Sartre, Jean-Paul, 86–87
Saturday Evening Post, 27, 75, 93
Scotland, 58
Scott, Sir Walter, 38
Scribner's Magazine, 134
Sensibar, Judith, 10, 21, 30, 42, 43, 48, 49, 50, 176
Shakespeare, William, 19
Shanghai, 60
Shelley, Percy, 130
Silent film, 140
Silver, James, 28, 78, 190
Sirk, Douglas, 142, 143
Slavery, 24, 27, 28, 74, 117, 163, 164, 176, 179, 193, 200, 218n8
Smith, Bessie, 116
Smith, Harrison (Hal), 82
Sohn, Clem, 133
Solomon, Stefan, 11, 115, 123, 218n15
South/southern, 24, 33, 65, 68, 76, 77, 78, 80, 87, 90, 92, 102, 115, 116, 117, 168, 176, 178, 179, 190, 194, 198, 199, 201, 203; gentleman, 26, 40, 124, 130, 132, 147, 148, 162, 164, 166, 167, 171; past, 28, 131; planter aristocracy, 9; politics, 84; status quo, 9, 18
Spanish Civil War, 83, 84, 90, 100, 138
Spiegel, Penina, 172
Spratling, William, 38
Square Books, 33
St. Louis Blues, 116
St. Moritz, 53, 64
Stack, Robert, 142, 143
Stalin, Josef, 100
Stallings, Laurence, 139
Starr, Hubert, 76, 216n5
State Department, 40–41, 55, 63, 78, 79, 100, 188, 215n6

INDEX

Stein, Jean, 10, 42, 46, 51, 53–67, 149, 193, 197, 216nn1–3
Stein, Jules, 53
Stockholm, 15
Stone, Phil, 22, 37, 43, 76, 77, 106, 190, 200, 222n16
Story of Temple Drake, The, 146–49; Stephen Benbow, 147–49; Toddy Gowan, 147; Trigger, 147–48
Sullivan, W. B., 177
Supreme Court, 77, 78, 178
Sweden, 55, 97

Tale of Two Cities, The, 95
Tarnished Angels, The, 142–44
Taylor, Elizabeth, 56
Taylor, Walter, 196
Tempy (horse), 58, 61
Texas, University of, 10
They Shoot Horses, Don't They?, 168
Thomas Crown Affair, The, 167
Tierney, Gene, 12
Till, Emmett, 178
Till, Louis, 178
To Have and Have Not (film), 84, 114; Mr. Johnson, 84
Toronto, Canada, 17, 22, 37, 94, 98, 101, 102, 192
Trotti, Lamar, 146
Troyat, Michel de, 133
Turgenev, Ivan, 44
Twain, Mark, 166
Twentieth-Century Fox, 114, 115, 117
Twilight of Man, The, 181–83
Tyner, Charles, 167

United States, 79, 82, 119, 143, 189, 196, 201, 209
Universal International, 142, 143
University of North Carolina Press, 175
Urgo, Joseph, 98

Van Vechten, Carl, 66, 116, 123, 125, 127
Vicksburg, Mississippi, 184, 185

View, The, 89
Virginia, University of, 7, 19, 22, 27, 62, 68–69, 102, 144, 147, 191
Virginia/Virginians, 59, 191
Vogel, Mitch, 166, 172

Wald, Jerry, 113
Walt Disney Ranch, 167
Warner, Jack, 93, 104, 144
Warner Bros., 12, 94, 103, 113, 114, 115, 130
Warren, Robert Penn, 26, 133
Washington, DC, 41, 100
Washington, George, 187
Wasson, Ben, 44, 47–50, 60, 147
"Water Boy," 120
Waterloo, 92
Watkins, Floyd, 28, 175, 178, 179, 203, 205
Wayne, John, 13
We Believed We Were Immortal, 209
Weinstein, Philip, 10, 20–21, 198–99
Wells, Dean Faulkner (niece), 149, 190
West Point, 93, 144
West Virginia, 119
White House, 97
White Rose of Memphis, The, 125
Wickham, Kathleen, 209–10
Wilkerson, Isabel, 201–4, 208
William Faulkner: American Writer, 197
William Faulkner and Southern History, 198
William Faulkner: Life Glimpses, 197–98
William Faulkner: Man and Artist, 196–97
Williams, Joan, 10, 13, 15, 42, 45, 46, 49, 51–52, 53, 54, 59, 60, 63, 149, 189, 194
Williams, John, 167
Williams, Tennessee, 53
Williamson, Joel, 9, 21, 79, 122, 177, 178, 198
Willkie, Wendell, 187
Wings, 140
Wingwalkers, 31–36
Wintering, The, 42, 51
Wiseman, John Edgar, 178
Wittenberg, Judith, 8, 9, 43, 196
Wolfe, Tom, 137
Woman's Home Companion, The, 145

World War I, 17, 22, 31, 89, 92, 93, 109, 110,
116, 131, 132, 143, 182
World War II, 11, 12, 15, 75, 84, 85, 93, 98,
102, 103, 110, 182, 188
Wyler, William, 167

Yale Bowl, 134
Yale University, 37, 76
Yankees, 38
Yoknapatawpha, 16, 23, 26, 39, 64, 90, 108,
131, 132, 154, 162, 163, 166, 195
Young, Gig, 168
Young, Stark, 27, 28, 200

Zugsmith, Leane, 82

About the Author

Self-portrait courtesy of the author

Carl Rollyson, professor emeritus of journalism at Baruch College, the City University of New York, has published biographies of Marilyn Monroe, Lillian Hellman, Martha Gellhorn, Norman Mailer, Susan Sontag, Rebecca West, Jill Craigie, Michael Foot, Dana Andrews, Sylvia Plath, Amy Lowell, Walter Brennan, and William Faulkner. His reviews of biographies appear every Wednesday and Friday in the *New York Sun*. He has a podcast, *A Life in Biography*: https://anchor.fm/carl-rollyson.